D0297043

BRILLIANT, BRILLIANT, BRILLIANT BRILLIANT BRILLIANT

BRILLIANT, BRILLIANT, BRILLIANT BRILLIANT BRILLIANT

MODERN LIFE AS INTERPRETED BY SOMEONE WHO IS REASONABLY BAD AT LIVING IT

JOEL GOLBY

MUDLARK

This book is dedicated to Sacha Fernando,
who gave me an iPad once. This is the deal.
We are even now.

Mudlark
An imprint of HarperCollins*Publishers*
1 London Bridge Street
London SE1 9GF

www.harpercollins.co.uk

First published by Mudlark 2019

1 3 5 7 9 10 8 6 4 2

A catalogue record of this book is available
from the British Library

ISBN 978-0-00-826540-3

Printed and bound in Great Britain by
CPI Group (UK) Ltd, Croydon, CR0 4YY

CONTENTS

THINGS YOU ONLY KNOW IF BOTH YOUR PARENTS ARE DEAD

My parents are dead and all I can think about is how to sell this house that they left behind. It's me and my sister in a room without curtains – we had to take down the curtains to decorate, so the sunlight is pooling in, and nothing looks more naked than a house stripped and moved around when the person who lived in it died, and no more is that so than in the cold, white light of the day – and we are painting every wall in this fucking place white, because my mother went decoratively insane before she died and discovered the Dulux colour-match service and went absolutely ham on that thing. And we've had three separate estate agents come in, with blazers that bunch around the buttons and a clipboard or iPad, and a special laser tool to measure the size of every room, surveying the corpse with cool detachment and weighing each pound of flesh for gold, and they say – all of them, in turn – they say:

'It's going to be very hard,' they say, 'to sell a house with a pink kitchen.' Which I admit is true.

My parents are dead and the kitchen is pink and the dining room, where she always used to sit, each morning, with a pale cup of tea and some cigarettes, is a sort of terracotta orange, with a gold line of paint stencilled around it at approximately head height. The front room is a looming maroon, a deep dark red the kind you haven't seen since a *Twin Peaks* hell scene, and upstairs the spare room is brown with bronze swirls crawling up the wall in the vague approximation of a plant. The house was always her project: whenever I would go home, she would explain with extravagant hand gestures, not moving from that dining room chair, smoke spiralling through the air, what the hallway would look like when she was done, and what she'd really like to do with my room – now a spare room – and what to do with the spare room that wasn't my room, if she had the money, and then ideally the garden, and then of course the kitchen, but—

And then she was dead and we had to paint over it all white to sell it.

My parents are dead and now I don't know where to spend Christmas. Like, can I go to Dad's? No. Dad's is out because Dad now resides on a golf course in Wolverhampton, a golf course that has no official idea about this because when we sprinkled him – a grey, dreary day in February, the first of his birthdays without him – the family neglected entirely to go through any legitimate ash-sprinkling channels, which is why we had to take two cars and kind of sneak down this side road and park nearby, hop through thick grass on a hill, then crouch among thin, leafless trees, passing around the big ice cream tub that had Dad in it, sprinkling that, and so of course he went everywhere, big billowing clouds of Dad all around us, sticking to boots and trousers, clots of grey Dad on the ground. So: can't go there.

Mum's is out, because Mum is a slick of grey dust long since lost to the waves who was last seen poured into a shallow hole on a beach in Filey. This is another thing they never tell you about death: how, logistically, getting rid of two-and-a-half kilos of ground Mum is a nightmare. Firstly it is never in an urn: the crematorium always presents it to you in a practical-looking if grey-around-the-edges plastic tub, with a plastic bag inside it as a rudimentary spill insurance. Then you have to get the old band together again, i.e. get all of the family to one chosen place to reverently pour dust on the ground. My sister did the hard work of organising this one, getting my two cousins, aunt, my cousin's two children and his dog, my cousin's son's girlfriend who I don't think ever met my mum so why she'd want to come to a beach in Filey to dispose of her I don't know but by then we really needed to up the numbers, a couple of Mum's old friends and also me to a beach in eastern England, the sky so white it was grey, not a scrap of sun, not a scrap of it, and we spent two hours in Filey slowly walking down to the beach, digging a small hole, dumping the ashes, finding a bin for the ashes urn (someone had to carry that thing for half a mile, swear to god), then fish and chips and home. Trying to think if I had an emotion that day. Don't think I had an emotion.

So anyway yeah: Christmas is tricky.

My parents are dead and my dad died when I was 15 and my mum followed suit ten years later. I had 'completed the set' by the age of 25, and they managed to split up somewhere in the midst of it, too: they never married but they argued like they had, separating when I was 13. 'I am an orphan!' I would say to people, as a joke, and they would go, 'you're not an orphan, don't be sil—' then realise that yes, actually, I am, and just because I'm not some grubby-faced *Oliver*-style orphan, flat cap and itchy tweed asking a man for oats, doesn't mean I'm not an orphan. I'm an orphan. Look it up. I am the dictionary definition of an orphan.

My parents are dead and my dad, especially, has fucked me over because he died before he could teach me how to shave. This is what dads are supposed to do, but he has been dust for four years before puberty kicks in enough to sprinkle me with whispers of neck hair, a formative moustache, general testosterone, so I had to teach myself to do it when I was in my first year at uni. This, for whatever reason, causes me enough shame for me to entirely lose my mind about it: I go to an out-of-town pharmacy to buy a razor and shave gel in secret (for some reason I am obsessed with the idea that someone will see me perusing the shaving gel aisle and go 'HA!' and point – there is a whole group of people I half-know with them, in this fantasy, and they all come round the corner to point and laugh at me, 'HA!' they are saying, 'HE DOESN'T KNOW HOW TO SHAVE!'), and I decide to discreetly do a practice shave – on my thigh, where, even in shorts, nobody will know I have done it – in my room.

So here I am with a wad of printed out 'how to shave' instructions from wikiHow, and a jug of warm water for rinsing, and a towel, and the door is double-locked, and I have shaved my left thigh entirely, entirely nude. It's horrible: eerie, actually, too smooth, weak and fragile to the touch, and so immediately after I am done have that sort of dark, grim, post-orgasm feeling of dirty regret: I had a pink, nude thigh and a jug of lukewarm hair water and a hollow feeling inside my body. The warm hair water is a problem – I cannot sprint to the shared bathroom to dispose of it in case the same crowd is there, pointing and laughing, calling me 'Jug Boy' or 'Baby Thigh' – and so, in what is easily my third or fourth moment of sheer madness in this entire episode, throw the water jug out of the window. The person in the flat below – a pathological smoker, who I think actually was probably smoking out of the window at the exact moment I threw a load of hair water out of it – starts immediately thumping on the ceiling, so I cower on the floor near my bed and stay there, still and silent, for 15 minutes in case anyone comes to my room. It's there – trouserless, afraid, silent, and with one perfectly shaved pink thigh – that I thought: *this is probably a low point, in my life.* I entirely blame my father for this happening.

I don't know: a small part of me feels cheated, I suppose. My parents were old when they had me – Dad, who already had my sister from another marriage, was 42; Mum, a first-timer at 38 – but still, when you sign up to push a baby out of your body and nurture it to adulthood, you are in my opinion signing an invisible contract: *I am going to live long enough to see this one through so it can learn to live without me before it has to*. It would have been nice for someone to teach me how to shave, or what an ISA is, or how many carbohydrates I should be eating (as close to zero as possible!) before they died.

My parents are dead and the cats are going crazy about it, lost in what's left of the house. The cats are brothers, Boz and Jez, big beefy thickset tabbies with loud mouths and who lean into tickles ear-first, great cats, wonderful boys, starting to creak a little as we've had them since I was 11 but otherwise great, good boys. They are staying with some friends of my mum's since the death thing happened to her and the friends – a couple – are sending us mixed messages about them, about how happy the animals are and the humans too. The husband is deeply in love with Boz and Jez: they sit on him, he tells us, they are very settled, they can stay with us as long as you need, if you are thinking of putting them up for adoption, he says, he is interested. The wife is calling us at odd times in the afternoon to tell us that actually the cats are deeply unhappy and we need to come get them, stat. Listen, I like being courtside on a slow-moving divorce just as much as anyone but right now, while I'm trying to pick funeral flowers out, it's less than ideal, so my sister decides to take the cats home to London to live the most luxe life a cat can possibly live in the two or so years they have left. When we take Jez, in a cat box, to the train station, it's the most he's ever travelled in his life. Do you know when a cat is really distressed – like, really, really freaked out – they *pant*? Honestly, it's fucking crazy. It sounds like a werewolf transformation scene in an especially bogus eighties movie. This cat is panting and panting and panting. The noises coming out of this box, my god. Anyway, long story short: we get on the train, sit at a four-seater table, and then Jez just immediately panic-shits everywhere. Just *everywhere*. Jemma has to take him into a train bathroom and clean him up with wet wipes like a baby. Boz is chill throughout.

My parents are dead and my sister has gone back to London for the weekend because 'this fucking shitheap fucking town is driving me deranged' (my words, not hers) (my sister did NOT say this) and so I am left, alone here, with the echoing floors and the still bristling ashtrays and my mum's phonebook, carefully handwritten and over-written and rewritten, years of house moves and name changes and marriages and divorce, with the names and numbers of all her families and friends. And it's me, my turn – my sister did this when my dad died, it is my turn to do this now – it is my turn to call everyone and tell them she is dead. The first person I call is my mum's best friend, Teresa, the best woman in the world, the woman who still even now sends me Christmas cards with 'NOT 2B OPENED B4 24/12/2017' written on them, mum's one best friend throughout her life, the one friend she loved throughout it all, decades she has known her, Teresa, decades she has known me, she has seen my dick as a baby and seen me have tantrums as a teenager and seen me grow, sort of, into an adult, and she is driving when she picks up, it sounds like, on the hands-free, and briefly she is pleased to hear from me because I've literally never phoned her in my life, she says it so surprised, so genuine, 'oh hi' she says, and 'how are you?' and then I have to tell her, and the words feel dry in my mouth because I haven't ever said them yet, 'Terri,' I say. 'It's mum. She's dead.' And Terri goes *no, no*.

That's all I remember: *no, no*.

Sometimes when I try and sleep I close my eyes and I can still hear it exactly how she said it: *no, no*.

With her voice kind of breaking halfway through. And there's a pause, and she says, 'I'll have to call you back' and I say yes, and then I just sort of sit there, holding the phone, just sat in the armchair, looking.

And that is definitely the worst thing I've ever had to do in my entire life.

And for the rest of the friends we just announce it via a Facebook status, because who can do that, really. Who can do that to themselves.

* * *

My parents are dead and I am drunk, so much drunker than everyone else around me, so drunk for a Wednesday, and it's so *obvious*, being that drunk, such an *obvious* way of coping, but here I am. My sister is in London still and the cats are at the friends' house and all my mates are at work and so it's just me, in the house, going crazy at the way this place seems to have deformed and changed in the time I've been here, the very shape of the rooms seem different, too quiet, and I try and start the day normally – I have opened my laptop and started a game of *Football Manager* and I am convinced I can pull Queen's Park Rangers up out of the Championship and into the path of glory, and a lot of that glory depends on the form of a misfiring Bobby Zamora – and but it's 1 p.m. now and I'm bored and still not dressed yet and, long story short, lunch is one ham and coleslaw bap, one small bag of Mini Cheddars, and a fantastic amount of beer and bourbon drunk alone. I have just discovered the boilermaker – a bottle of American beer chased with a greasy shot of bourbon – and have decided it is fantastic. By 5 p.m. QPR have been relegated because I'm trying to play five men up front, and I am roaring.

So we're out tonight, everyone out tonight, even though it's a Wednesday and not typically an out-tonight kind of night, but because I have requested it and because my mum is dead everyone is going along with it so whatever, and when I arrive at the same pub we all go to – Wetherspoons; shout out to! – everyone is there slowly sipping their first pints and someone turns to me with a note of surprise in their voice and says Joel, they say, you're so *drunk*.

And I say: hell fuck shit fuck yeah I'm drunk! And I order another two boilermakers (two.). And I would say this activity continues for roughly three more years.

My parents are dead and the fridge is, too. I cannot believe this: the day my mother died the fridge in her house also decided to expire, so it's just this lifeless white box and we have to keep milk for tea in this foil-lined freezer bag on the side, and let's be honest about this system: it does not actually work. Already, my health has deteriorated drastically as a result of my mother's death – two weeks alone in a house with no fridge and no store cupboard reserves has left me stringing meals together from whatever I can buy that day from the nearest decent supermarket a mile away, microwave friendly a plus, or whatever I can muster in desperation at whatever time I wake up from the local corner shop (one dreary grey Sunday, with no other shops open and nowhere to turn, I end up going to the Spar and my dietary intake for the day was 1 x entire thing of fromage frais, 1 x entire packet of Cheesestrings, 1 x apple, 1 x pack of popular prawn-and-maize snack Skips, no other vitamins or minerals). I am eating in pubs, a lot. I am eating a lot of sugared cereals. I feel like hell. I feel like garbage. I would pay up to £1,000 for someone else's mum to cook me a meal and tell me it's okay.

My parents are dead and I don't know what my dad's face looks like any more. I know what my mum's face looks like: I can look directly in a mirror for that, imagine myself with a grey chin-length bob and a fag on the go, yelling at the tennis, by which I mean to say I have my mother's exact face (my sister, too, has her mother's exact face: our shared dad had weak genes, clearly). But his face ... not so much. Every early January I am vaguely reminded of his death – he died on the fourth, early in the year, which obviously made it double-sad because that was so close to Christmas (see *ibid.*, re: already being very marred), which marred the occasion somewhat. The last Christmas present he ever got me, since you ask, was a Dreamcast console, which I discovered ten years later when we were clearing out Mum's house, and when I found it I just squatted on the floor and held it and looked into the middle distance and Thought A Lot About Stuff, which you do a fair amount of when both your parents are dead – and I realised with a jolt this year that this January marks 15 Januaries without him, equal in number to the 15 Januaries I had with, meaning I have now spent more of my life without a father than with. And those memories are becoming blurry now – the things he did, the way his voice sounded, gentle but melodic, sort of, the way he smelled so bad because he was a smoker, and the way the car smelled so, so bad because he was a smoker, and all the smoke – but his face. His face. I just can't picture it. Sometimes I go to my sister's house and idly flick my eyes over at a bookshelf and there, buried among knick-knacks and shells and Asian-looking scrolls from her time in Malaysia and in amongst all that crap, boom: there's a perfect sharp photo portrait of my dad, the one I took when I was about eight, when, after school, I went with him to the local college nearby, where he knew the photography lecturer who let him use the dark room there; and there, in the empty hours of the evening, he'd sit and make a shallow pool of chemicals slowly splash, and, alchemy-like, black-and-white photos would emerge; and I would spend most of these times bored out of my mind, or playing with something – a Gameboy, an off-brand single-note Thunderbirds-themed electronic game, a Tazo – until, once, he set the camera up for me – steadied it on the tripod, gauged the aperture and ISO, stood me on a box and trailed a shutter release wire down to me, then sat in front of the camera, *click*. And then he went to the back and developed it – out of the canister, into the pool, slick paper pushed into the bath with tongs – and then, what seemed like hours later, there: the last photo of him ever taken. I had just eaten a Kinder Egg and had chocolatey fingers, and there, in my excitement, I grabbed the photo, smudging the back – my tiny fingerprints still mark the back of it – and I remember the photo. I remember the chemical smell. I remember the Kinder Egg and the slow, short walk home, pink sun setting in a red sky. I remember the Hoover repair shop we always had to walk past on the way there, and the name of the photography lecturer who gave Dad a key to his studio, and I remember the winding cast-iron staircase I used to sit on and play with. But I do not remember his face.

My parents are dead and all I can think back to is the Christmas I figured Santa wasn't real. Because I kind of knew – you always know, before you *know*; children are obsessed with Santa, entirely, and strive to solve the puzzle of him even though they don't truly want the answer, and as a result are constantly searching for clues as to his existence or non-existence; and plus also a bigger boy two years above me in school called Daniel told me, and I mostly believed him – but it is cold and the night is sharp and jet-black, and I'm sat huddled on a bench at the train station with my dad, hands both in our pockets, waiting on Christmas Eve for my sister. She'd been off living in London, nineties London, which I can only assume meant taking acid before cutting your own hair a lot and literally nothing else, and the train is delayed or we are early or whatever and my dad is making small talk asking me what I wanted for Christmas. He was always very clear-eyed, when my sister was coming to stay: rare, half-yearly trips, just a weekend here or there, and he would always be on his A-game for it, make sure he was sober and sparkling, and he nestled in near and said, And So What Do You Want Santa To Bring You For Christmas.

And I don't really know, I say.

What If He Bought You A Camera?, my dad asks. And I say—

—and this haunts me, every time i think of it, in the many years since; if i could take back one moment and swallow it away, push it all in my mouth like a piece of paper and chomp it down and swallow it, take it all back, i would, but i am stuck with the scar instead; and it will come to me, in dark blue-grey nights when i can't sleep and when i'm walking thru supermarkets and when i'm on my commute and when i'm just minding my own business on the sofa, and it will come to me in the high moments as well as the low, and it will knock all the air out of me all over again, and i go—

—'Ugh. *No*.' And my dad turns to look away and says, Okay.

And so of course the next day I open a carefully wrapped shoebox with, inside it, a small, pristine, second-hand camera. And the note from Santa is in my dad's handwriting. And he says he hopes I like my present. And that is how I learned that Santa wasn't real.

(I just wanted a Megadrive, that's all. I just wanted a Megadrive.)

My parents are dead and do you ever think about the moment of death? The actual moment of *death*? Not your physical body collapsing beneath you, or your liver finally failing in its liver hole, or anything biological, physical, like that: do you ever think, of that last second of life, as the air eases out of your lungs? Do you ever think what it is like to be in that moment, and know it is the end? There is no peace there. That is a moment of sheer horror. You know that your body has failed you and you are trapped, for the rest of your life, in the prison of it. And then the edges grow blurry, and the words begin to fade, and the light grows pale and the darkness comes to replace it. And then— just as you never knew you were born. You die.

My dad is dead and we are at his flat, clearing out his things. It's a small flat, a stubby hallway that opens out into a sort of double room and, behind it, an equally sized living area; off that, a box-shaped kitchen, and from the hallway, a small bathroom. I am telling you this because I know the flat inside-out, as I did then and I do now, because I used to stay here every other Friday until I didn't, and since I've been here last it has filled with another layer of accoutrements. In the last couple of years since my parents split and he moved here, my dad has mainly preoccupied himself with drinking, and with stumbling into town a couple miles to do a loop of all the charity shops, on the search for geegaws and trinkets on a rhyme and reason known only to himself. You look at this flat, and any interior designer will tell you there's no overarching theme here, no throughline to the knick-knacks – here, for some reason, is a brass bugle; here a small tin car; some wooden owls; a tiny pot statue of an elephant; here is a deck of cards inside a decorative box; here is a toby jug with a monstrous face. We pick through the crap (an awful lot thereof) and chuck it; the few items worth keeping are distributed amongst us, for memory's sake. All I have to remember my dad by is a cowboy coffee pot, a fist-sized wooden ball studded with faux ivory, a pair of binoculars with an honest-to-god swastika on it, and a cast-iron skillet.

And then a curious thing happens, which is: Dad's best friend turns up. Only none of us have ever met this best friend, ever. And he says it – 'I was your dad's best friend' – and he explains, through the tears, this old wizened toothless man in a flat cap and a wrinkled face contorting with emotion, that he used to come over, with the dog – the dog, he gestures to, straining on its leash – and they would talk about things, about the wind and the day and the lay of the land, and then he – and this man is gulping, crying, with an emotion none of us, dead at the nerves, have felt for days – and he just wanted to say – I— found— him— – gesturing to the hallway he was found back-down and grey in, and – he— was— a— good— man— – and all I am thinking here is:

Who the fuck is this dude?

My parents are dead, or at least my dad is, and my mum and I don't really talk much anymore but whenever I see her she demands I play Scrabble with her, because she is very good at Scrabble and enjoys beating me at it a lot. I do not have the exact statistics to hand but her unbeaten run at Scrabble goes back at least 15 years, because my mum is the kind of Scrabble dickhead who plays 'XI' in the corner on a triple word score like three moves from the end, conjuring 48 points out of thin air, and also a lot of the times we played I was a literal child, but whatever.

The point is I am 21 now and have a degree and I have won by 12 points and this information has shocked her to the core. 'No,' she says, touching each tile, counting and recounting, the entire board, top to bottom. 'No, it's not possible.' And she looks up at me across the table—

—and i remember that the only other board game we have ever played together was the night my dad died, when we just stayed up in silence on silence playing cards, until the cold part of the night turned something blue then grey then red as the sun came up in the morning, and she said 'well', and 'I guess we best get on with it', and she rang work to tell them she wouldn't be in today, and rang school to say i wouldn't be coming in today and didn't know when i would be in ever again (it would be six weeks until i went back there)—

—she looks up at me and goes, 'You cheated. You must have cheated.' And the torch is passed between the generations. And I am the family champion of Scrabble now.

* * *

My parents are dead and I am trying to buy a beer basket online. A beer basket is a beautifully packaged wicker basket with beer in it. Ribbons, that sort of thing. An outer cellophane shell. Inside, to cushion the beers, is that sort of cardboard shred that hamsters have in their cages sometimes. It is a nice gift. I am buying it for my neighbour because he found my mum's lifeless body on the floor of her bedroom and had to call an ambulance about it.

Mum had cancer, so we sort of knew this was coming, just not when. There are two kinds of death of your parents: ones you know about, and ones you don't. I have to tell you some information about this that is going to make me extremely sound like I believe in horoscopes, now. Makes me sound like I have some Real Opinions About Chi. Like I have written a letter to the government before about the medicinal power of weed. This is what I am going to sound like right now:

Both times, when I got the call that my parents were dead, *I already knew*.

When we got the call about my dad, I was 15 and asleep, and the phone rang about midnight, 1 a.m., and a phone ringing at 1 a.m. is literally never good news, so I sort of swum awake and watched the yellow light of the hallway hum and blur, and heard distantly the sort of wobbling sound of my mum's voice through many walls and a stairwell, and even though he wasn't sick or anything I just *knew*, clunk of dread in the ol' bottom of the stomach, and then my mum came and sat on the edge of my bed and said 'It's your dad, Joe—' my family call me Joe and I hate it '— it's your dad, Joe, he's gone,' and I just. I dunno. I cried so much I yelled.

And then when my mum died ten years later, again I remember such clear weird little details of it: I was out drinking the night before and woke up in the most drunk sleep pose ever (entirely face down, face entirely enveloped by the pillow, and surrounded by a tacky pool of your own saliva, and honestly sleeping for six hours in that position I don't know how *I'm* not the dead one) and the first thing I did was look at my phone because I am a millennial and I remember it being early, even for me – in the 6 a.m. hour, still, an hour I am incredibly unfamiliar with – and I had three missed calls from my sister and so I knew already what that means, and I called her quickly – still face down, somehow, I did not turn over for this phone call – and she said 'Yeah it's your mum she's—' – and a little pause – '—she's gone, mate', and I remember saying 'okay' and crying exactly one tear – such a pathological number of tears, it was out of my left eye and I remember it dropping with a soft thump onto the pillow beneath me – and I said 'okay,' and then, 'what can I do?'

And it turns out one of the major things I can do is buy a 'sorry you had to find my mum dead!' beer basket for the neighbour. I am searching online for somewhere that delivers next day, and I cannot decide which beer basket seems more appropriate – the £35 version, eight craft beers and one tube of salted snacks, or the £55 version, all that and more? I am torn because obviously finding an actual corpse is probably quite a bad shock but also I am poor and 25 and my parents are dead and now I'm the only one left to provide for me and also I have a funeral to pay for and £55 for some beer and some ribbon is a lot. I spend like 15 minutes hovering the mouse between the £35 option and the £55 one. What, truly, is the price we put on the act of finding our mother dead in her bedroom on a mild June morning? I sigh and I click. It turns out it is £55.

My parents are dead and so I can tell you from experience that literally nobody alive knows what songs you want playing at your funeral, so if this is important to you then put some sort of system in place now, because here's what happened with my dad—

'What ... does anyone know what music Dad liked?'

'What CDs does he have in his house?'

'He literally has one CD and it's Eric Clapton's Greatest Hits.'

[*Extremely tedious half-hour while everyone tries to remember out loud a single instance of them seeing my dad enjoy a song*]

'I think he liked jazz so let's bang some Miles Davis while we lower him into the pit.'

'Cool.'

And with my mum—

'This again. What's in the CD pile?'

'Tom Jones and Cerys Matthews from Catatonia, *Baby It's Cold Outside* CD single.'

'Inappropriate.'

'*Jiggerypipery*, the self-titled album by Jiggerypipery, who are a local tour band who make what the back of the CD describes as "fun bagpipe music".'

'A hard no.'

'And U2, *The Joshua Tree*, on tape cassette.'

'I do not understand how someone can live sixty plus years and this is all they have to show for it.'

We ended up playing the soundtrack from the musical *Sarafina!* for reasons I cannot recall now. For the record, I see my funeral as the only time I can force my friends to sit and endure my music tastes – the AUX chord is always snatched away from me at parties because obscure lyric-less drone music does not exactly get the vibe popping, so I literally have to wait until I die to take it – and so I want Ratatat's *Germany to Germany/Spanish Armada/Cherry* movement from the first album, *Rome* from their fifth album, then whichever 14-minute-long Fuck Buttons song is in my Spotify most played library when I die. Follow these instructions to the letter or I shall haunt you all forever.

My parents are dead and suddenly the home I grew up in has shifted, imperceptibly enough to feel alien, to feel like a house, now, rather than a home, to feel like four cold walls and a roof. The fridge doesn't work. There's no food in. The cats are not pattering about. My sister, deranged with the repetition of administration and grief, has gone back to London to work. It's just me, alone here, padding around this place I own now, feeling as if I'm a ghost.

I got trapped in a wardrobe, here, once. This was when my parents were alive: I remember, actually, it was a rare moment of peace for them, a searingly white-hot day and I watched them, out of their bedroom window, my face and nose pressed tight against the net curtain, and they were chatting and repotting plants and seemingly both in a good mood, so I left them to it – I was, like, six at this point, maybe five – and so I turned around and went to play imagination games in the spare room at the back of the house, and ended up clambering into this old wardrobe – my mother, a sort of amateur seamstress, had stuffed it with old plastic bags of rags and fabric ends and half-done pieces of knitting, which were sort of slippery and fun to climb – and then the whole thing started to creak and tip and long story short it collapsed on me, vacuuming me entirely to the floor.

Now: a normal child, in this situation, I imagine, would scream. Yell or something. Thump on the wardrobe panels. Beg for a fraction of help. But I think I just accepted that *hey, I guess this is how I die*, swaddled in dozens of clothes bags, trapped in pitch blackness beneath a wardrobe. It was about 20 minutes before they came inside and found me, muffled steps up the stairs turning to quick sharp noises of alarm before my dad heaved the wardrobe off me, and I remember both their faces staring down at me, and the light pouring in, a combination of extreme did-my-child-die and just bafflement, and my mum just said: 'Why didn't you *say* anything?' and I replied: 'I just didn't want to be any bother.'

I just remember that story a lot because whenever I try and recall my parents being together in the same room and not mad at each other that's all I can ever think of. Me politely resigning myself to living the rest of my life out as a wardrobe boy, RIP, 1987–1992.

My parents are dead and I'm shopping at Tesco for vol-au-vents. Planning a wake is like planning the most vibe-less party in actual existence: all the same motions as planning an actual party (invites, finger foods, the chilling of drinks) but none of the buzz or excitement, extremely low chance of anyone getting laid. In my trolley is: a tray cake, feeds 15; a number of 3 for 2 party foods, including cocktail sausages; a light and refreshing mix of own-brand lemonades and colas, as well as a respectful two (two.) boxes of beer. My sister is off in the far reaches of the shop buying lasagne supplies – my mother had this tradition where she would throw a party every Christmas and invite everyone round (and she was the exact type of woman to call such a party a *soirée*, to give you a bead on my mother), and for whatever reason her showstopper party food was 'a lasagne', she would make like four or five of these great, heaving lasagnes for people to eat great huge cubes off from slowly oily-going paper plates – and my sister intends to honour that tradition, God Bless Her Soul, by making her own lasagne, which everyone will tell her at the party in a quiet voice – *it's a very good lasagne, thank you* – but with all the unsaid context being *but it's not Hazel's lasagne*, and I think my sister knows this, deep down. Anyway we are politicising the lasagne.

The point is that I am tired, so tired, it has been two weeks of admin and grief and sorting and nothingness and it's still not over, yet, and I am taking a brief moment of respite while my sister weighs up beef vs lamb mince to lean on the trolley and stare at the freezer aisle and sigh, and someone says Joel, they say Hello, they say, How Are You.

It's the mum of a girl I did not really know at school (she, the girl, was a good five or six rungs up the attractiveness ladder than me – I was an extremely obese smooth-faced 40-year-old mum-of-four looking kid for most of my adolescence, with a voice that seemingly took five years to break, and school hierarchy is defined by exactly two axes – who is hot, or at least if not hot then who get tits or a beard first; and who is hard, and the hard boys get with the tit girls and form these sort of royal allegiances, and kids like me get Really Into Videogames And *Robot Wars* And Metal Music – and so despite sharing a classroom with me for five consecutive school grades did not, in fact, know who I was) and also a former colleague of my mother's, which is why she half recognises me more than I do her. 'It's Jackie,' she says, 'I used to work with your mum.'

And her face crumples and she goes: 'I heard about the cancer.' And I nod. And then she goes: 'How is she doing?' And I realise she does not know that my mother is dead.

And so now I am stranded here with a trolley full of wake food and a dilemma. Do I, really, want to do this in the middle of a supermarket freezer aisle section? Do I really want to have to explain what all the food is for, and how and why? We can pretend that I went through this

– that I, like a lightning flash, rapidly weighed up the pros and the cons and decided logically on an outcome. We can pretend that happened when it did not. Instead, instinct kicked in and

'Yeah,' I said. 'Not so great.' Technically this was not a lie. And Jackie said: 'Oh, well,' and said, 'give her my best.' And I walked away thinking: that was a very strange thing that I just did. That was a very unusual thing to do.

My parents are dead and there is always cake at the funeral. It's weird eating cake and being sad: at my dad's, his ex-wife, Annie, had made one of the most astonishing cakes I'd ever eaten, a dense low chocolate cake with a mirror-finish ganache that shone like glass, and I was two slices, maybe three slices in – I was, as aforementioned, an especially large shapeless teenage boy with a sweat problem – when one of my mum's cousins who I had never met ushered me over to his armchair. And he said, *do you not think you need to lay off the cake?* And I thought: today of all days, dickhead. Today of all days you come and tell me this.

Funeral guest lists are unusual affairs: you are as surprised by the attendees as the non-attendees. A throng of my sister's closest uni mates – all in the first great flush of their early twenties and ostensibly with better shit to be doing than this – were at my dad's; his lifelong best friend, Don, left the voicemail we left him telling him the news unanswered. At my mum's funeral, none of her side of the family attended, including her closest cousin, Josie – but clearly she was popular at work because an entire office's worth of people lined up to shake my hand and tell me what a good laugh she was. Only after death do you see facets of the living you once knew through the eyes of those who knew them away from you: you learn who thinks them kind, who considers them wise, who considers them a best friend. They, all of them, line up to tell you how they were capital-G Good: we are, all of us, washed of sin when we die. When we live we are jagged and complex and fucked up and we oscillate between joy and despair, and all of that is flattened out in death, all of those wrinkles uncrumpled. We go into the ground as saints.

My parents are dead and forms; forms, forms; forms, forms, forms. There is a form to declare death and you have to pay for each printout, which means you have to predict exactly how many corporations and banks and agencies are going to ask for certified proof of death and then pre-emptively pay £12 for them to have it, and we umm and ahh and ask for four (you need two, at most: if you take anything from this, just know that everywhere takes photocopies, and save yourself £24). Then you have to, as in our case where there is no will (while I am here handing out advice: if someone draws you up a will and you go through the hurdle jumping of defining exactly who gets what in a will and how the will should break up, and where everything goes after you die, and all you have to do to verify that will is sign it, exactly once, please sign it exactly once, and do not leave it, unsigned, for two years, on the table next to you among a big pile of post, *Mum*), jump through the various hoops to invoke probate, a sort of de facto all-of-this-dead-person's-shit-now-belongs-by-blood-to-you ritual where I had to go to a local family court, get knife searched on the way in, then swear godlessly on a sign of the cross to say that I am the one true heir to a £90,000 terrace near Sheffield, nobody else may make claim on my land. The bank wants to know she's dead, the electricity company. I stop chasing the £800 left in her building society account because the constant administration of it was too exhausting. The government sends me a letter to tell them they overpaid her pension, i.e. made payment into her account exactly once post-death, and now they would like that money back, now: I tear the paper up and scatter it into the bin. I am warned that people might wheedle out like cockroaches from beneath the family fridge: someone, somewhere, some distant cousin, might try to make a claim on what thin gruel there is left, and to be prepared for it. They mean legally, but I want it in blood: I am angry, so angry, I am ready to meet anyone head on, if anyone even steps to me and tells me they want a penny of what's mine I will tear at them until they are just a mashed pile of red, I will punch and punch and punch, I need this, I need them to come out, I want so bad somebody to take this out on, I need it.

My parents are dead and one day, three years later, I go back there, to the house, after we've sold it. This is a mistake: I'm watching from sort of afar, in case an old neighbour sees and recognises me and we have to do a whole awkward thing, and everything feels juddery, at once familiar and not. The house looks more or less the same – steam rises from the exhaust vent on the boiler we had put in a few years ago; the smoke bush my dad planted 20 years ago still looks somehow both fragile and overgrown in the front garden – but it's not. It's late October, cold but not freezing, and, on the doorstep, there's a pumpkin, carved for Hallowe'en. We never left a pumpkin out, even once. And then suddenly I am overcome with the realisation that this isn't mine, now; that another family exists in this space, fills every corner of it with their own existence, their own sofa positioning, their laughs echoing on the walls they now own, their voices shouting upstairs for dinnertime, their crap filling the basement. I feel like a ship on the sea with endless deep blue beneath me and nothing holding me up. No anchor, no home. Someone else's pumpkin makes me lose my entire mind.

My parents are dead and my friends are trying their best. My friend takes an afternoon off work and drives me out to the countryside, out far away from the grey jagged misery of the town, and I wind the windows down and let the warm June air rustle my hair, and I inhale bugs and lungfuls of green, wholesome air, and I put my hand out of the window and wave it through the wind, and then we stop at a pub overlooking green rolling hills, starched yellow almost in the sunlight, and we both sit down with amber ales and he tells me he thinks he has cancer.

'What?' I say. 'What?'

And he sits stiff-backed in double denim and says: 'In my bowels. They did a test. I'm waiting on the scans.'

And I say Jesus, I say Jesus Fucking Christ. What is with everyone getting cancer?

And he says I know.

And we drive in silence back to the town and we line up more beers in another pub and meet some friends and he tells them he thinks he has cancer ('In my bowels,' he says. 'Blood. Bad blood, that black blood. They did a test. I'm waiting on the scans.') and he starts crying so much the landlord very quietly asks us to leave the pub, because quote, unquote we are really bringing the vibe down, and then the next pub we go into we are also asked to leave because of the crying thing, too. And at the funeral a week later I ask him if he's coping okay and he says a cheerful 'Yep!' and then proceeds to not ever mention cancer or die over cancer at any point over the next three years, and I figure there is something, about death, there is something that brings out the weird little crevices in all of us.

My parents are dead and it's a year or so later and everyone thinks that I'm fine including me. I'm cat-sitting for my sister, my boys, my big beautiful boys, but there's something wrong with Boz: he's thin when he used to be plush, he's quiet when he used to be loud, he keeps coming up to me, shaking and feeble, just leaning on me with all the little weight that he has. One morning, before I leave for work, I find him after calling him for breakfast, and there he is, shaking under a shelf: I coax him half out, bring him a small plate of biscuits, swaddle him with a towel. Boz has been my best little mate since I was eleven and he was six months old, and now I look into his huge orange eyes and I know that he is dying. *Moww*, he says, and I say *moww* back, and I cry, and cry and cry and cry, and kiss his little head, and cry and cry and cry, and I'm crying now, and I cry and cry and cry and cry, and I suppose that's when it all hits me – me, on the floor, cat biscuits on my fingers – that's when it hits me most of all.

* * *

My parents are dead and I'm starting to get to the age where my friends' parents are dying, too, and I feel I should know what to say to them. And I never really do: instances of grief, I have found, are unique, two never coming in the same shape, and they can be piercing and hard-edged and they can be like passing through deep dark treacle or they can be like a long, slow-passing cloud, it can make everything grey or everything sharp, it can hit you like a truck or it can hit you like cholesterol. There is no one single catch-all solution to dealing with the worst life has to throw at you because life has such a habit of swinging you curveballs.

But what I do always say is: oh man, this is going to suck.

And I always say: you need two fewer death certificates than you think you need.

And I say: snakes will come up from the grass and you will want to hurt them.

And: at one point you are going to become keenly aware that everyone is judging you for the exact way you outwardly behave when someone close to you dies, and I need to tell you that that is a nonsense. You are going to feel a dirty little feeling of guilt. If there's a long illness involved, there might be this horrible, metallic-tasting feeling of relief, one too hard and real for you to admit to yourself is there. You will do weird things and behave weirdly and not even know it is happening. You will offer up a portion of your psyche to the grief gods and say to them in the rain: take this and do what you want with it. Suddenly your body is not your own, your mind, your home. There's no right way of dealing with it but there are a thousand differently angled wrong ways. You'll cycle through all of them.

I'm on my fourth Christmas without parental guidance now, and I suppose I am okay. There are still times when I feel unutterably alone – times when all I need is my mum's roast, or a voice that knows me on the other end of a phone to tell me things will be alright again, or what I need to do to make things alright; times when I'd give anything to go for one pint with my dad, or drive around in his smoky old Volvo listening to Fleetwood Mac. It's weird what you miss: every holiday we had, when I was a kid, was foreshadowed on the morning of travel by my dad getting the shits – every single time, without fail

– and our journey to Cleethorpes or Scarborough or Whitby or Filey would be delayed by Dad, in the bathroom, making the air sharp and sour, groaning through the door, and Mum, on her tenth or eleventh furious cigarette, hissing, 'Every. Bloody. Time. Tony! Every. Fucking. Time.' through her teeth, and I don't know. Holidays don't seem the same without this consistent element of intestinal chaos beforehand.

I picked up his camera, recently. I think a lot of people my age and of my generation get this delayed obsession with film – that gauzy, blurry, physical quality of it, haunted eyes reflected back from a flash bang, a fraction of a second of light that could have exploded – just for a moment – a day ago, or a week, a year, one hundred, more a frozen moment in time, somehow, than anything digital – and I asked my sister to dig out his old Nikon. I turn 30 this year, a moment that will be marked with me living more of my life without him than I ever did with, and it was curious, looking into that bag, reminding myself of a time left behind me: an old emergency pack of Rizlas, the gnarled old piece of tights material he used as a lens cleaner; the ephemera of a life left behind. The bag *smelled* of him. I held the camera up to my face, put the eye where his eye had been, nestled my nose where, years before, he would have squashed his. *Click*. You wonder what they would make of you, now. *Click*. How they might be proud of what you've become. *Click*.

THE MURDERER WHO CAME TO TEA

Dad taught me how to make a prison bomb once. I do not think my mum ever knew about this. This was not on the family curriculum. But we were playing cards one day when I was ten, and, 'Oh,' Dad said, as if recalling some vital lesson all fathers teach to their children that he had somehow neglected, 'right: you know you can make a bomb out of this?' And I said: I'm listening.

You can make a prison bomb out of a pack of cards, Dad explained, if you cut all the little red pieces out – the hearts and the diamonds, and any red ink-like paste that might be smeared on the back – and mush them into a wet paste, which you cram down a radiator pipe or some such. When the pipe heats up – it's an inelegant art, and results vary, so don't, like, sleep close to it, especially not head-first – some chemical reaction will happen, which causes it to explode, dismantling the wall behind it and through which you – he motioned me in a very confident way, as if to say, 'You, my sweet large son, are destined for prison'

– through which you escape. And that's a prison bomb. And *that's* rummy.

I didn't really question this at the time because dad was always talking about war stuff and cannons and stuff, and also because he went to prison once. This, again, was one of those strange things that was never explained to me as being abnormal – Dad got stopped for drink-driving once and given a warning, and then he was stopped again and given a fine, and seeing as we were poor and couldn't pay the fine he did three weeks in prison, one week maximum security and then another fortnight – after they realised how truly meek and unthreatening he was – in an open prison somewhere near Leicester. 'How was prison, Dad?' I asked, when he came back again. He said: 'Not bad.' He genuinely looked quite healthy. Prison wore well on my father.

We didn't talk about prison much after that, mainly because it was such a pathetic stretch he did – I mean I never even had to draw a heartbreaking crayon-coloured picture of our family, labelled 'MUMMY', 'DADDY?', 'ME' about it – and also because Mum very strictly forbid us talking about it (she was really mad about that time he had to go to prison). But one day I answered the phone – one of my pathological childhood obsessions, for a while, was snatching the phone up and answering it in my politest sing-song – and a strange voice on the other end growled: 'Is that Joel?'

Yes, I said.

'Hello Joel,' he said (imagine the voice is more prison-y than that. You are not reading it prison-y enough, and I can tell). 'Hello, Joel,' the prison voice said. 'I've heard a lot about you. Is your dad there?'

And I said sure, who is it.

And he said, John.

And so I yelled up the stairs, D–AAAA–D, JOHN'S ON THE PHONE.

And my dad appeared before me like death had learned to shit his pants in fear.

'Yeah,' my Dad said, shakingly, as I watched. 'Yeah. Yeah. Yep. No I'll— yeah. No I'll come to you. Yeah. Yep. See you there.' And then he hung up and turned and swivelled into a crouch down next to me and said, Don't Tell Your Mother.

I'm not saying who told her but she found out.

It turns out Dad had made friends, in prison, as he was wont to do as he was a very mellow and agreeable man, especially friends with his bunkmate, John, who murdered someone. 'Yeah come over,' Dad said into the bunk above him, confident this man would never be released from prison ever in his life. 'We'll get a drink. Kip on the sofa until you sort yourself out.' And then John *fucking got parole*, and instantly called *the only phone number he had on his person, which was my Dad's*, and *asked if he could stay with us, promising not to do a murder again*. The row between my parents that night – the Red Corner fighting 'can a murderer stay on our sofa' and the Blue Corner fighting out of 'absolutely fucking not' – went on so long our neighbours kept flicking their bedroom lights on and off in a really passive–aggressive way, slamming their flat fists against the shared wall that ran over our alleyway.

John never stayed, in the end – 'Because of the murder,' I imagine my dad saying, over the pint they eventually shared, at a pub far, far away from our house, and I like to think John was a gentlemanly murderer who waved his hand and said 'I understand' – but I always like that my dad even tried it: that he thought a murderer could stay with us, for anywhere between one day and six months, really says a lot about him, his gentle trusting nature and his inability to operate anywhere within the sensible laws of society.

I often imagine how I would do, in prison. Quietly, I think I'd thrive. The Boys there would at first be suspicious of my smart mouth and bookish ways, and look to teach me a violent lesson, but I think after the first two or three beatings they would take a begrudging shine to me – 'He does reading,' they will say, proudly, to their bunkmates, 'He's helping me write a letter to my lawyer' – and that, over time, would evolve into a quiet sort of respect. One day a young upstart would try and beat me with a metal pipe on his first day to prove some sort of point, and the more seasoned inmates would jump to my defence – 'Leave him alone!' they'd say, 'He's just a harmless little soft cunt!' – and I would say Thank You, Lads, dusting my prison uniform off, going back to my eccentric little hobby of cutting all the red bits out of cards. And then one day, just like Daddy taught me, I'd blow every one of those fuckers up to kingdom come, and sprint off into the night, hooting and hollering with delirium, until the police shot me to death with Tasers. But I still wouldn't fucking invite a murderer to dinner, would I? Because I'm not *mad*.

TWITCH.TV

#.

I got to tell you that there is something singularly amusing about watching a Dutch teenager swear in a flurry of American slang. *Fucking shit bro, fuck man*. Jord is swearing. *Fucking shit man, my mom*. Jord just got down to the last five of the game – 100 players whittled down to a handful over a grinding 35 minutes – and the circle draws ever tighter, pushing those last few remaining players in, and they are all concentrated on this one small patch of bushgrass, and Jord is just lining up his shot, he'll go through the back of the head of this guy then hop over and loot his ammo then use it to take out the final two players a little over the ridge, this is a very high tension thing – and then his mum stumbles in and the mic is abruptly muted and we watch, thousands of us, in silent horror, as Jord's entire head is shot to pieces while he pliantly talks to his mum. He turns back to the screen and sees himself as a mess of blood and ammo. *Fuck man, my mom,* he explains. *Fuck*. He rubs his eyes and regains composure.

No man, she— I don't mean that. She means well. Exit to Lobby, new game, the tide washes in with the moon.

OR: JASONR needs to piss. It is midgame – that gauzy time when the initial flurry of desperate gun-hunting and easy-pickings inner-city kills have quietened down, and so now it is a case of picking your way through the expanse, picking up improved helmets and gun sights and vehicles, taking tactical positions up on hills and the roofs of houses – and he is swimming across a small river to get to the other side of the island. But he isn't: Jason has left his character automatically swimming – 'I gotta pee, man' – and everyone in the chat is deliriously tense in his absence. *I seen Jason die like this*, one chatter says. Another: *it's a long shot but he can take him out*. Jason's teammate, some guy a thousand miles across the country, pings to no one on the audio chat. *Jason? Jase. Jase*. He's gone a really, really long time. He bobs in the water. When he returns from his piss I am once again allowed to breathe.

OR: Shroud is falling apart. 'My eye is twitching guys, I don't know why.' The chat moves so fast you can hardly see it: it's caffeine, the chat says, or you need special blue-lens glasses to play in. Shroud is hardly watching because he is focussing on just *ruining* the brains of the schoolyard of players who have landed around him, so his fans take it into their own hands: donations of $10 or more get read out over the screen by a robotic voice, and they use it to communicate with their god. 'I'm not buying those blue glasses,' he tells one donor. Another message flashes up on screen: you have a magnesium deficiency, it says. You need to buy supplements. Shroud mulls this over while he kills two guys, perfect headshots, boom. 'Yeah,' he says. 'Maybe you're right.' He stares at the screen without blinking for five more hours. What sustains him also kills him.

OR: Shroud, again, mid-game, again, and he's talking about his living arrangement. How he couldn't rent this place – he gestures around him, the immaculate unfurnished flat wall behind him – because he had no credit history. But it turns out the landlord's daughter knew who he was, how he made money, how much of it he banked, so they agreed to let the apartment to him, figuring he wouldn't make much noise anyway. Boom, *pshht*, headshot out of nowhere. 'Well, didn't see that,' he says, reloading the game all over again. Piss, eyes, moms, rent. Heads exploding without warning. Periodic reminders that our gods are still mortal.

#1.

I have to tell you that I am really into watching people play videogames now. I want to be clear about this: I own the means with which to play videogames myself. I have a console and a controller and a TV and games. I can, if I want to, play the videogames. But that is like saying I have a football in my garden, so why do I have to bother watching

Messi. Yes, I can play videogames. I can take back the means of control. But also I am very bad at them, in a way I cannot communicate to you. I can play videogames, but it is actually far better to watch people who are good.

Twitch is a website where you watch other people play games, and I did not understand it until I got Really Into Watching Other People Play Games. The game I am obsessed with watching is *Playerunknown's Battlegrounds*, which Jord and Shroud and JASONR are fantastic at, and I am appallingly bad. *Playerunknown's Battlegrounds*, in short: a 100-man battle royale set across a digital island, where you parachute in and loot empty buildings until you find enough guns and lickspittle armour to mount an attack on your fellow players. The game's active area slowly shrinks – this adds a vital layer of urgency to proceedings, to stop people camping out and games lasting eight to nine hours each – until, after about 35 minutes, the once island-sized game map is crushed into the size of a single field, and it becomes a kill-or-be-killed hellscape. The first time I played it I died within one minute and proclaimed the game to be 'bad' or 'shit' (I forget which). Second time I made it until about three minutes in, before I was cleanly dispatched by an uzi for an overall ranking of around #89. My friend Max then took over, and came #2 overall, after a 40-minute stand-off, a Jeep chase, an exquisite sniper take-out and this one time where he threw a grenade into a room. The final battle saw him and one other fight for supremacy around the edge of a hill, and he was taken out by a single bullet to the side of the head. Here is an impression of me, sat on a computer chair at Max's shoulder, trying not to breathe too loudly and so put him off his aim: '[*Hands held over mouth, breath held, voice coming out strangled and high pitched*] Fuck! Shit shit shit! Fuck!' It was the most exhilarating gaming moment I had ever seen. I mean, Christ man. I live a relatively empty life. It was possibly the most exhilarating *anything* moment I had ever seen. So you see now how instantly I was hooked.

But as we have discussed I am terrible at the game (my simple mind cannot, however way I try, get my head around the W–A–S–D keyboard movement system, and for now *PUBG* is PC-only), so instead I watch Jord play it on Twitch. Or: I watch Shroud on Twitch, because his American time zone means it's easier to watch in the evenings (at weekends, when I want to wake up and watch someone playing videogames who isn't me, I watch American streamers who stay up deliberately late in their time zone to catch the European early morning audience, and they all wear caps and have obnoxious catchphrases, and I universally hate all of them). I watch some guy called JASONR sometimes, and though I don't like him as a *human*, I respect him as a player: all three of them have this preternatural reaction time, a kind of hardwired cold-bloodedness and resistance to panic, unerring accuracy with digital rifles even over long distances, and also this *relentlessness*: they wear their rare losses lightly, so when their heads explode in the middle of a grey-brown field they, instead of wail and gnash with the sting of loss, boot up the game and go again. Essentially: the mindset of highly tuned professional athletes, but in the bodies of slightly awkward nerd teens. Twitch is a curious beast: a YouTube-shaped streaming platform that technically can be used to broadcast anything but is almost exclusively used for showing people playing games, Twitch was bought for $970 million by Amazon in August 2014 and is now worth an estimated $20 billion, with its own subcurrency tipping system – the 'Cheer' – slushing around its network. Fans of streamers can pay $1.40 to buy 100 'Cheers' which they then donate to their favourite gamers through various in-chat messages (the gamer themselves will get around $1 for every 100 cheers – Twitch needs to take its vig) and emoticons: for a sneak peek at the future of capitalism, there is a single emoji that costs $140 to enact. Alternatively, fans can donate directly to streamers – tipping the odd $5, $10 here and there, or subscribing for a fee every month, thank you bro, thanks for the sub, *thank you guys for the donnoe* – with more money going directly to the gamer's coffers. So to reiterate: Twitch is a website where you can *watch someone else play a game* and, if you really want to, *you can pay the person you are watching to let them let you watch them play a game*. At no point in this interaction do you, personally, get to purchase and play the game. You only watch. Some Twitch streamers are multi-millionaires. It has previously been impossible to tap into why.

#2.

I know why, and I and I alone have figured out why. In the adolescence years 13 thru 17 – a four-year long feeling of emptiness and antsiness and crushing, overpowering horniness I am going to nominally refer to as *Wanke's Inferno* – I would go to my friend Matt's house and watch him play videogames. It wouldn't matter what time I would go over there – 2 p.m., 10 p.m., 2 a.m. – Matt would be awake, and playing videogames. This is because Matt was a goth, and goths are always up playing videogames. Also his mum was a nurse who worked nightshifts so his house was always best to scratch at the window if an existential crisis hit at 1 a.m. and you just needed to be out of your house and in the vague presence of some company, which very often happens when your body is pulsating with the dual needs to i. grow, constantly, in every direction and ii. be so horny your head might explode. Everything seems happy and sad at the same time when you are a teen. Psychically it's like putting your head in a washing machine, *for eight years*.

Here's what the back of Matt's head looks like: an at-home dye job is growing out, so at the crown of his head is a digestive biscuit-sized circle of his natural hair colour, somewhere between blond and brown, while the rest of his hair was dyed black (see: goth) with a stripe at the front that was electric blue (also see: goth). The stripe didn't last long, actually – it is hard to maintain an electric blue stripe of hair at the best of times because it requires bleaching the hair and then dyeing over the top of that bleached hair in the colour of your choice, and bright colours wash out quickly, and being a goth on pocket money is the exact polar opposite of the best of times, so after a while the blue fell out and there was just a sort of pale blonde streak remaining. I remember all of this vividly because for an entire summer of my teens I looked fixatedly at the back of Matt's big goth head while he played *Quake 4*, *Unreal Tournament*, and, for some reason, this extended six-week period where we linked a SNES up to an old CRT TV and compulsively played *Dr. Mario* until the sun came up through the trees.

I mention all this because going to a friend's house and watching them play videogames is exceptionally nourishing to teen boys. I mention all this because all those half-conversations I would have with the back of Matt's head while he coldly racked up headshots were some of the best and also least consequential of my life. I would lay on his black bedsheets (goth), play with a skull candle of his (goth), flap at the blackout curtains (goth goth goth), occasionally disassemble an old Warhammer model of his (nerd) or read a comic (nerd) by Jhonen Vasquez (goth), and Matt would still be that, spine curled, hand on the mouse, headshot after headshot, while I unloaded. It was as close to therapy as two teen boys can get: chatting, and chatting, and chatting, every worry and every gripe, every girl we liked and every hope for the future, who we wanted to be, what we feared, how scared we were to grow up: all without a scrap of eye contact, conversation occasionally just falling into a lull, of grunts and occasional laughs, as heads exploded and arms came off in geysers of blood. Occasionally I would fall asleep on a Sonic beanbag on his floor, and have to be wearily stirred awake again at 4, 5 a.m., when I would wander home in my shirtsleeves through the chill. As I grow older, I am more deeply aware than ever that, essentially, a very large part of me has always wanted to retreat back into the nerve-jangling terror womb of adolescence, whether in search of a hard reset, or a time when life was consequence free, or just to be 17 again and actually learn to drive this time. I feel most men, given the option to go back and revisit their teen years with an adult mind, would for some reason jump at the chance. It was a time when your body is lithe and willowy and full of potential, and way less hairy. The most exciting thing that can happen to you is you can distantly see a girl you are in love with – and who is unaware you are alive – at the mall. It is a horrible, terrifying, high adrenaline time to be alive and I miss it with every atom of my body. Watching my friends play videogames emulates that feeling of distorted comfort all over again. Doing so with some Dutch guy called Jord over Twitch allows me to wallow in a black bedsheeted pit of nostalgia from the comfort of my desk at work.

#3.

Twitch taps into a new media landscape that makes absolutely no sense to fucking anyone, but that seems to be the way things are going, and Twitch is only one strange facet of that. Example: I recently had lunch with a friend and he told me about his obsession with Dr. Sandra Lee, or 'Dr. Pimple Popper', a woman with an immaculate bedside manner and a preternatural gift for lancing cysts, who lives both in her doctor's office and also on YouTube. Every video she has ever done goes like this: a floating, eerie mid-zoom of the boil or zit or massive tumour-esque mass she is about to explode, which she prods at with rubber-coated fingers, purring and describing it in a cheerfully clinical tone. Then: then a jump-cut to the boil or whatever swabbed in surgical cloth. And then, using either her fingers or precise metal tools, she slices it open and squeezes out all the yellow gunk inside. It is horrible and fascinating: watching poison ooze out of humans, thick custardy torrents of it, then stitched neatly up and dabbed over with surgical spirit. My friend, a neat freak with OCD, says it taps into his compulsive need for things to be clean, tidied, free of chaos. 'I watch them while I'm eating my breakfast,' he says, the maniac. 'Muesli, yoghurt, zits.'

OR: I found myself in a cab recently having one of those conversations you only seem to have when you're shouting from one end of the car to another, and in it I was explaining the concept of ASMR. ASMR, or 'autonomous sensory meridian response', is this tingling effect some people get in their ears when they hear certain sounds – paper crinkling, soft finger clicking, whispering – something close to synaesthesia. YouTube has thousands of hours of videos dedicated to ASMR triggers, and a small-but-dedicated audience hungry for more, but obviously it's very hard to just whisper for 30 minutes straight, so you find these performances quickly veer into something very weird – they are all recorded at 4am, when outside static noise is at its lowest, and the performers all do these weird drama class ad-libs, talking to themselves through various whispered scenarios. So like: one guy does this bit where he is an extremely rude waiter, talking down to you about a reservation you didn't make uninterrupted for *40 fucking minutes*. Or: there is this one guy, Toni Bomboni, who looks sort of like a *LazyTown* villain come to life, and I once watched a video of him in the scenario of 'a gum store', where he would chew and taste various bubblegums on your behalf to help advise a very serious gum purchase you (the viewer) were going to make, again something that went on, whispered, for like three-quarters of an hour. So I mean go to TV and say, 'Hey: I've got a half-hour video of a lad chewing gum to himself and urgently whispering. You uh … you want that?' and TV will say: no thank you. But the Internet has carved out its own weird niche of anti-media. Some people just like watching people do mad and boring shit.

Some people like to watch skin erupt, or maniacs whispering. I, for example, I can only relax to headshots.

#4.

As best I can tell there are four or five species of Twitchers (I do not know if 'Twitchers' is a word or the accepted term: we are just going to have to assume that it is), which can be categorised as thus:

— Extremely Hyperactive Kid Who You Just Know Got Put Bodily Into Some Lockers At School: these are of course my least favourite Twitchers, because they are boys who fundamentally did not fit in to the intended hierarchy of the world of school or work – they were down at the bottom, punching fodder for jocks and so on, not smart enough to be genuine nerds, not physically dextrous enough to fight anyone off, doomed forever to be henpecked and unhappy – but then who found their niche (streaming videogames to an audience of millions) and so jumped up through their expected social stratas and became as obnoxious as possible in as short a period of time, so they have adopted the sort of bro-y discourse of actual bros, and say things like 'fam' and 'you guys' and 'wuh–POW!' and '[*every single irritating sound effect a human being can make with their mouth*]', and gurn to the camera, and develop their own little catchphrases and routines, and behind them is a plethora of sort of wide-tyre nerd culture ephemera – anime posters, figurines from popular adult cartoons, Monster-branded green neon-lit mini-fridges, extremely complicated gaming chair/gaming headset set-up – and then they act in front of it, and they are extremely annoying, these people, on the surface, but also very much you can see not even very deep within them to see the vulnerabilities and frailties within, and I just know that every single one of them I could make cry with an accurately timed 'your momma' joke, and that's no way to respect another adult, is it—

— Quiet PhD Student Type Who Just Loves Exploding Digital Heads: these ones are my favourite, because they transcend the idea of performative streaming – i.e. the idea that streaming videogames is about anything other than the videogame and the skill they possess at the videogame – that being a personality is secondary, tertiary, to having quick mouse response times and unerring accuracy with a sniper rifle, and these are the guys who take it closest to a sport. There is a narrative, in sport, of showboaters and not: the lads who have hot new hairstyles, and tattoos, and take selfies on Instagram, and still ascend to the very top of the game (in football: Neymar, Beckham, C. Ronaldo), and they infuriate your dad because of it, and then you have those who don't, head-down-and-score-a-lot-of-goals lads (again football: Messi, Shearer, Xavi), who your dad adores. That's the split in sports: that being good at sport – at being one of the five very best people on the planet at kicking a football – but also having ego around that, at being happy to be nearly supernaturally good at something, is somehow profane. In sports, I love these showboaters: when it comes to watching them play shoot-em-ups, they tire me out. Give me a quiet Dutch lad who is killing 40 minutes before he does his homework any day of the week.

— 'The Character'. Some streamers dress in wigs and wraparound shades and eighties-style leather jackets and the like and maintain all these catchphrases and go-to sayings and stuff like that and in one way I very much admire them for developing a character and sticking to it, unbreakably, like a mid-eighties American shock jock, and in another far deeper way I cannot watch even one minute of them playing videogames, holy jesus, I am never in a thousand timelines going to be wired-out on Red Bull enough to find that funny—

— Girl Streamers, who unfortunately have this horribly uphill battle to Prove Themselves To Be Sincere, the gamer boys who are so primed to watch girls in like calf-high socks and pigtails and full-face anime-inspired make-up kill dudes in battle royale settings and do kawaii peace signs to the camera being sort of bait as well as red rags to these dudes, dudes both wanting very much to sexually conquer them – the chat that runs alongside Girl Gamers being, essentially, pornographically explicit – as well as mad at them for liking their safe little male thing, intruding into their world, so Girl Gamers are seen as a sort of strange curiosity in a male-dominated sport (even for male-dominated sports e-sports is a male-dominated sports), but also I find the associated energy that goes after them fundamentally fatiguing, so I cannot watch them for very long, and that is my cross to bear, sorry ladies—

#5, OR: THE AUDIENCE WILL EAT ITSELF EVENTUALLY

Like religion, the audience makes this something bigger than it is. Without a flock, preachers shout to an empty room, and Twitch is similar: streamers have a symbiotic relationship with their audience, they shape them and are shaped by them, a constant feedback loop with a clear hierarchy, gods and believers. The geography of the classic Twitch screen goes a little like this: down to the left-hand bottom of the screen, you have a fixed three-quarter view of your chosen gamers face, blank with concentration: to the right, a chatbox trickles constantly along. In the middle of the screen, prime real estate, is where the bulk of the gaming action happens, and occasionally our mighty overseers will flick their eyes over to the chat – 'What we saying, chat? Where's that sniper at?' – but mostly they are fixed on their jobs, which is to explode people's digital heads. And so there is this sub-economy of attention that goes on: for subscribing to their favourite gamer, fans' names are briefly displayed on-screen, where they often earn a shout-out; by donating five or ten bucks, they can have a message displayed in the middle of the heads-up display, right where their hero is aiming, as close as they can get to god. So here's where you get these weird little one-sided conversations, as followers yell praise to on high: 'Thanks Shroud, you're the best!' they say. Or: 'Hey Shroud: what hair product do you use?' (They want to be him the same way kids want to be Ronaldo, the way men want to smell like David Beckham.) You see how weird humanity can get when left alone for too long in the same room. 'Hey Shroud,' one donor says. 'Noticed your submachine gun shooting rhythm matches the drumbeat to an intro on my favourite anime.' This person is insane. 'That deliberate? :)' Or: you gain insight into who is watching, and where, and why: 'Hey man,' one donor writes. 'Stationed in Afghanistan right now and missing my games. Watching you keeps me going. Rock on.' In many ways, Twitch is a long-distance friendship simulator, the humming sound of male bonding. A big ding, an animation, a series of catchphrases and in-jokes, long developed with a community that is at once guarded and open: someone has donated $3,100. The gamer reels back in his chair. 'Wow,' he says, barely flickering with emotion. 'Hey man, wow. Thank you.' Without the audience, the Twitch streamer is nothing, and they run the gamut from fanatical to removed, but always, there, there is this bubbling economy: in a world where artists struggle to sell honest-to-goodness CDs, and where movies are torrents and books are downloaded, Twitch streamers just sit there and shoot, their own little sub-niche of entertainment, and their fans are breathless to hand them money for it.

#6.

And so obviously, I pay to watch a man shoot. I've been watching Shroud for weeks, the grace of his movements, the way no ounce of motion is wasted, as slick and refined a professional gamer as it is possible to be. I watch highlight reels when he's not online and find myself re-watching explicit kills on my lunch break. One day, I see Shroud, midway through a seven-hour stream, do the most audacious move: he throws a grenade from about 200 yards away then runs into the building just as it tinkles to the ground and explodes, slipping through a concrete bunker window and violently wounding the two players inside, who he finishes off with a single one-two pelt from his shotgun. I literally go into work the next day and describe all this to the IT guys as if we were talking about a football game. There is something hypnotic, about it, something soothing – something that takes me back to the womb of adolescence, sitting in a room silent but for the occasional jagged explosion sound, the pierce shrill of digital screaming, a punching noise run through two cheap portable speakers – takes me back to 15, staring at the back of a head, rapt with it. Twitch, on the surface, very much doesn't make sense – the entire model of it seems wholly unsustainable, like selling one-way tickets into the heart of the sun – and that maybe in five years, or ten, gamers will have to drop their handles, go by their real names, slink into the corporate world of work. Or maybe it's something else: a weird cusp of a mega-economy, one that will create celebrities and gods for generations to come. All I know is, I sign up to connect my Twitch account to my PayPal account. And that I wait for the right time when Shroud is looking at the screen (a lull between two games, when, after a top-three finish that ends with an outta-nowhere sniper kill, he clicks back to the lobby to reflexively find another game). And then I push the button on donating $10. 'Hey Shroud,' I say. 'Thanks for the headshots.' And he turns to the screen and reads my name aloud. And I feel like I have been touched by god.

RIBS

Show me a boy who didn't once between the ages of 13 and 21 try and suck his own dick and I will show you a liar. My method, which I was convinced was the one to finally crack this case, was to lie on my back lengthways against my bed and, raising my back and my legs against it, slowly push my lower half against the solidity of the bed frame, slowly folding myself in half like a dick-sucking sandwich or falafel wrap. I mean obviously this did not work. All it really did was left a perfectly straight purple bruise perpendicular to my spine that didn't go away for weeks. But I think I tapped into something, there, in the grey-dark of my bedroom at night, desperately trying to press my dick down into my mouth: I unlocked a certain spirit of adventure, the same one that pulsated through more heroic men before me, the ones that unlocked pyramids and discovered America. The same yearning to push myself to the very limits to see if I could suck myself off is, in many ways, the same urge that first sent man to the moon.

RIBS

In secondary school my friends and I passed the same tattered biography of Marilyn Manson around between us, because we were all similarly obsessed with the curious black-and-white streak of a man shocking America top-to-bottom at the time. This was around the time Manson released his mainstream-puncturing *Tainted Love*, which feature him in an electric-blue hot tub – one eye milky and blind, long wan body, jet black bob, arms longer and more slender than any non-horror movie human deserves to be, winding those limbs and hooking them beneath the shoulders of the hottest video girl ever committed to film, a girl who was all kohl eyes and double-Ds and who stuck her pink tongue out luridly when Manson touched her, possibly the coolest and most erotic image I had ever seen, then, and probably still have to date – and we longed both to be him and know all about him. And, too, Manson was the recipient of a rumour that passes like a torch down from generation to generation of schoolkids who just discovered cumming for the first time: that he, surgically and at great expense and cost, had four of his ribs removed so he could better suck his own dick.

A part of me misses the innocent version of myself that could believe this rumour. (Prince, purportedly, did the same thing; Cher supposedly had hers removed to have a smaller waist; if you are a lithe pop star, just know that schoolchildren are going to speculate about the length of your ribcage.) Now I know more about human sexuality and the sheer allure of rock stars and/or anyone famous and creative, I know the truth of the matter was: *Marilyn Manson didn't need to suck his own dick because he had so many people willing to suck his dick for him*. Sucking your own dick, conversely, is seen as some great feat of sexual braggadocio, when actually it should be seen as similar to being one of those IT nerds who upgrades his usual hand-job technique to work in a Pocket Pussy®: 'I have given up on convincing another human being to touch my junk,' the Pocket Pussy® owner is saying, 'the touch of this rubber fuck toy is the only joy I will ever know.' A cursory glance at the search string 'do you have to remove your ribs to suck your own dick' paints a bleak, stark truth of the rumour. 'Manson did not get that done,' reddit user zaikanekochan says plainly. 'Grow a bigger dick.'

I was at university the last time I tried it – my method this time was to bob my head down towards my crotch at great pace, like a sudden cobra strike, hoping to catch my body off-guard and accelerate straight from head to dick – but sadly, obviously, it didn't work. I had another realisation, there, stripped to my pants in the grey light of my bedroom, neck cricked down towards my crotch: talk to some girls, maybe, go outside, stop expecting flexibility to somehow secretly develop within you, maybe convince someone else to take this job on. Ribs are there to protect your heart and lungs, obviously, but they also act as a sort of built-in rev limiter: without them, mankind would become a dick-sucking ouroboros, dick to mouth and mouth to dick, and we wouldn't talk to women, or procreate, or do anything, really. If I could suck my own dick I wouldn't be writing this, right now, because I'd be too busy sucking my own dick. In the Bible, Adam gave his rib up to create Eve, and there weren't any explicit passages about her sucking dick but you have to assume it happened at some point. That's the sacrifice, there: God showed us the way before we even knew it. And, I suppose, this is what I've learned about myself: that I'm glad I'm not Marilyn Manson, ribless and pale in the smoked-out back of a 1999-era tour bus. That I'm glad I have so many ribs. And hey: I guess this is growing up.

LIST OF FEARS: A LIST

In no particular order:

1.

Bridges. This one is justified: when I was an early teen I had a sit-bolt-upright-with-the-cold-sweat-dripping-off-you nightmare where – on an old grey concrete bridge that connects Chesterfield town centre proper to the train station nearby, one that runs over an A-road and so is extremely fun to spit over – I was walking along the bridge, in a dream, and then for whatever reason and in a perfect one-two-three motion I put one foot on the kerb of the concrete, grabbed the railing with both hands, jumped off the edge of it and exploded on the road like a melon. In the dream the remaining pulp of me got run over by a truck, one final indignity, and I don't think it's unrelated that ever since then I have been very cautious on bridges. This isn't so bad: I just try my best to walk as close to the exact centre of it as possible, so whatever kamikaze autopilot that spins like a top inside of me at all times doesn't tilt over and override all sense and logic and I just leap forever off the bridge, to death, but it does make me wary. If you can't trust yourself, who can you trust? Who can you *trust*? But yeah: the main takeaway of that nightmare 17 years ago is I'm really very irritating to go for a nice meander along a canal with.

II.

Speaking of nightmares: for some reason the greatest and most frightening nightmare I ever had was when I was five years old and the blood-red velvet curtains that were in my bedroom (apparently I grew up in a fucking haunted Victorian mansion owned by an eccentric doctor and not, like, a normal terrace in a red-brick street in the Midlands?), so yeah the blood-red velvet curtains formed in their wrinkles a face, enormous and frowning, and in a deep voice the velvet face shouted at me for not tidying my room enough and for generally being a Bad Boy. I think it says a lot about my formative neuroticism that the main nightmare I had as a child was not a Frankenstein monster or some vampires but my own curtains telling me off for being naughty, but the result was the same, and that result was: I pissed the bed in fear and woke up screaming. This necessitated a particularly high-stress intervention by my father who had to unhook two heavy velvet curtains from the rings about my bed at 3 a.m. while shouting and surrounded by the ammonia-like smell of fresh piss, plus all the sheets needed changing, and though I'm not saying I'm *scared* of curtains exactly, I would say I am very *careful* around them, because I know now what they are capable of.

III.

Dogs. Listen: I am fully aware that dogs are fundamentally perfect wholesome little animals, essentially human hearts full of love and made dog-sized – just pure heart-meat, dogs, right to the core – and that being afraid of them is ultimately absurd when their primary function is to love and adore. I get this. However, when I was a small meek child at my mother's knee on a rare trip back to London to see the old friends she had left behind there a decade before and introduce them to the grown child that had ruined her life in such a way that she had to leave them to raise it, I was taken to a large grand house where all the adults drank wine and smoked and laughed very loudly, which when you're a small meek child is a high-stress situation anyway, because all you really have is a box of orange juice and you're in the kind of adult house where they have absolutely no prearrangement for children ('Oh you want … something to. Do. Okay: would you like to read this encyclopaedia?'). When I was there, amongst the smoke and the adult cackling, their medium-sized Rottweiler jumped towards me and barked, and I instantly realised that dogs aren't hearts with fur on at all, they are pure prime muscles constantly ready and prepared to jump up vertically and bite you on the dick, and my instinctive reaction to this was to sob – obviously, I thought, the dog was going to gnaw my dick off in one smooth primal bite, and I would have to live a life without it, a sort of modern eunuch, and they would call me Dog Dick Boy – and then everyone had to stop drinking wine and smoking and instead calm the hysterical child down, and in the cab home there was definitely A Silence between my abruptly sober mother and I, and it was pretty clear that me being suddenly afraid of dogs had entirely ruined the evening, and I'm not sure our relationship ever truly recovered from that, really, and I have been cautiously wary of dogs ever since. Cute, yes, but very capable of biting you on the dick.

IV.

Maybe I just have a fear of losing my dick in some sort of dick accident, actually.

V.

Sudden rushes of fear were an oddly common phenomenon of my childhood. As a kid I deeply loved escalators, almost to the point of mania: every time we encountered an escalator, in a store or mall, I would demand to ride it up then down, then beg to go up then down again, a lone passenger on the world's lamest rollercoaster. Then, one time at the big M&S in the centre of town, I sprinted towards the escalator filled with glee that quickly turned to horror: watching as my mother went up the machine ahead of me, I realised suddenly escalators were just stairs made of monstrous metal teeth, ferrying you unrelentingly towards the top of them, where you would be crushed and gnawed to death by the spiked outer workings of the machine, at which point I stopped abruptly, foot hovering over the killer belt beneath me, and started both yelling and crying at the same time, a little like this noise: 'HUAAAAAAAAAH.' I kept sort of yell-crying while my mother floated up away from me, bent backward screaming 'WHAT?' and 'WHAT IS WRONG?', until a kindly woman lifted me up above her head and carried me, gurgling and shouting and crying in one perfect triptych howl, to the top of the stairs, and the rest of the shopping trip passed otherwise without incident. Again: I'm not now afraid of escalators exactly, but I am very cautious.

VI.

(Other things I loved deeply as a child to the bafflement of everyone around me: hub caps, the protective-cum-decorative plastic shields on the wheel rims of cars, which I developed an encyclopaedic knowledge of when I was a kid because I liked cars but couldn't see from my short height any particular part of them other than the wheels, an obsession that led to a point where I would collect discarded hub caps we would come across in the street and I was able to identify vehicle make and models only by their hub caps. Sample conversation from my childhood:

'Hey Dad! Dad! This Volvo has newer hub caps than the one on our street!' and my dad would say, wearily: 'Yes'.) (I have since almost entirely gone off hub caps. They leave me cold.)

VII.

The way other people handle and prepare raw chicken. No judgement – I'm not exactly briefed on the correct code of hygiene around chicken myself – but quite often if I am watching amateur cooking shows I see people do things with raw chicken that strike me as ludicrous or insane, like using a wooden chopping board or rinsing it haphazardly under a tap, and it's made me constantly on guard about how any chicken I have eaten has made itself to me. A useful question I like to ask before any meal I eat: has anything happened in the preparation of this food that might cause me, violently, to shit myself? It's not a healthy way to live but it's the way I choose to.

VIII.

I do fear wardrobes falling onto me and the subsequent coffin-like encasement in them and the obvious analogue for death that comes attached to it, after that time a wardrobe fell on me as a kid and it felt like my end had come. I remember feeling like I had died, but also very much feeling quite calm about that, but it's made me afraid of precariously balanced wardrobes since, and I think that's fair: I suppose we are, all of us, constantly shaped and smoothed by the fears we accrue as we age. A lot of our fears are completely justifiable, and as a result we hold them close around us, like rosaries.

IX.

One very specific fear I have is that a number of television personalities who I have spent a lot of my time detesting because of small perceived micro-aggressions against me – the guy from the GoCompare adverts, for example, or Jamie Oliver – are actually incredibly sound in real life and I would get on with them really well, and an ongoing fear fantasy is that I meet Jamie Oliver one day and he's really nice to me – 'Cor,' he says, with that big tongue of his, 'yeah you're really sound – let me get you a pint!' – and not only do I have to sit through the drink with him but I also have to admit, privately, to my biggest critic (myself) that I was wrong all along, and that Jamie Oliver is sound as fuck. I think that's me projecting a fear, actually: I'm not afraid of Jamie Oliver being sound, am I? That's simply impossible. I am afraid of being fundamentally, deeply wrong. I am afraid of the embarrassment that comes with backing down on an opinion I have that is only important to me.

X.

At the time of writing (Oct., 2k17) I am in the midst of a break-up, and while largely that is good, I suppose one enduring fear is the main one that comes with break-ups, i.e. the fear not that a person you shared tender words and embarrassing little nicknames and fragile plans for the future with now keeps texting you to call you a 'dick' or 'dickhead', but that the break-up – the final, actual act of breaking the bond of the relationship you are in – has now actually severed and deleted various alternative timeline futures for you, and the one you are left in is the one where you never know happiness again. So for example: one alt-universe timeline that has shot off into the infinite void was the one where you were happy and became married and had two perfect little cherub-faced children, and you spent your weekends barbecuing and doing maths homework with a toddler that looked like you both. Or: so for example the future where you both grew old and gnarled and knew each other perfectly because you had over the years hewn gaps out of each other that only the other could fit in, one bulbous old ying and one haggard old yang, so that in this (now deleted, forever) future you could communicate with each other without even words, just with gentle looks and hand touches and knowing nods, and you would die together, ancient hand in ancient hand, watching the gauzy sun set beyond you, rocking back and forth gently in armchairs on a porch. The fact is that there are now a hundred thousand timelines gone – holidays you had, drinks you enjoyed, expensive meals and cheap ones too, Christmases you will no longer have, birthdays that go uncelebrated, dogs and cats that lived entire wholesome lives within your joint care – because you basically had one argument over Netflix that got a bit out of hand. It is just you, now, alone as alone can be, that all future companionship has been deleted forever, from this point in your life onwards – so yes going off-piste a little but that prospect seems like a low-hum kind of constant soaring fear—

XI.

I mean not to be too drastic but I am 30, now, that age where friends around you suddenly morph and change from the young adults you thought you knew into sort of sincere and responsible, like, people, and some have bought houses and some have had weddings and some, even, have grown ripe like an apple and birthed a baby, an actual baby, an actual *child*, and named it something beautiful and interesting and unique, and now every time you try and see them now they are like 'yes well but: *but my child*' or 'yes I suppose Tuesday at 7.30 on the absolute dot could do it, although I shall have to leave again at around 9 p.m., to feed as aforementioned my child', and sometimes they hand you it, the child, and expect you to know how to hold it (I don't!), and then they talk to you about child things – the child has teeth now, it can hold up its heavy torso, it grunts and makes noises. And you ask: how can you do it? How do you hold a child? And they explain: sometimes, they say, at night, when they feel at their absolute lowest – it is a full-time job, they say, on top of another full-time job, and then so of course we also need to fit that in with our actual, they say, full-time job

– and they say that in the depths of these despairs, all those nights of staccato sleep, all those months without sex or friendship, all those pills and injections and doctors' appointments and nappies and schedules and sometimes, the child, the child will just *piss* on you – in amongst all that one time there will be some moment of marvel, often at 2 a.m., they say, where the child is taking feed, and it is a quiet moment, just you and the child and a small sterile bottle of milk, both of you just cooing in the lamp glow (the lamp is a special child-friendly lamp, soft orange light, you cannot expose a child to a normal lamp, the lamp cost £49) and for a moment the child will look at you, up at you, and it will realise that it is you, who they are, that you are they and they are you, and you are the caregiver and the lifegiver too, and there will be this pure perfect moment of recognition, and the child will giggle, a little, and at once every hard edge in you erodes, and every moment you doubted who you were has gone, and you know, now, what it is you were put on earth to do, it is to raise this child, make it strong and wise and give it every opportunity, and love it so hard you grow to love yourself too, and they turn to you (you in this scenario being me), and they say, like, *so when are you going to have one?*, they say, *any lucky ladies on the horizon?*, and you have to admit that you ran out of Super Likes on Tinder this week so you haven't spoken to a human woman in six entire days, and no it's not going very well actually, life, though I don't really want to talk about it—

XII.

You know like will I ever find someone to take on half the burden of my very specific mania, that sort of thing—

XIII.

Rats, mice, hamsters, gerbils, or essentially any small animal that it could be said 'scurries'—

XIV.

Actually perhaps I fear the uneasy motion of scurrying – all those arms, those legs, whirring away, hands meet feet meet hands meet feet – than the actual animals themselves, though rat tails I'm not particularly a fan of either, those long rancid worms—

XV.

I read once that every muscle in your body has the potential energy to break the connecting bone it rests on – every muscle is primed with absolute strength, or something, and the only thing stopping that muscle clenching the bone within it to dust is your own brain – and that made me not just worried of every time I cramp up or over-clench a thigh muscle while stretching at the gym (although I am, deeply, afraid of that: how embarrassing would that be? To concurrently break every bone in my body while trying to plank at Fitness First? All the musclebound weightlifters around me wondering why I start screaming and collapsing at the same time? I just go down like someone deflating a sex doll? Nobody calls for help?) but also made me very aware that my body is essentially a high security prison that contains my brain and skeleton, and one fuck-up from me – if my brain malfunctions or I get too scared and just clench my entire body too hard – and I will kill myself, instantly, my legs, arms and ribs all clicking in two like twigs—

XVI.

Consider major surgery for a moment. Major surgery is this: medicine puts you into a deep and painless sleep that allows doctors in masks to open your body up with *knives*. Are you *kidding me*. At this point, I don't even fear major surgery, I fear any illness or accident that might lead to me having major surgery, because I know already I'm going to have to explain in a plain and unwavering voice to whatever doctor offering to peel my body open and fix the mess inside of it that no, actually, at this point I think it's going to be a lot easier for me to just die, rather than this, thanks very much for the offer though I appreciate it, but the entire concept of what you are offering to do to me – ostensibly for my wider health! – fills me with such an overwhelming dread that I literally consider death a smoother and more hassle-free option—

XVII.

You open your eyes in the shower and there is a figure in there in the bathroom, with you, either standing in the shower or just standing in the room, reflected gauzily in the steamy mirror, and they are cloaked, the figure, and holding a knife of some sort – either a to-the-point sort of hunting blade or instead a curved hook or scythe, and they raise it, and for a brief second you wonder which part of your soft naked flesh they are going to slice into first – and sometimes that is a fear, irrational as it is, one that has me with my eyes tightly wound while I shower, afraid to open them and see, as if the figure there is lurking and waiting for me to recognise them before slashing my throat open, to death, that is a fear, I suppose—

XVIII.

That one day my bank will phone me and in a stern voice tell me exactly how many consecutive days I have been in my overdraft.

ADULT SIZE LARGE

I recently lost three-and-a-half stone, 22 kilos, and in doing so went from an Adult Size Large down to an Adult Size Large. This pissed me off enormously: fat melted from the wattle around my neck, my torso leaned out and became slender, my entire waist melted down through two (two!) entire jeans sizes, and my top half inexplicably remained the exact same dimensions according to the t-shirts I was buying in every single store on earth. Reader: what the living fuck.

My friend Sam is an Adult Size Large, and yet he is at least 60% more lean than I am through the torso, perfectly proportioned limbs and body, BMI so immaculate it could be holy, perfect example of health and beauty, capable easily of fitting into anything down to a size S and up to an XL. He is essentially a shop mannequin model with kind human eyes. He wears the same size t-shirt as I do, and I feel like I am staring at a blackboard full of calculations that lead to an equals sign followed by a question mark. Here is my central thesis: how is this man the same size as me according to our tee? I am like twice as wide as him, torso-to-torso. It makes no sense.

Or, so: my sister came to me recently. My sister, like yours, has got into exercise lately. Everyone's sister eventually gets to this stage. Everyone has a healthy sister. Perhaps your sister is a brother, or an aunt. It does not matter: they are running a half-marathon this autumn and want your support. My sister, like yours, got into triathlons, then just cycling and swimming, and now just swimming. She went insane at a running store and bought a load of unused all-black exercise wear. Would I like it, she says, to sit around the house motionless and typing. 'It is Adult Size Large,' she says, and offers me the pile. There is some good stuff in here, man. Nike and et cetera. I take the running gear, which fits me like a glove.

One night I came home drunk off the back of an exceptional Arsenal win and found my then-girlfriend like a tiny long-limbed creature in my bed. 'Put this Arsenal shirt on,' I said, staggering into my wardrobe. 'You know I have lingerie,' she said. 'Like: loads of lingerie. You never get me to wear it.' It does not matter what lingerie you have: the single sexiest thing a naked woman can put on is i. a man's work shirt, with the half smell of the day still on it, rendered flower-like and fragile by soft moisturised skin and the everlasting dint of breasts, ii. an Arsenal football shirt with 'ARSHAVIN 23' across the back, Adult Size Large.

I do not understand this. If you are on a bus or a train

look around you. Many, many people wear clothes the wrong size for them. Men's jeans are fantastic for this, because they have the exact size of them printed on a visible label on the back of them: I recently saw a man rocking 36-inch waist jeans with an (at a guess) 30-inch waist proper, so he had to cinch his belt blood-stoppingly tight around him so the jeans would fit properly. But on top: Adult Size Large. Or: men buy jeans that balloon out from the calves and somehow envelope their entire shoes. Men wear jeans, but do not understand them. They buy coats they can get their arms in, no more thought goes into it than that. And they all buy Adult Size Large, and they fit into them, and unless they are particularly unbroad or bird-chested it fits them more or less fine.

And I am screaming at the night sky, now, outside, so my breath turns to fog on the cold of it: if we are all Adult Size Large, then why do we have so many differences? I feel that somewhere in the grey unknowable magic of this size there's something approaching peace: Adult Size Large transcends race, and sex, and gender, and age and height and weight. Adult Size Large is the t-shirt that more or less fits everyone. Can we not come together and appreciate that? Put down your guns, brothers. Unprime your bombs. Deep down, we are all the same. Come, unite with me, in the fields of peace. There is no need to fight anymore. We all have more or less the same-sized torso. I don't understand how but let's try and work it out.

24 STORIES FROM THE MIDDLE OF THE DESERT

I'm staring at a poster in the camel museum. At the centre of the poster: a large, cartoon impression of a camel. Out from the camel, in little squiggling offshoots, photos of camels pulling various different-but-extremely-similar camel faces. Gaze into the eyes of a camel and you will see nothing but glassy tranquillity staring back. Gaze into the eyes of a camel and it will calmly blink and chew cud. But no, this poster says. Camels contain multitudes. 'APPEAL OF CAMEL PERSONALITY,' it reads. 'Family Bond', 'Sensitive', 'Loyal', 'Smart', 'Defending'. The next attribute is portmanteaued into one with a backslash: 'Bossy/Leaders'. And there, hovering up around the original cartoon camel's ear area, a single word, in rigid black: 'Fear'.

Everything is camels and camels are everything, here at … the King Abdulaziz Camel Festival, Saudi Arabia!

* * *

CALL: Why were you at a camel festival in Saudi Arabia?

RESPONSE: Because it was there, and when something is there, it is human nature to go and look at it.

CALL: What is a camel festival like? What is a camel festival?

RESPONSE: I don't know exactly because the camel festival I went to started being constructed in March 2017, i.e. six weeks exactly before I arrived in Saudi Arabia to come and look at it, so necessarily was entirely incomplete, and actually on balance I saw far fewer camels than you might have expected me to, on the whole, seeing as I flew all the way to Saudi Arabia to go and see camels,

CALL: What actually was it then?

RESPONSE: It was basically just a big car park with a load of camels in it. I flew seven hours and drove two. That's what it was. It was a car park full of camels, in Saudi Arabia.

CALL: Would you highly recommend the camel festival as a fun continental tourist retreat?

RESPONSE: No I wouldn't go so far as to say the word 'highly', no.

* * *

So I am in a tent, later now, trying to understand the appeal of camels. At my feet: a discarded tray-plate of grilled chicken, Gulf Sea prawns, rice, fruit, *om ali*, a pudding that is essentially cornflakes soaked in milk and warmed up with some cashews in it; to my right, a small cushion-plinth on which is resting two (two.) disposable paper cups of Arabian coffee and a larger plastic cup of sweet chai. The sun is blurrily setting and the sky turns dark from blue. There is a boy whose job in the tent is seemingly to bring me tea and coffee whenever I hold up a hand to say 'tea' or 'coffee'. When he is not bringing me tea and coffee he just stands on the balls of his feet, staring covertly at the TV. There is something unusual about seeing a huge, clean-new HD TV plugged into a tent: in amongst rugs lining walls to deflect the searing heat of the sun, one perfect clear window, a slash of tech amongst the sand. On the television is an old BBC Two show where modern-day families live life for a day as either a slave or a lord in a *Downton Abbey*-style home, dubbed in Arabic. Earlier: a British nature documentary, where for some reason the monkeys in it were dubbed to have voices, and somehow, despite speaking Arabic, here, the monkeys have British accents. The refreshments boy brings me some more chai. I have been in the sun for ten hours and I am delirious. The monkeys are British and the camels are beautiful.

'It's like,' the translator, Ali, is telling me. 'It's like … young men, you know? To show off they have some money … it's like: a camel.'

I say: 'Right.'

'So it's like … horses. Or: falcons. You have falcons?'

'No we do not.'

He is incredulous.

'You don't have *falcons*?'

'We don't have falcons.'

'Ahhhh: that's why you liked the falcons.'

Earlier we saw some falcons and yeah, alright, I'll be honest: I lost my shit about the falcons. I liked the falcons.

'Huh.'

For a moment we both pause in the heavy, heavy heat, trying to think of a British equivalent to camels that aren't horses or falcons. 'I guess,' I say, and I am thinking of Instagram, and how the people I follow who are in a good place in their life use it, and what they show off about, and how they might mark the occasion of their good fortune and express it through ownership of an animal. 'I guess ... dogs? Pedigree dogs? Like a bulldog?'

Ali thinks for a moment, strokes his beard.

'Yeah I mean I guess,' he says. 'Yeah. I suppose.'

But no. What I am learning is in Arabia, camel-liking is some curious mix of football fandom, Crufts, *Max Power* masculinity and hump acknowledgement. That camels aren't like dogs, or horses, or falcons. What I am learning out here, in the heat and the sand and the flies and the dates, what I'm learning is this: there is nothing. There is nothing Quite Like A Camel.

* * *

There are two types of camels in Saudi Arabia, black camels and white camels. It is, if you go deeper, more nuanced than that (there is an oft-repeated never-fact-checked eskimos-and-snow type factoid about camels – 'In Arabic,' people say, 'they have over 1,000 words for camel!' which no, they don't, but it's certainly true that there are up to 40 types and sub-types of camel, and there are words for that, same way we have words like 'pug' and 'Labrador', but in Saudi Arabia they don't go around yelling, 'The British people! Those lardy fools. Those pastry pigs have over a million-and-a-half words for dogs!'), but for now – knowing in advance the onslaught of camel information I am about to hit you with – it is easier if we just divide into the black camel from the south (*majaheem*) and the white camel from the north (*maghateer*).

Camels have two stomachs. Camels walk like this: right front leg and right back leg, then left front leg and left back leg. Get on all fours and try and do that now. You can't. No other animal on earth walks like a camel. Camels: camels can consume 30 gallons of water in 13 minutes, then not drink again for several weeks. When camels exhale, their nostrils are designed to capture tiny droplets of moisture from their breath and recycle in back into their bodies. There are 1.7 million camels in Saudi Arabia, so 3.4 million stomachs. There are 7.1 million camels in Somalia. Camel hair can be weaved into a rough fabric that is useful for making rugs and desert tents out of. Camel meat can be consumed. Camel milk is thick, frothy, and warm from the teat. Look into a gawping camel mouth if you want to see a brief glimmer of hell. Camel feet are just two fat toes with hard nails and a thick wad of skin like a shoe beneath it. Camels are designed to experience extreme heat variations – both hot and cold, as the day turns into the cool night – and are barely ever sweaty. A camel can spit enough in one go to entirely cover the top half of you – you, a puny human in a t-shirt – the entire top half of you and your body. This is all by way of saying that camels are freaks, basically, absolutely irregular cunts, and not as you thought before just lumpy horses, and that, in a way, is why they are celebrated and revered, and that is why I am in Saudi Arabia to look at them.

The King Abdulaziz Camel Festival takes place 140 km north-east of Riyadh, and is known colloquially as the 'Miss Camel' beauty pageant. This isn't exactly true: the camels paraded here are judged on a variety of factors, which we will get into, which all together can be added together to make some vague approximation of 'beauty', but calling it 'Miss Camel' suggests camels in thick rouge and red lipstick, stiltedly walking on stilettos, turning on the spot at the end of a catwalk and shuffling back behind a glittering curtain while a Donald Trump type, half-hard and glimmering beneath the stage lights, whoops and hollers in horny delight. But instead it's just a racetrack in the middle of the desert (there is literally one stand; the rest of the track opens out into an expanse of nothing, as deep as the sea) with a load of camels racing in a pack over it, *chunter–chunter–chunter*, and four men with clipboards nod at them appreciatively. You know when you go to a party and it's just, like, popping? Something intangible and electric in the air. An unsynthesised form of excitement you can't emulate or explain. A *vibe*. So, right, you know that feeling? Now imagine the exact opposite of it. With camels.

It's like this where, for three small hours in the morning, camels rove forwards and back, while a sort-of-full but-not-actually-very-full set of newly erected bleachers rumbles with the stomping of a few hundred men in thobes. I am allowed onto the track for a bit to take photos – camel herders with plastic neon sticks gallop to the front, making high *ya–ya–ya–ya!* whistling sounds as the camel pack moves calmly behind them, parading in front of a handful of distant judges, sweeping past them once, twice, three times maybe, then hurdling off into the distance, all while a crowd of a few hundred men hold their hands up to their eyes to squint and watch them in silence. And that's it. 11 a.m. and it's done. Everyone files out to the camel festival village, to look at pictures of camels instead of actual ones. Some people just file back on a coach and go home. That's it. That's the camel festival. Also this goes on for six weeks. What is anyone getting from this?

* * *

So early morning at this camel festival, that's when the actual camel festivalling happens. This is before the sun comes up and sears the ground beneath it: though camels can cope in extremes of heat and dryness, humans can't, so if you want to watch some camels on parade, you take an early breakfast and get out there between 9 a.m. and 11. The thing is, I'm still getting my head around the logistics of this: as a guest of the camel festival, I'm sleeping here at what's known as a barracks, a sort of grim grey prefabricated building a short drive from the central camel village. The rest of the King Abdulaziz camel festival stretches off around me: a small central hub, the aforementioned village, a tarmacked space that can be walked from one end to the other in about three minutes flat, home to a bustling trinket market, a camel museum, an observatory (???). Then, up beyond that, you have the parade grounds: an arching racecourse-type structure, with a grey-white stand and spaced railings that lead out into the desert, where paddocks await the prizest camels; and then ... and then I mean there is just a massive, *massive*, Disneyland-sized car park, which is almost entirely empty. And that's *it*.

So what I don't understand is this: did this crowd of camel-liking men, here at 8 a.m. in the morning, did they drive here from Riyadh today? Did they get in a Jeep or on a coach at six actual a.m. and drive here to look at camels today? Or did they sleep here, in tents and barracks unseen, and wake up still quite early to whoop and cheer at camels? And where did they go again after they had looked? A few piled on to a coach, I saw them. A few milled around the village section before the heat of the sun made being outside unbearable for more than a few minutes. Who. Has. Come. Here. To. Look. At. The. Camels. Apart. From. Me.

Where. Are. They. Going.

Where. Are. They. From.

Does. Anyone. Actually. Like. Camels. That. Fucking. Much.

* * *

'Yeah so I've been learning about camels. I've only seen, like, six camels though. I saw the camel museum, I saw some facilities at the village. I drank some camel milk. But I didn't see a whole lot of camels. So I'm trying to understand the appeal, and I think I'm getting there, but I want to see some actual camels tomorrow. Are you into camels?'

'No.'

'Okay.'

/ INTERVIEW ENDS

* * *

Saudi Arabia is banking on people liking camels that much. Not just the Saudi people, though it is for them – 'Tradition,' a financial officer tells me, 'it's not just for foreign people, it's for us. The younger generation. We don't care about those kinds of things. Others, they, you know, they're city guys, they don't care about camels. If you forget your past then you don't have one.' – but also a hub for camel-liking nations that surround Saudi – Sudan, Egypt, Yemen, UAE, Bahrain, Iraq – to come and gaze. The King Abdulaziz is part of Saudi's 'Vision 2030' project, a sort of country-wide civil service-led scheme to start the engine of tourism in the country by pouring gallons and gallons of petrol into the tank of it (money. In this analogy that means 'money') and yank wildly at the rip cord, hoping some errant spark will judder the whole thing to life.

They probably need to sort the visa thing out before that becomes a reality, though. Traditionally, entry to Saudi Arabia has been a case of getting on an aeroplane and riding it through a series of loopholes: a visa is required for every visitor, non-native female travellers must be met by a sponsor at the airport, anyone who has ever been to Israel before is going to have a really rough time at the airport, &c. &c. &c. Theory dictates that these notoriously strict guidelines have been loosened recently, to reflect the friendly new face of Saudi Arabia, but in reality nobody at the airport seems to have ever seen a visa confirmation message in their life and seem intent on holding me – tired and crumpled from a seven-hour flight, body melting in that way bodies only melt when you take them from the skin-tightening air-conditioning of an aircraft cabin and put them in the pregnant dry heat of an Arab country at night – and long story short I have to wait for two hours on a sterile hospital waiting room-style seat while three lads in a back office hold on to my passport, occasionally scrolling through WhatsApp on one iPhone before dipping into a pocket to retrieve another, slightly more cracked iPhone, then scrolling through WhatsApp on that, and then deciding finally I can leave and begrudgingly stamp the paperwork – *that was there on the desk next to them all along* – to allow me to do that. It is five o'clock in the morning and my taxi glides across new tarmac like it is ice, and the sunrise here is gorgeous, inky blue night ceding to orange, hazy day, like someone took a big thumb and smudged the two colours together, and the air is crisp and cool before the day has started enough to heat it. Sunrise here is astounding: it makes you pensive, reflective, sad and quiet. It makes you want to take every visa worker in the airport and bury them where they'll never find them, out there in the sand.

* * *

At breakfast a man tells me he used to live in London, for several years, although can't remember where. 'Somewhere west,' he says. I ask him if it was Shepherd's Bush. It wasn't. I am out of ideas. It's hard to elegantly move away from someone in a Bedouin tent – you are both sat on the floor, so you have to creak up into a standing position then move all the way over to the other side of what is the same tent, so I just don't – so we sit in silence for a while, both looking in opposite directions, quietly eating fruit. Later – hours later, as I am stood on the sand photographing hundreds of camels – he stalks up behind me and yells 'EALING!' at my shoulder, and now we are friends forever.

Here's what my mate says about camels:

A GOOD CAMEL, AS PER A LAD WHO USED TO LIVE IN EALING FOR A BIT BUT NOW LIVES BACK IN SAUDI ARABIA, WHERE CAMELS ARE

— Small ears (ideally ones that point sort of up, though pointing back had been mooted as beautiful as well);
— Shapely neck w/ low dip;
— Hump is a smooth shape but goes sort of 'back'???? Not sure very hard to describe;
— Big lips;
— Docile demeanour.

Do you have a camel, I ask. Yes, he says, one. He keeps it in the desert, at some stables. He hasn't seen it for a few weeks since he's been working here. He pauses. 'Being around a camel …' and he grapples in the air for a bit, searching for the word. 'It's just nice.'

* * *

Things you will see discarded in the desert on the drive from Riyadh to the camel festival, a list: single grey-black tyres, warped and worn in the heat of the sun; pairs of shoes, quite often, for some reason; an entire pushed-over barrel of oil, a small slick puddle of purest jet black against the sizzling orange of the desert sand; that's it.

* * *

'What kind of camels do you like?'

'I don't understand the question.'

'What camels do you like? What kind of camels do you like?'

'Like black ones? White ones?'

'Yeah.'

'I kind of prefer the black ones. They are handsome and shiny like a good horse is.'

[*Laughing, for some reason*]

'Maybe that means you are an angry person. The black camel is the angry camel.'

I have just had my fortune read by my camel preference.

'The white camel is the lovely camel.'

'Okay.'

* * *

I'm sharing the drive with a journalist from Dubai who has covered camels and camel festivals every conceivable way in the past ten years and speaks fluent Arabic and is speaking it, very rapidly for two straight hours, in the car ride over there, and who is completely bored of camels by now, oh my god. 'Ugh,' she says. 'Camels, camels, camels. My boss wants an angle beyond "This Camel Sold for $1 Million!", but ...' – she gestures at a camel. 'You know.' What is this whole camel thing about, then, I ask her. 'Money,' she purrs.

* * *

This spot in the middle of the desert was chosen for its historical significance: it's a sort of perfect meeting point between the north, west, east and south of the country (the south, known by the quietly horrifying nickname 'The Empty Quarter', which just really sounds like there are lots of haunted skeletons, half-eroded into the sand, that live there, guarding crowns and lavish old jewels), so was traditionally a useful point of trade. That doesn't quite explain why there is nothing here, nothing surrounding here, no trace of life before this, just desert, in every direction, newly criss-crossed with slivers of tarmac and this camel village, but I'm rolling with it. Here is where new tradition crashes into the old: save for a few baby camels who were whizzed in folded in the back of a Toyota pick-up, most of the 30,000 animals on display here walked to the venue over a period of a few weeks. There were fears, years ago, that camels would start to die out in the Gulf, replaced in terms of practicality by SUVs and cars – that, without the need for the ships of the desert, camels would fade away, and with it an irretrievable facet of the country's tradition, but instead it sort of boomed in a hobbyist way nobody could have predicted – and now, if nothing else, the festival proves animal and machine can still live together, out here, in the sand.

* * *

I'm hanging out in the media tent trying to find WiFi (there is no WiFi) (obviously there is no WiFi; I am in a fucking *desert*) when a softly spoken man comes over to me to quietly tell me that sorry, he doesn't speak English. 'That's okay,' I say, loudly. 'Thank you.' He offers me Arabian coffee from the Arabian coffee table. 'No,' I say. 'Thank you, though.' The man who cannot speak English says, slowly:

'You smile. Like ... a British footballer.'

Thanks!

* * *

The first camel I see is an extremely sick small three-day old baby that seems an awful lot – an *awful* lot – as if it is dying, lying weak and prone under a small flap of cardboard while its owner lifts and rubs his head, makes little *kth–kth–kth* noises into its ear, flopping it back down again, its neck lolling sickeningly in the heat. The journalist who knows how to speak Arabic bends and talks to him: 'My friend is a vet,' she says, calling on speakerphone. 'He can help.' She yells into the phone for what seems like ages before a harsh, digital voice rings back. 'Acupuncture,' she says, to the camel owner. 'He needs acupuncture.' Everyone seems chill about the dying camel. The camel guy picks him up and flops him down again. I am telling you this camel is fucked. Acupuncture cannot help it.

* * *

Now we're in a tent drinking camel milk. Camel milk, in review: it is just milk but it's warm because it just came out of a titty and also it froths up like crazy. I didn't not like it. It was milk. Whatever. Drink the milk, enjoy the milk. There is always something holy about milk. It is the liquid of life. A body can produce a nourishing meal. It makes babies thrive. Milk is magical. Later, in the Bedouin tent, a man who understands more English than he can speak asks me if I drank the milk. Yes, I say. Very nice. He erupts with laughter, as do all the other tent lads, filed around the edges of the rug, the room shaking. I am lost in a sea of foreign giggles. Ali, the translator, helps:

'Because it— it makes you have a reaction.' He gestures his stomach. 'Some people.' It makes you shit? 'Yes.' But I didn't shit, I tell them. I am wearing tan-coloured trousers. If I had a very urgent camel shit you would know about it. I didn't shit myself! Ali does not translate this. 'Eh, it's only some people.' Tell them I didn't shit! 'It's like, ten per cent of people.' I turn to them, shake my head and gesture my stomach, scissoring my palms in front of it. I didn't shit! I didn't shit! There is no explaining this. They definitely think I did shit.

I just do not understand why you would give someone shit-yourself juice, in welcoming them to your country. That's all.

* * *

Here is a camel-parade fact that I cannot fit in anywhere else: sometimes, in amongst the parade camels, replete in festive decorative dress and being ridden by a guy with a neon cane yelling *ya–ya–ya–yai!*, there is a Toyota with a baby camel folded up in the back of the pick-up section, driving past. 'Why?' I ask. 'Why?' And it is because the baby camel's mother, who is on parade, cannot bear to be more than a few yards away from her child, so they have to drive the baby near her, sort of like dangling a treat to a cat. And that is my camel fact.

* * *

ALLEGED PROPERTIES OF CAMEL MILK: A LIST

— Good for calming the stomach;
— Good for the immune system;
— Also good for diarrhoea;
— Makes foreigners shit themselves near instantly;
— Anecdotal evidence suggests a sort of half-Viagra dick effect as well;
— Low sugar.

* * *

MORAL QUANDARY

Say you have a camel and it's really fucking pretty – good hump, small ears, big eyes, beautiful coat – but its lips suck ass. That is its one flaw. Like: this is a really, really pretty camel. But it's got those thin little I'd-like-to-speak-to-the-manager lips. Got nothing going on in the lip department. It is, for all intents and purposes, lipless. Just lip skin and nothing in between. The lips are AWOL. You know you are entering a camel contest where lip size is a measurement of beauty. But what you got here is just this entirely lipless beast. You cannot win without lips. What do.

SOLUTION

You are Kris Jenner and the camel is your beautiful daughter and you inject it in the lips with silicone. I am serious about this: the King Abdulaziz festival is forced to take a hard line on doping, which includes lip fillers for camels. In future festivals they have plans for a purely anti-doping judging committee. Says Dr Fahd Abdulla Al-Semari, festival organiser, all-round go-to camel don: 'The point is this, like a sport, you have people who mess up the camels. They use silicone, they cheat. We spotted three cases, so they were removed. It's very delicate: we now have a special committee to formulate a system on how to prevent these things. Like what happens in some sports where men use drugs, like in the Tour de France, or swimming. So we are serious about this now, it's a concern for us. So we created a special team.' Your lipless camel is Lance Armstrong. Your lipless camel is Yulia Efimova. Nothing Is Pure In This World, Not Even Camels.

* * *

Nobody can get my name right, a rare novelty, so I'm asked what my surname is in case it's easier for them to pronounce. 'Golby,' I say, and the group lights up. *'Gol–bee, gol–bee,'* a young guy who works for the festival says, pointing to his chest. 'It means "my heart" in Arabic,' someone whispers. So that is what they call me for the next two days: *my heart*.

* * *

Like Dubai, Saudi has no scent, and is entirely under construction but studded with great wealth, the way you imagine New York would be one year to the day after an *Avengers*-style alien attack. In Arabia they drive how you want to drive, if you weren't curtailed by pesky traffic laws: they overlap and weave like a closely contested Mario Kart race; they straddle lanes and drift aimlessly between them. Wing mirrors are a notion. Right: you know that chase scene, in *Matrix: Reloaded*, that goes for like 15 minutes and was, for a time, the most expensive car chase ever filmed? That. That is how everyone drives in Saudi Arabia.

* * *

Bedouin culture is something I can get behind. Basically, at the end of every day – or, actually, quite often during the day, when it gets too hot or you straight can't be arsed with it then you sit with a flask of sweet chai and a golden urn of dates and work your way methodically through both of them – everyone gathers in these tents, extravagantly rugged arrangements in a simple boxy shape, small low cushions lining the walls with a central space in the centre, the low cushions studded by larger, squarer ones that work like tables, and you just sit and eat and the TV is going and you chat shit. I don't chat shit, obviously; whenever someone enters the tent, kicking their shoes off at the door, they hold up a solemn hand and say 'salaam alaikum' – 'what up, dudes' essentially – and everyone parrots it back apart from me because no matter how slowly and how many times I am taught how to say it I just cannot seem to contort my mouth and prime my brain to say *sa-laam a-lai-koom*. But everyone else seems to be having a very fun time, chatting shit, telling long, winding dad jokes, everyone laughing. Someone does an impression of an engine that for me goes on far too long but everyone seems to love. Bedouin.

The guy half-slumped next to me leans over and explains that he is sorry, he doesn't speak English, he wishes he could. It is fine, I say, please don't apologise, it's not like I speak Arabic, come on. But then he takes his phone out and shows me an app on it: if we both speak, slowly, into the microphone, the app will take our words and translate them, and we can have a rough conversation. Big up the future, because this app rules:

how old are you
29
what is your country
england
are you married
you sound like my girlfriend

And the Saudi lads are loving it, loving it, banter is the universal language, there is no doubt about that—

And he asks me how I like Saudi Arabia so far and yes, good, but also I am still annoyed about being held at the airport that one time so I explain through the translator about the visa, the two-hour wait, *the fact that the same guy who just stamped my visa went and very slowly checked my passport at airport security some ten yards away, like my dude have you not seen enough of my passport yet*, and they are all rolling their eyes and groaning sympathetically as if to say 'right?', as if to say, 'visas'.

I am assured, though, that I am actually relatively lucky, and I am one of the recipients of the new, cuddly-faced vision of the border – up until only a year ago, things were tighter around here, with the religious police (or Hayaa) in full force: they were able to break up same-sex pairings if they didn't like the look of them, publicly shave men's heads if they deemed their haircut too inappropriate. In 2012, Hayaa members were accused of causing death by dangerous driving after chasing a vehicle that was playing loud music; their powers were finally stripped after a viral incident last February where a woman was assaulted outside a Riyadh mall. Even here at the camel festival, you're aware of the quiet, watching hands of enforcement: to enter the festival proper you need to drive through various armed checkpoints; we later cruise past an endless run of barracks that, I'm told, are home to the 1,000 security, police and firemen here to keep the festival in order. There are 30,000 camels here, 1,300 owners. An audience of 400,000 visitors spread over

42 festival days. About one armed guard per 9.5 visitors per day. It feels a bit much.

'Ah, it's for the king,' I'm told, a wave of the hand. King Salman bin Abdulaziz is scheduled to close the ceremony, waving to a plethora of assembled dignitaries: behind me, as the camels parade in the morning, a team of builders furiously saw and drill his VIP stand together, raising with sheer force of will a camel festival out of the sand. When the $30 million collective prizes are handed out at the close of the ceremony, the big wins will go to Prince Sultan Bin Saud bin Mohammed and HRH Prince Abdul Al-Rahman bin Abdulaziz Al Saud. I'm back in the tent with the man and the app:

'We love the system,' he tells me.

Pause.

'Sometimes,' he adds. And the whole tent shakes again with laughter.

* * *

Before I leave here it is my destiny to get on a camel. Camels, I am warned, get up from a sitting position in the most insane way imaginable: back legs stand first, tipping you all the way forward, then the front legs unfold, swinging you back to some form of equilibrium. I am anticipating some sort of waltzy rollercoaster experience, but it's smoother than that: the camel beneath me is placid, calm despite the great weight above it, walks around the designated camel walking area with a peaceful trot, a kind of louche gallop. There is something very all-seeing about being on a camel, the same way standing up on a bike makes you that bit taller and more omniscient than humans are meant to be: you look down and survey your surroundings, you take in the details, you gaze to the horizon. I have drunk of the milk and seen of the parade and I have not understood camels. I have seen them stand up and I have seen them lie down, I have seen them spit and I have seen them dying. I have seen black camels and I have seen white camels. I have had a thousand identical conversations about camels, and what makes camels good, and why everyone is so bang into camels. I know of camel ears and eyes and lips and humps. I have toured around a camel museum. I have stared at the stars from the camel observatory. I have flown seven hours and driven two into the dry heat of the desert to see as many camels as it is possible to see. I have not understood camels. And now up here, soaring, I *get* it: camels are just chill, weird, useful little monsters, statuesque ships passing in the desert night, absolutely mad fuckers who love to give milk and meat and life and a form of transport, they love to gently rock up and down, lips flapping, hump steering backwards. I get it now. Camels are sound as fuck. I mean they're no dog, are they. But they're still quite good.

SWOOSH

I often think about death, most particularly those awful throbbing seconds before it, that tiny glance of moment where you – you, your brain, you id and your ego, they all realise together that this is the last breath, and flood your body with adrenaline – that creeping feeling up your body, toes to throat, of the last of the life of you escaping. And I always think: *that sounds bad*. Dying, I think, I could cope with. But the few seconds of panic just before death: no, not for me. That doesn't sound fun at all.

Thankfully I have devised the perfect way to die, and all I need is a basketball court, like 200 guns and a bunch of lasers.

So first you get a basketball court. I figure like a basketball court at a secondary school over summer, that sort of thing. Somewhere you can really let loose, and also die. Where you won't be interrupted or anything like that. Put some bulletproof metal down at the half court line. That's when you get your 200 or so guns: rifles, pistols, anything with a decent medium-range, anything that can splatter shrapnel through your head and guts. Aim all the guns at the half court line. Figure out some sort of relay system so they all go off at once.

And here's what you attach that trigger to: the basketball hoop. But you use detection lasers or whatever so, if the rim shudders or vibrates in any way, the guns do not go off. *The guns only fire if you get a perfect swoosh.*

Please, take a moment to imagine your death:

You, having driven your car off the end of a pier in a jealous rage after you find your wife in bed with her lover, whisky drunk and crying, crying and snotting, and veering, you steer the vehicle off the pier and into the sea, where the cold water hits up your nose like concrete, or—

You, having turned up two minutes to closing at Chick-fil-A, order their most expensive and complex chicken meal, the one that means the already overstretched and overworked staff have to fire up the fryers again that they had just started wiping down to make it, and they hand it to you with surly brows 15 minutes later, and yeah yeah the meal is good and everything – big up the Polynesian sauce – but also something seems off, somehow, you swear one of the patties was pink in the middle, and so it turns out to be, a crippling case of E. coli, you bent and doubled by your toilet, all night and all day, depleted of fluids, I mean it is spraying out of both ends of you like a Catherine wheel, and you are exhausted, and coughing, and pale, and losing you are pretty sure blood, and there is the acrid taste of vomit in your nose, and you are going light headed, dizzy, and hold on, is this it, are you d—

You, having lost all your riches on a single 32 red blackjack bet at a high rolling casino, you out of your mind with that one, you thought it would be a thrill but you lost it all, you flew to Las Vegas for this, you were seduced by the glitz and the glamour and the free Scotch and the low-plunged dress-wearing women, how will you tell your wife the house is gone, how will you look her in the face, and you are on the top floor of The Palazzo, full tux, and you think you will flutter to the ground but in practice it feels overwhelming, the ground rushing up to meet you, no stop, you didn't mea—

Or my way, where I spend a relaxing hour or two trying to score perfect swooshes, because scoring a perfect swoosh is the most awesome feeling not only in sport but in all of life, it is a hundred thousand orgasms at once, it is winning every lottery in the world, and yeah alright it's taken me a few hours of rim bounces and straight up air balls to get here and I'm sweating a little, slightly clammy, but I can feel myself warming up, it's coming, and bounce, bounce, arch the toes, bounce, this one feels good, oh this one looks good, oh it's marvellous, oh my god, it's dipping, it's dipping, and—

Swoosh

And for one perfect second I feel elation.

And then the guns explode my body into atoms.

Who in the world knows best how to die? It is me. I know best how to die. Golby: 3; Life: 0.

PCM (PER CALENDAR MONTH)

0.

When I was a kid my mum considered the entire house her project. My mother had, and RIP, but the worst taste in interior design ever in the world. The front room was painted a deep, ominous red. The dining room was a sort of dirty terracotta with a head-height gold line – less than an inch thick, like a twinkling string – running the entire circumference of the room. The kitchen was white, then wood panelling painted blue, then a lurid pink. The staircase, her final masterpiece, stripped of wallpaper and left bare for years while I was a child, before one day I came home as an adult and, oh, it was vomit yellow. My bedroom was cobalt blue until I was allowed to paint it neon green. When I abandoned the nest it was wallpapered in a turdish brown. We painted over all of it when she died, to better sell the place to normal people. Layers and layers of white.

In a way I crave that now, living as I am in my ninth

consecutive plain white room. Paint colours are a mark of ownership. You do not get to paint walls as a renter, not without express written permission and a promise to paint it back over, white again, when you leave. White walls, they tell you, are a blank canvas on which you can project yourself: put up prints, they say, hang pictures with special adhesive hooks that don't leave marks on the plasterwork. Be here, they say, make it your home, but leave no trace of yourself behind when you go or we will take it out of the deposit. I now understand that unusual craving to paint a bedroom cream w/ ornate streaks of orange. For ten years now, I have lived under a singular monster, a hive brain with many bitter limbs. For ten years I have lived under landlords.

1.

The first landlord I ever had was called Nigel and used to come over on the first of the month every month – knuckles on the door but then immediately keys in the keyhole anyway – to demand his monthly rent was written, in front of him, and handed to him as a cheque. Like: direct debits were invented, then, my dude. They already existed. We might have been students but even we knew this. We could have wired the money to him every month automatically. There was no need for him to be here, at the door, at 8 a.m. There was no need for anyone to knock on a door at 8 a.m. He would knock on my door, first, because I had the downstairs room (in student house-shares, in small grey northern Welsh towns, on terraced streets pebble-dashed with student house-share after student house-share, where all the back gardens were grey-tiled over with weeds leafing up in between, and on top of that, bin bags full of old chicken bones and beer cans, in those homes there is no concept of a shared living space, a leisure room: only an additional room that could be rented out as accommodation, and that was my room). Four of us lived there and he went around collecting the cheques from each, then wordlessly sauntered off. At one point over Christmas of that year he hired builders to erect a plasterboard wall that dissected our open living room/kitchen space and instead turned it into a smaller living room, a smaller kitchen space, a small narrow corridor between the two, slightly less space than we had before because it was now taken up with drywall, and also one of the main windows and therefore main sources of light was now blocked. He told us this was to comply with fire regulations. I do not believe him. I believe he made our home uglier and less functional for perverse reasons beyond fire regulation. I believe he did it out of spite. He kept 100% of my deposit, £280 pcm.

2.

My second ever landlords were an eerily smiling couple renting a dissected student house around the corner from the first. Student housing in small university towns is high demand/low supply, so to get the best places you have to band together with your friends as a sort of impenetrable gang, but our group had disbanded: one guy dropped out, one guy moved in with some girls in the vague hope he could sleep with one of them, and one guy punched me full in the face, the pub has the CCTV footage, after I made a tame joke about his goatee beard, which to his credit he maintains, the beard, I just checked on Facebook, he maintains it even now, a decade or so later (a *goatee* beard). This meant I was left with no choice but to move into a sort of waifs-and-strays house-share, where I had to live with no-mate third-year students who cooked plain boiled rice at insane hours of the night then ate it, alone and insanely, in their own bedroom, while somehow using all of the broadband supply at once, occasionally leaving their bunkers to leave passive–aggressive fridge notes that detailed every noise made after 9 p.m. in the last fortnight. It wasn't the best.

The landlords were very keen to stress when I was viewing the house that they were Reasonable People, which I have learned to now take from landlords as an immediate red flag that actually means 'I am insanely deranged', but I didn't know this then; I was but a young bear cub, tiny and clear-eyed and full of trust, and plus desperate. There was a back room in the house that was ostensibly a garage but had been cleared and roughly plastered and, we were told, when we returned after summer's end (you will see a recurring theme where university landlords would change the very structure of our house for no immediate reason to us but meaning they could charge more rent to the next cohort and that we, the current renters, would have to put up with the building sounds and building smells and the building dust being marched through our house followed by builders, we would have to put up with the inconvenience for someone else's reward), would be a gleaming new lounge, with sofas and carpet and a large TV, and curtains and no drafts and a coffee table off which to eat our dinner. This was a lie. When we returned the garage was in more or less the same state although maybe with slightly more tools in it, and on odd Tuesdays or Thursdays the landlord, Mark, would turn up and start sawing and swearing and playing a game with himself where – as best I can tell – he would repeatedly drop a jigsaw into a bucket of old nails, from a large height, repeatedly, for hours, while swearing. Very little progress was made on the whole thing despite the regularity of him standing in our garage-lounge and trying. And then so one night around January, when at 8 p.m. he still hadn't left our house, still sweating and swearing in the lounge-that-wasn't-a-lounge, we asked him as a household when the work might be finished: and he went absolutely full-throttle mental, jumping at us, me in particular because I was tallest, and screamed directly in my face, 'IF YOU WANNA FUCK OFF, THEN FUCK OFF!', only there was as aforementioned no more available housing in the entire city, so we didn't fuck off, and we had to go through the humiliating ritual of this spurned man, his chiding wife standing behind him, turning up a few days later to shake our hands and manfully apologise, and long story short the lounge ended up getting finished about eight weeks before our tenancy was up, and it was a shithole, so what exactly we were paying that extra £50 a month for all academic year I don't know. £340 pcm, 100% of the deposit withheld.

3.

If the universe is just it will, just once, let me watch my landlord die. Or a landlord, any landlord. But I would like it to be my own: I would like it to be one that wronged me. And as they die, their heart rage-exploding in their chest, their body under too much fiery pain to make a noise, every muscle contorted and engaged, every nerve alight, as they collapse to the ground silently at my feet, eyes pleading, arms extending in desperate prayer towards the sky, I will watch them, blinking, I will watch them and enter a near zen-like state of calm. I once practised literal meditation with a Japanese monk at 5.30 a.m. at a temple in Kyoto, with the small splashing sound of koi in an ornamental lake behind us, maple leaves dipping into the glassy water beyond, mosses and greens, quiet bonging sounds, the tinkle of the first morning wind in the bamboo. It was a transcendent, beautiful experience. My mind jetted out towards the edge of the universe and back towards my exact centre. I found a note of peace I don't think I've ever found before or since. And I think I could eclipse that if I just watched one landlord – one! That's all I ask! – collapse and die in agony. I do not ask for much.

4.

Third landlord didn't ever happen because, after moving to London and spending so many months in my sister's spare room that she and her husband – hard-working successful human beings living and killing it in the toughest city on earth, empathy and patience close to angels, charitable people, pure souls – even they got kind of tired of living with a 21-year-old manchild who exclusively ate breakfast cereal and did not clean that breakfast cereal up after he had eaten it, and also took 20-minute showers and almost violently needed a haircut. Three months into my first job in the city I went to look for rooms and found one sort of nearby – I would be the second room in a two-bed house-share that was otherwise occupied by two extremely normal PhD students who were almost unbearably in love and clearly had a thing for decorating their flat and rooms with objects they had found travelling, which was also annoying. (There is an entire strata of people in London who are just extremely normal PhD students called Tom, who wear the most unforgivingly cut jogging bottoms around the house and their only hobby is always 'cooking', and their dissertation and deadline schedule seems to directly only coincide with the, like, one night out in three months you come home roaring pissed at 3 a.m., and they are always in love with an exceptionally clean-faced girl who is round your flat all the time, and the two of them, for fun, like to do things like *playing frisbee*, and it is impossible to spend any time living in this city without having your own PhD Tom, and they are among the worst people to live with, and I include the guy I lived with for a year who partied once a week like clockwork and rolled home to do this gigantic, immovable drug shit, this enormous cocaine shit every single Sunday morning, medically unflushable, the shit, and I consider him a better housemate than this city's thousands of Toms.) Anyway, it never happened because the landlady did such a deep dive into my finances to see if I was capable of mustering the £550 a month that she made like three calls to my boss, not just asking what I earned and how often I was paid but also my job performance, was I likely to be fired anytime soon (I was), and asked for two years' worth of bank statements, like she wanted to look at my finances harder than I ever have before or since, and by the time my boss pulled me to one side and said, 'Hey,' like, 'can you get this crazy lady to stop calling me?' I decided to find somewhere else, because if a landlord is so fucking annoying that they jeopardise your very employment *before you even move in* then imagine how they are gonna react when you tell them there's mould in the bathroom. No thanks, Susan. £550 pcm n/a.

5.

You are in the hire car and I am in the passenger seat. I have planned this meticulously. We both wear black hoodies and black jogging bottoms. Scarves around our faces. I have been wearing gloves all day so as not to leave a fingerprint on anything. CCTV will never pick us up. We rented the car in cash, no paper trail. The registration number can never come back to us. They will never find us. I brick the window of the estate agents while you slow, then we peel away, laughing. We do this two weeks in a row, three. Every time they have to board the window, then pay for the entire pane to be replaced, then do it all over again. Shatter the glass. Peel away. We are costing them thousands. We are costing them every penny they took from us then more. And then, one final hit, once more with feeling: a Molotov cocktail, a Jim Beam bottle stuffed with petrol and lit with a fabric wick, thrown at pace through their front window. And Michael Naik on Church Road, Stoke Newington, goes up in red red flames. I watch as it turns orange, then vivid yellow, then grey down to ashy black. I watch the flicker then the smoke then the shocked-out corpse of it afterwards. We cannot return your deposit. I'm sorry you're unhappy with our service.

6.

So third landlord proper was entirely absentee, and as a result I never met him and harbour slim-to-no ill will. For whatever reason, this guy bought a three-bed flat in Muswell Hill, London, and then just immediately moved to LA, where he seemed to both forget the flat existed and the concept of inflation did too, meaning we were paying near pre-millennial rent on this place, which is a double-edged sword: on one edge, you do not have to pay as much rent as anyone else in the city; on the other edge, any time you need something fixed in the flat the dude responsible *lives all the way over in LA* and any attempts to alert him to the fact the flat exists might remind him that he owns it and, dominos fall, he then raises the rent. So yes, on one hand: I did especially enjoy only paying £280 a month rent. On the other: when our boiler broke down one winter it got so cold that when I got home from work one night I *put more clothes on* and then had to sleep in those three layers of clothing, beneath a duvet, wearing gloves, and then woke up crying (??? somehow???) and had to go and move back with my sister for a fortnight until it was fixed. Like: the house got so cold it was colder than just being outside. Somehow the boiler broke so bad it reverse engineered the entire place into a refrigerator.

The landlord's proxy was his father, the most Irish-looking man alive, a sort of sinewy human knuckle of a man (you know when you go to a restaurant and they have an offal dish? Is it a liver, or a brain, or a foot, or something? And you umm and ahh about ordering it because you like the good meat, the glamour meat, but you're feeling adventurous and go okay? And you order it and it's the ugliest but most unctuous piece of food you've ever eaten? Okay imagine now the pig's foot dressed w/ gravy is somehow wearing old Sergio Tacchini sportswear and has a hearing aid). It's this guy called Pat who would occasionally bowl into the flat, looking through failing eyes at an errant radiator or dead boiler or swathe of black flecked mould, then sit on the sofa and tell us in the broadest pissed Irishman accent possible about his day, his life, his dry home life, his errant LA son. And then he would ease himself up after like 20 minutes and creak down the stairs, and we wouldn't see him again for like four more weeks, and the problem with the mould or radiator or whatever would not be fixed, because he almost certainly forgot about it as soon as he left the building, possibly before. One day the woman downstairs died and we only really knew because it'd been a couple of days since we heard her yelling at her kids. I would say this was easily the best flat-share arrangement/landlord situation I have ever had. £280 pcm rising to £330 after two years.

7.

Hold the landlord's skull and feel it give way beneath your fingers. I feel like I know the density of the human skull. I can tap on my own and guess the thickness. It is full with liquid-heavy flesh. Grab the cheeks near the jaw. Ignore the screaming, the yelling. The landlord will try and get its arms up between you and its face. Dismiss the arms, twist them behind the landlord, bend and snap them. Grab the cheeks, position the thumbs over the eyes. Pick the landlord's head up. You know how thick a landlord's skull is, you know your own skull. Pound it against the pavement – *pound, pound, pound* – until it opens like heavy fruit.

I can imagine what colour the inside of a landlord's head is and so can you. It is purple-pink that cedes to grey. And there, deep in the dome of it, look closer: black spores, specks like mould, hundreds of them, thousands. Feel the landlord's eyes and soft face ooze through your hands. Feel the mash of blood and flesh beneath you. Nothing but gurgling and a soft wheeze. *How could you do this*, you think to yourself. *I have become a monster*. And then you hear it, soft as a heartbeat, beneath you: the landlord has survived the attack. It is leaking but it is sentient. And it hisses, there, with its last dying breaths: *this is going to cost £400 for professional cleaners to tidy up*, it says. *This* will *be coming out of your deposit*.

8.

'I've moved you before, right?' Dimitri says. 'Last year. Muswell Hill?' I have a guy, now. My guy is Dimitri. Dimitri is the best man-and-van guy in London. He just absolutely does not fuck about. The dude can pick up, like, five different bags at once. He can somehow hold a fruit and veg box full of books under one arm and, like, a sack full of clothes wrapped around my PlayStation in another. Dude is lifting my TV all of his own accord. He clambers up and down stairs at twice the speed I can. I try and help him but I suspect I just get in his way. Dimitri texts like this when he can't make it and he has to send one of His Guys (Dimitri has guys): '£150 for two hours will get u one helpful driver.' The driver is helpful because he can lift the approximate weight of a full-grown horse while also avoiding parking fines. Dimitri has helped me move so many times now that he recognises my face, despite the fact that he only sees me once every 15 months or so, and despite the fact he probably helps move two to three people in this city per day. 'Hey, look at this,' Dimitri says. He helped do some van shit on a Katy B video last week. He is careening through traffic while trying to load the video up on his BlackBerry (Dimitri still uses a BlackBerry). Grainy footage of supercars pirouetting in a car park. 'You see that?' Dimitri says. Cars veer past us. He lifts all my stuff into my new room in 20 minutes flat. I legitimately have a closer bond with Dimitri than I have with some of the people I consider friends in my life. He does not know this at all. I pay him in cash and tip him a tenner for beer.

9.

Listen it's my own fault but I moved from a three-person flat-share to a five-person flat-share, so that is five people needing to use the shower in the morning and five people needing to cook individual dinners between 6 and 9 p.m., and five people who cannot fucking seem to remember to buy toilet paper and five people all using the butter and pretending they didn't use the butter and five people who variously consider getting in at 1 a.m. on a weekday night is acceptable and five people you need to know are dead asleep or not likely to rattle your door handle when you masturbate and five people who decide Hey Guys, Sorry

To Drop This On You, I'm Moving Out and five people you have to once every six months like clockwork hold open auditions for to replace, meeting as you do the best and worst of London's flat-share-seeking singles. I have seen it all: the girl who close to sobbed on the sofa because she'd just broken up with her fiancé and asked in a quiet voice if we'd all like to bake together one night a week (we did not); the close-to-silent secondary school teacher who flinched at the word 'homework' like you were shouting 'CHARLIE!' at a Vietnam vet; the extremely unblinking Dutch guy who wanted to build a pizza oven in the garden, presumably to char our bones in once he had methodically killed us all; the guy who only has one question, yeah: do you guys mind if my band practises here one or two nights a week?; the guy in advertising who can only afford to slum it in this house rental because he so visibly spends all his money on cocaine; the guy whose only hobby is cycling who cycled here and is wearing cycling gear, sweat-slicked cycling gear, here on our sofa, we all gave our Sunday up to talk to this.

Of the five of us, crucially, nobody could quite decide who of us was the 'House Dad' in charge of all the grown-up shit, so we all intermittently e-mailed the property agent separately about the faulty boiler, shitty bathroom, the pilled carpeting on the stairs, the draughty windows, to the point that they would ask us to stop. When they did respond, the answer would always be the same: yes, they'd say, yes they can send Someone out (their Someone is an extremely shoddy building team who are always the same three guys who leave our front door banging open whenever they work and are borderline useless but clearly a friend of the guy who runs the property agent, e.g. they repainted all our doors but did not strip the paint from the previous door-painting and so just painted over it instead, leaving in some cases the doors now too thick with paint to close, and also they painted one of our main windows like, entirely shut, like even if I painted a window I would not do that and I am, building-wise, close to remedial, so what does that make them) but we will have to raise the rent again because this work on the house (i.e. fixing it to a barely liveable standard) now 'upgrades' the house in line with market rate ('market rate' of course being a fake idea because the market is dictated by invented numbers by the same property agent issuing the work), and anyway you all need to change your direct debits to reflect an extra £60 a month, starting this month which we are already three days into. I did not get my deposit back from this one because the guy the remaining housemates sat on a sofa and interviewed and accepted they could live with couldn't move in for three more weeks so he emailed me to say sorry mate, he couldn't pay for this month's rent because that just wouldn't be fair mate would it mate? Even though he accepted on the room, mate, so the property agent deducted my deposit entirely to cover his lost rent and thinking about it I get so mad I think my veins might explode—

10.

(£445 rising to £595 [!!!], bills not included, deposit one-and-a-half month's rent, oh my god)

11.

Here's my fantasy: I am a sniper and landlords are the prey. I assume I am good at things I have never tried, and sniping is no different: laying passive for extremely long periods of time, making small and precise movements rather than large and athletic ones, breathing slowly, pulling the trigger at once calmly and with great eerie force, watching a head explode a thousand yards away like a balloon full of shaving foam: yes, I can do all this, this is something I can do. So in this fantasy I am the sniper, and for whatever reason, four fields away, a series of captive landlords (they have been starved, for days, the landlords, so they are somewhere between desperate and insane), the landlords are given an opportunity: run the length of the field without me exploding their head with a bullet and they will be given their freedom. And so they sprint, the landlords, cutting each other up, trailing wildly, zig-zagging, and each one of them, with clinical precision, I shoot and then kill: sometimes I let them run, really run, get as close to the finishing line as they can, and then, *p-oom*: a mile away I make their head explode, and their last vital moment before they die is one of desperation and hope. And the weirdest thing, the most curious thing:

every time I strike a landlord directly in the skull with a 13 mm bullet, instead of shards of white bones and grey-pink mash and instead of veins and blood, a steaming plume of red, weirdest thing: their heads instead explode in a shower of money, and not just any money, it's every deposit I ever lost: it's the month deposit in Bangor, the second; the first deposit I ever gave to an outgoing letter instead of to the property company; it's the money I lost because the guy who moved in after me couldn't move for two more weeks, and because of his mistake I lost close to a thousand pounds: it's all of those cheques, exploding and burning in the air. And bodies slump headless to the floor—

12.

I was in kind of a rush to move and a friend of a friend was looking for a person to move into his flat, and during the size-each-other-up meeting we bonded over our shared love of Arsenal and the fact that both of our mothers were dead, plus there was a very sweet female kitten living in the house too, so I agreed to move in the next week. Two complications were: this guy owned the flat, making him both the landlord and the housemate, which cut down on admin fees but also added tension; plus as it turns out after five months of living together we were entirely incompatible, as humans, and a loud row about the recycling bin turned into him emotionally pleading with me to move out a few days later and leaving a faux legal letter he had written himself on the kitchen table asking as such, and this time the reason I lost a chunk of deposit was because I'd put some pictures up on temporary hooks in my room and the sun had bleached a weird dust line along the top of them, and when I had tried to wash the stain off with sugar soap it'd just spread the stain, so all the walls were white smudged with grey, which fair play that one was entirely my fault but my main goal in life right now is to hang a picture on a wall and not end up having to pay anywhere between £250 and £400 for the privilege, I mean truly, is that so much to ask—

13.

Imagine if a landlord just got to their car and it exploded, though. One second it is a car and a landlord and their arm is reaching to the door, casual, they do this every day, and then next: the next moment the sky is lit in a plume of orange and hot-white and yellow, and before the sound has even hit you – the sound is of crunching metal and that sound of pressure coming off machinery (like this: *snrr*), and then the sound of dust going up and then settling, and the scrape of iron on concrete, the fizzing sound of fire hitting the air – before the sound has even hit you (you, watching from a safe distance through binoculars), before it even hits you the landlord is dead. Imagine. Imagine that.

14.

'What, *again*?' I cannot tell if Dimitri is mad or disappointed. Once a year or so I give him £150 to haul the same boxes and bags up and down the same flights of stairs. This time the move is short, to a two-bed in Clapton. The landlords, again, vouched that they were Good People, and they lived in the flat upstairs, though when we went to see the property they did a viewing with a few other people at the same time, two couples who excitedly started saying how much they wanted the flat and how they would overbid on the quoted rent price to make sure they could have it, and the landlord took us to one side and whispered that, if he had to pick, he would pick us lads – you're good lads, he said, I like you – but the others had bid £25 more a month, could we match it? To which my housemate said 'how about £50?' and the landlord said 'how about a hundred?' and my housemate said 'how about £50' and the landlord said yes – which made me all really think it was a scheme, a complicated scheme, to get us to pay an extra £25 a month each. Our flat was essentially a long hardwood corridor with London's smallest bathroom and two double rooms attached, and I lost the coin toss for the good room with the nice view, so I spent the entire year begrudging every single penny of the £825 a month I was paying to stay there while staring out of a window at nothing outside.

More or less the landlords were fine, I suppose, apart from one time when – the night after we had a party, which we had spent the morning hungover and clearing up from before settling down for the Euro 2016 final – the landlord stormed downstairs, picking up and dumping the recycling bags we'd set outside, yelling to himself

'NO!' and 'WRONG!' and 'IT'S ALL FUCKED UP!' before yelling through our window – the window keeping him mildly inaudible, so he looked like a silently screaming cat – and made us come outside and sort the recycling so it was two to three feet further over to the right. Still not entirely sure what that was about but I suppose we all have our middle-of-our-life mental collapses in different shapes and ways. When I moved out they returned 100% of our deposit, a human history first. Would I still like to watch them, grey and motionless, die in a hospital? The eerie digital shrill as a heart stops beating in its chest? Would I? Would I? *Eeeeeeeee—*

15.

Maybe it is just something that happens at you, when you approach 30, that you notice interior design trends where before you hadn't, I don't know: I just know that one day I woke up and I thought it was okay to sleep on a mattress that didn't even have a sheet on it, and then next day I woke up and I had this strong primal desire to buy some cushions, and a candle, and some sort of decorative tray, if maybe I could put my things on a decorative tray? And there are two trends, in interior design, right now, Year of Our Lord 2k17: Hygge, a sort of Scandinavian-derived idea of capsule cosiness, which basically as best I can tell involves buying a large mug, making herbal tea in it, and then curling up among soft lighting in a heather-coloured blanket; and then there is a sort of intense minimalism favoured by Instagram lads who wear torn black jeans and have sparse monochrome rooms, and wear snapbacks and do a strange curled eyebrow-pout at the camera, and everything they own is black or white or charcoal, which of course is a form of black, and I thought for a while that, hey, maybe I could do that: maybe I could cosy up a single corner of my room, maybe I could only buy things among a limited colour palette, maybe I could live an organised life. And then I realised, suddenly, one day, that these interior trends weren't a choice, or an option: they were a *reaction*, that having fewer things (minimalism) makes it easier to move house with them, once a year, every year; that having a pack of four or five go-to items that act as a cosiness shorthand then bypasses the need for you to have a truly cosy house. It is easier for Dimitri to haul your idea of cosy up the stairs if it can all be packed neatly into the same box. And this: if you were born in the late eighties to early nineties then the closest you can get to ownership of your home – the only way you can, truly, tap a vibe and imprint an identity on it that is unique only to you – is to have, like, six black things on a shelf, or a £60 eiderdown from John Lewis. All the bricks are taken. All the bricks are owned. Pay what's left of what you have to the landlord above you.

16.

I get in, with my landlord. That's the plan. I get friendly with them. 'Hello,' I say, at their doorway. 'I made you brownies.' It is, I explain, a gesture of friendship. To a cosy relationship going forward over the 12 months of our contract. I am cooking, my food says but not my mouth, I am cooking for you to win your favour. I want to keep you sweet, my cooking says, so you do not raise my rent again. We tiptoe around the landlords. We not only have to pay them all our money but we have to be nice to them while we do it. In case they sting like a snake and incite retribution. Smile sweetly and be polite, or that's £100 extra a month, again, in line with the mythical market rate.

The joke of course is my brownies are poisoned. And the cookies after that. The rice krispie treats, the pound cake. Not obvious poison – I'm not an idiot – but a slow poison, a dreadful one. The landlord wakes up one day and loses a tooth. Hair comes out in clumps. 'Where has,' the landlord pants, 'my energy gone? My vigour?' The only thing that used to bring the landlord any joy was draining me of £900 a month, but that immediately goes to medical bills, for complex tests. Doctors are baffled. 'We don't know what's wrong with you,' the doctors say. 'But something within you has soured.' The landlord pulls the mirror in the palatial bathroom in their own home and sees the weak remains of them staring back. 'I am dying,' they say, sobbing weakly now. 'I am dying, and I know it, but nobody can tell you why.' I knock on the door with a malt loaf. 'Come in, come in,' the landlord says. 'Your contract is nearly up this year, but if you sign on again early, we'll only raise your rent up 15%.' I acquiesce. Sometimes I slip into their house when they are sleeping. Their lungs and heart have deteriorated at an astonishing rate. They make great, rattling, horrid sounds as they sleep. Draw weak long breaths, vile landlord, while you still can. Tiffin, scones, mince pies. I watch as their skin goes green-yellow and sallow. I watch them wrinkle and contort. I watch their organs expand and bloat. When they slip away, weak and wheezing, I am there to watch it. 'Hello,' their son says, the next week. 'I am the landlord's son. I am your new landlord.' He tells me that, given the circumstance, he has to raise the rent. I understand, I say. Would he like an almond slice?

17.

I know the best place in the woods for a grave. You have to dig it deep, is the thing. This is so often where people slip up: they dig a shallow, barely there, low little grave. Dog walkers go past this thing like two, three days later, and there, look: a human hand just peeking out of the dirt, reaching up for forgiveness. No: deep, deep, miserably deep, so deep and dark you need a ladder to get out of it. The night I kill the landlord (single bullet, base of the spine, then up again to the head, all pain and all silence) it is raining, thundering: the car slips and slides in the mud. The landlord body is wrapped and taped in a polythene tarpaulin and dragged through the countryside. The rain comes down in white diagonals through the black dark. When the body hits the bottom of the grave it makes this noise: *flump*. When the body hits the bottom of the grave it makes this noise: [*sound of bone distantly cracking through dense flesh*]. It's hard work to pile the soil back in but I do it, I do it, my arms and shoulders on fire. By the time I leave the sun is just rising over the horizon. The rain has passed, now, but the air is cool and brisk. Take a lungful of it: one, two. Watch the morning break white over the orange trees around me. Nobody will find that body until it's bone.

18.

A property agent is informing me in a tight voice that it costs them £150 for them to cut me a new set of keys.

19.

The sound a landlord makes when you rip their eyes out with your thumbs is, 'I know a builder who could fix this but he probably won't be available for another six to eight weeks.'

20.

The sound a landlord makes when you nail their toes down into the wood floor beneath them is, 'this isn't the definition of normal wear and tear'.

21.

The sound a landlord makes when you slice round their knees with a box cutter and prise the patella out with your clawed hands is, 'the tenants before you didn't have parties, I'm not sure why you have to have so many parties'.

22.

The sound a landlord makes when you snip the webbing between their thumb and forefinger with kitchen shears is, 'there's been a break-in but your contents aren't covered by our insurance so you're going to have to pay for a new front door'.

23.

Between 1986 and 2012 circa five million homes were built in the UK, and as per 2014 figures just over half of these are now owned by landlords. Or, context: in 1994 the number of private landlords in the UK was estimated in the tens of thousands, and today that figure is two million. In 1988 the Housing Act deregulated the rental market and created a legal structure that sided hard with the landlords. In 1996 the buy to let mortgage boom gave landlords a financial upper hand on buying up property if they weren't personally going to live in it. They say there was a sort of housing crisis in the eighties, because housing was so affordable, that people rented for some sort of perverse pleasure: to see if they liked an area, to see if they liked the relationship they were in; and now we are sandwiched around another crisis, on one side sub-prime mortgages and on another a dangerously inflated property market. Millions of landlords did this. In the nineties they wanted more people to buy houses and they made it so easy nobody can buy a house anymore. Inch by inch, ill-thought laws have created a new underclass, a sub-species, landlords under whose yoke we now must live. Landlords get to win twice over: they get to pull our salary out of their wallets, and they get to drive up the price of housing stock by making it scarce, so when they finally sell they sell at a huge profit. We lose double and get told to suck it up. When the war comes I'm going to be at the front of it, heart on fire, strafing bullets into the landlords in front of me.

24.

I'm at a party but I can't open the back door to let some air in. 'It's the landlord,' I am told. 'He doesn't want cigarette butts out on the balcony.' I am at a party and the bathroom is streaked with black mould spores. 'It's the landlord,' they say. 'He won't let us open the bathroom windows.' A cheap fan embedded in the wall screams above me. 'You have to hit it with the flat part of your palm,' I say (this is my house). 'The landlord won't replace it.' *Tchnk, tchnk, tchnk,* until my hand goes sore and the screaming stops. I have to hide my embarrassment at the state in which I live when it's not my responsibility. I have to pay hundreds of pounds each month for the pleasure and not wretch in the landlord's faces. 'Turn the music down,' I am warned, at another party, at a high building towering over London. 'Last time the neighbours complained to the landlord.' The landlord is always here, the bogeyman over everything we do. Always there. The spectre of him, watching.

25.

Ten years ago I walked into a prison but I didn't know it. I had this fevered, diva-like dream – I wanted to live in a house, rather than beneath an underpass, in a cardboard box – and I followed through on it. I walked through the double-locked gates and past the guards and jeering prisoners, and I walked into a small blue room with woodchip wallpaper, and a single bed and a desk falling apart at the seams, and a clothes rail in lieu of a wardrobe, and some leftover magazines from the previous tenant of the flat. And there I signed in blood a deal with the devil himself: in exchange for up to half of the money I make every month, you will provide very basic shelter for me, and occasionally fix pipes when they inevitably leak. And the devil laughed and said, *sure*. The devil went, *though how are you going to save for a deposit on a flat of your own if you are paying all your money to me?* The devil went, *once you start paying rent, you can never truly stop*. Items I have lost moving house: a navy-blue perfect fit shirt, a Timex Weekender watch w/ limited edition strap, a stack of *Viz* magazines, my *Rocky* DVDs (my *Rocky* DVDs!), a mirror. We leave remnants of ourselves in every building that forgets us. There are people dwelling in the rooms I once owned right now, different steps on the same awful ladder. We're all chained in. And I think: when I was 21, I wasn't this bitter. And when I was 23, I was full of hope. And I desperately long to be that person again – paying £450 a month! Can you imagine! The luxury! – then I realise there's a reason I have shed those people like a shell. If you escape your twenties in London without at least once moving in with a partner you're not quite sure you love but know the situation will save you rent, then you have dodged a bullet that has shot me and others like me. If you get out of here with anything left in your overdraft then you are, by my accounts, some sort of blessed saint. And the circle starts again: I need a new flat, soon, I need to check Dimitri's availability, I need to prove to another vile landlord that I can afford their exorbitant fee. Once again my lips form a horrible *O* around their sour teat. All I long to do, in my entire life, is choose what colour a wall is painted. Not magnolia, or off-white. Not cream. Red, red, brilliant red. Deep red like the blood in the veins of every landlord who has wronged me.

HOT SAUCE CAPITALISM

I guess I didn't really know who I was until I discovered chipotle-flavoured Tabasco®-brand hot sauce. You know what Tabasco® sauce is: it is the wire-red sauce in the apothecary's bottle that kicks things up in a tangy, vinegar-y way, and if you ask me it is a very *obvious* chilli sauce but then it does the job and you know exactly, with Tabasco®-brand original sauce, you know exactly what you are going to get. Chipotle-flavoured Tabasco®-brand hot sauce is an entirely different beast: first, it is an extremely ugly brown, and if you don't shake the bottle it is likely to go grainy and kind of gross, like a grey-brown rim of sauce pieces will stick to the bottle in a sort of tide: look past that. Flavour-wise it is at once hot and smokey and kind of barbeque-y and kind of not, and honest to god I can and do eat bowls of plain rice with just some of this sauce on, I could just eat toast with that and no butter, this stuff is nectar, when we say the gods drank ambrosia we envision a creamy sort of almond milk thing, white and innocent and full of mother's milk-like charm, but actually ambrosia is here, on earth, available in small long-tipped bottles, and it is called chipotle-flavoured Tabasco®-brand hot sauce, and it is heaven.

So we all recognise now that chipotle-flavoured Tabasco®-brand hot sauce is the best commonly available table sauce on the market. We all recognise that. When I now bring it to people's new houses and flats as a welcoming present, despite the retail price being very low, it is a very thoughtful and perhaps impossibly perfect present I am giving them. 'Here,' my gift says, for me. 'I have bought you the gift of deep and delicious flavour. Cherish every drop of it.'

The point is how this sauce changed me, and the journey it took me on as it did. Because I thought I was a completed and finished human being, before chipotle-flavoured Tabasco®-brand hot sauce. The first time I tried this sauce was at Chipotle Mexican Grill, the burrito bar, and from the first taste of it I was altered as a human: I stole it, for a kick-off, the first time I'd stolen in my life, and continued to steal bottles from there because it was impossible to find in the wild. The sauce did not exist in shops, despite me checking every sauce aisle I ever walked down for *three entire years*, and yes I did think about bulk-ordering it online but the shipping cost was prohibitive, and so chipotle-flavoured Tabasco®-brand hot sauce became my white whale – apart from the bottles I continued to steal from Chipotle Mexican Grill, obviously, my stealing techniques getting more and more brazen and sophisticated as the years went on. I went on detours, to try and find this sauce. I took buses across the city to large supermarkets I thought would have it. Red bottle Tabasco® sauce? You can buy that anywhere. The weak, bad, green jalapeno version? Also commonly available. The deep brown super-heat Tabasco®? I know where to get it even though I don't want it. But chipotle-flavour eluded me, drove me to the brink of madness, until: until I chanced upon eight bottles in the corner shop in Stoke Newington one day. I bought all eight. Direct quote, from the shopkeeper, as I bought eight bottles of chipotle-flavoured Tabasco®-brand sauce, exhibiting euphoria close to tears: 'What the fuck, man. That's so much sauce.'

And now, finally, years after discovery, it seems Tabasco® has the logistics in place or whatever enough so that enough shops, now, stock chipotle-flavoured Tabasco®-brand hot sauce in enough supply so I don't have to bulk buy it when I stumble upon it, and so you can more or less find it now, if you want it, it is in a lot of supermarkets but not all, it is available but not widely so. I will take that, for now. For me that is a little victory. I no longer have to steal from Chipotle Mexican Grill. But then one day I realised that essentially my soul and chipotle-flavoured Tabasco®-brand hot sauce were palpably intertwined, and that's when I had a bowl of rice and we had run out of sauce and I couldn't find any nearby, and the rice and meal as a whole was disgusting, and I realised that maybe 80% of the meals at home I had cooked in the past 24 months had been chipotle-flavoured Tabasco®-brand hot sauce augmented, and that now I am broken, in a way, and cannot enjoy regular meals without it. Yes: I have small portable bottles of chipotle-flavoured Tabasco®-brand hot sauce that I now take everywhere with me. Yes: I have a back-up bottle of the sauce in my cupboard, and another back-up bottle of sauce behind that. I feel like I am among the top ten consumers of this sauce out of everyone currently alive.

Adulthood is a lot about realisation, and this sauce made me learn a lot about myself. It made me realise I am in a thrall to brands. Adulthood, I've found, is about finding the specific brands of the various things you like and then holding them close to you like glimmering fragments of gold that will never be snatched away, and if the packaging is changed or the brand is in any way discontinued then the grief of this is akin to losing a pet and you start a small but focussed letter-writing campaign. So: Aussie-brand Mega Shampoo, but not the conditioner. Sure For Men compressed antiperspirant (red edition). Adidas Original black-on-white tube socks. I have longer relationships with these brands than I've ever had with, like, a woman. Oral-B Pro Expert toothpaste and Calvin Klein size L trunks. Reebok Workout Lows, the perfect summer trainer. There is an argument, a strong one, that says brands soften and distort the raw deal at the centre of every capitalist exchange: that the temples they build around and in front of them, the projection of themselves as smooth-faced business empires, this false feeling of friendliness and trust: it masks the fact that you are paying them their costs plus a thick wedge of profit every time you buy something off them. I think adulthood is also about ignoring that fact if you find the right shampoo, if not conditioner. Chipotle-flavoured Tabasco®-brand hot sauce made me realise that: yes, everything is a lie, most particularly everything at the heart of any exchange of money. But I have spent a lifetime collecting my precious, precious brands, and if they discontinue them I riot. If Tabasco® stop making that hot sauce I'll fucking kill.

WAYNE ROONEY IS THE MAIN ANTAGONIST OF MY LIFE

The primary memory I have from my time playing football is the feeling of my glasses crunching across my face. This is a sensation you cannot replicate, right now, a feeling unique to a nine-year-old boy toe-poking a half-inflated Mitre at your face, while you (me.) wear Specsavers' kids' range spectacles, already Sellotaped at odd delicate angles due to being previously crunched from saving previous penalty kicks. (I know all this because I am very bad at dodging footballs, and also played my primary years of football in goal, where the ball would be very deliberately kicked towards my body or my head, and it was my job to take that hit without dying, which I often – bafflingly, and against all accepted training – did with my face.) The sensation goes like this: a soft *boomf* feeling, of the ball – with just a little bounce to it, a little elasticity to take some of the sting out – making contact with the face. Then the glasses go, immediately skewed diagonal and wonky, slashed across my forehead, curling round my ears, as my cheeks – still rippling from the force of the impact – try and struggle away from the more structural bones of my face. And then, finally, the sick *crunch* of the nose: cartilage bending without snapping to the very limit it can go to without breaking, the sound and feel of squeezing a handful of cornflakes. The sensation would normally be followed by: my entire face flushing pink then red. The sensation would normally be followed by: three to four nine-year-olds, jogging over to me, staring down at my dazed face. The sensation would normally be followed by: me, splayed like a starfish, staring up at the blue-white sky. I was not good at football. I was never good at football. And yet, despite myself, I still very deeply love football.

* * *

Wayne Rooney is good at football. He is known for this. Go to Wayne Rooney's Wikipedia page, right now, and see for yourself: he is listed as the top goalscorer in the history of the England team, the top goalscorer in the history of the Manchester United team, and he has a career that began at 16 and has been recorded in precise HD for every moment since. He has had at least two hair transplants and has one wife and three children. He is also, as he begins to wind down as a professional athlete, something else, something crucial: a totem of the very ageing process as it affects me and, to a lesser extent, him. Wayne Rooney has been one year older than me for as long as we have both been alive, and has been a success about it for almost half of my life: watching him score in a professional football match against Arsenal at 16 was like watching the hard boy from the year above somehow score a screamer past David Seaman, an adult and my hero. Our age proximities make me hate his successes all the more vividly: throughout his career, I have been able to think of him as a projection of me, what I would be if I practised more and was more genetically athletic and could run fast and actually had killer instinct enough to shoot, ever, when I got the ball, instead of laying a weak pass off to just slightly behind a team-mate's feet. I feel like every football fan has a player like this in their locker: someone who came through when they both were teens, who both enjoyed a boom twenties during the same era, then both started to get lower back pain and slow down a bit more around the same time. As Rooney's career comes to a glorious end, so I'm put in an odd-feeling position. And what I am saying is this: Wayne Rooney has been, distantly, teasing me, constantly, for 15 straight years, merely by existing. Wayne Rooney's entire playing career has been performative antagony of me, Joel R. Golby. What I am saying is: as the Wayne Rooney era finally comes to a close, I have to confront the fact that some of my dreams are dying. Wayne Rooney losing his touch is the moment I realised I was no longer young. I hate him for this, and more.

* * *

15 June 1996, 4.34 p.m.: the precise time I fell unrequitedly in love with the game of football. This was the moment Paul Gascoigne scored the most impossibly perfect goal of all time at Wembley against Scotland, finishing a passage of play that started a minute earlier, with David Seaman – lurid yellow kit, porn-lite moustache, a pair of pure-white Reusch goalie gloves the size of frying pans – beating out a Gary McAllister penalty for a corner. If you type in the time and day and coordinates, there are ways of seeing a map of the constellations in the night sky on the day you fell in love with your partner, or the day your child was born, or more likely this: the day Paul Gascoigne galloped on to a lofted Darren Anderton assist, pinged the ball in the air perfectly over the Easter Island head of Colin Hendry, then laser-pulsed it past Andy Goram for England's second goal, before splaying himself prostrate and pink on the technicolour green while Alan Shearer jetted Lucozade into his mouth. The sky above Wembley that night: Cassiopeia, Cepheus, Camelopardalis. I went to sleep dreaming of the ball floating – eerie and weightless, just for a second – above Colin Hendry's boulder-like head and skull.

The next day I set out to become David Seaman, because I fundamentally misinterpreted who the hero was of that game. Over the rest of the summer I developed a sort of strange, pink sunburn combined with a sort of permanent grubbiness from diving around in dusty dirt, and I embedded every joint of every limb – elbows, knees, but also ankles, wrists – with a sort of deep-set green-brown residue that you can only really get by inexpertly diving after a shot from another nine-year-old. In the field behind my house, which bumped and bobbled and skidded with dog shit, I had my glasses shattered across my face nine, ten, fifteen hundred times (look carefully at my face, now, as an adult with all his dreams broken, and you will see two perfect rectangular soft shiny scars by each temple: this is from having the arms of my glasses rammed into my face by free kicks, again and again and again and again). Every two weeks we would have to wait patiently to one side while a tractor slowly cut the whole field down from weeds to grass. Slowly, with patience, I learned to do three kick-ups in a row.

My friend Charlie and I fell in love with football at roughly the same time, so decided obviously to start a football team, a legacy to live long after us when we die. After a lot of soul-searching and thinking, that team was called 'Dunkers United' and consisted of me (goalkeeper), Charlie (general … outfield … player), and that was it. It is difficult and near to impossible to sustain a football team with only two footballers, especially when both of them are nine years old and appalling at football, but that didn't stop us: trips to Charlie's now included playtime dedicated to extending the Dunkers United brand, designing logos up in various jotters, and basically just kicking a football around in Charlie's back garden and shouting 'DUNKERS UNITED' whenever one of us scored. Charlie's brother George asked if he could join Dunkers United but we refused (too young, weak skillset). A boy called Paddy (fairly cultivated left foot, actually), from up the road, asked to join Dunkers, and when we agonised even mildly over the decision he decided that fine, he said, fine, he would start his own club, even better than Dunkers United, with even more players. One evening I found an old yellow goalkeeper training top in a pile of clothes my mum's friend had bought over that her son had outgrown, and, using some purple thread and one of my mum's needles, carefully stitched the word 'DUNKERS' into the collar of the fabric. The transformation was complete. I was David Seaman, lurid yellow and purple dream. Only David Seaman didn't get his glasses smashed into his face every time he mishandled a cross. David Seaman never had to stop a game early and walk home to his mum's house with his nose bleeding. David Seaman actually owned a pair of goalkeeper gloves.

* * *

Wayne Mark Rooney, England's Rose. His first autobiography is as fascinatingly unenlightening as you would expect from a peak athlete at the age of 20 – it's clear his ghost writer, Hunter Davies, had to crack the stone of Wayne Rooney and wring him for blood, because this is legitimately one of the better anecdotes from his childhood, written again at a time when his childhood was less than a decade away from him, and even there this is about as much as he can remember from it: 'There was another girl I can remember who had Down's Syndrome. She was two years older than me, and the only girl in the school we allowed to play football with the boys. She was a very strong tackler, always kicking my ankles. One day she held on to my fingers so hard I couldn't get away. I had to pull and pull, and push her away, but she still held on tightly to them. In the end I fractured one of my fingers in trying to get it free. But she was a nice girl, and I still sometimes see her and hear about her when I'm back visiting in Croxteth.' Or: Wayne Rooney, on making his Everton debut at the preternatural age of 16 years and 298 days: 'Following the game, I didn't go to the players' lounge. I was too new to know how all that worked, and I didn't really know all the first-team players, not properly. After my dad had picked me up and taken me home, I just went out into the street to play with my mates, in the normal way on a Saturday evening. Then I went to pick up Coleen. Yes, just four days earlier, on 13 August after I'd played in a testimonial game at Goodison, I finally managed to get off with her.' Wayne Rooney, on his inexorable rise from nine-year-old with promise to 16-year-old first teamer: 'I was doing well at Everton's Centre of Excellence, just loving it, and getting excellent assessments each year.' That, I suppose, is the magic of Wayne Rooney's story: there was no special alchemy, some template that could be read closely and repeated, again and again and again, until the England XI is filled with an entire line-up of gifted 17-year-olds with precocious centres of gravity: he just *was*. Wayne Rooney's early life, as he tells it, an entirely ordinary carousel of Scouse birthday parties where someone's mum does a nice spread, not really being that bothered about school but behaving when he was there, and then kicking footballs, constantly, over tarmac. At some point in his development between nine and 14, Wayne, against the grain of the usual boyhood footballing talent bell curve, just kept accelerating up and up through the age classes, never really impacted by injury or a plateau of talent, and then just, oh, one day he scored against Arsenal to break their 49-game winning streak and write himself into history.

When you are very bad at football, (me.), rare moments of brilliance are recalled with an incandescent, crystalline clarity. One of my first try-outs for the school team in Year 5 resulted in this: 30 boys, facing off against each other on a grey chain-link tennis court, headmaster Mr Oates with the whistle. From kick-off, the ball shuttled back to me, and everyone swarmed after it (ten-year-olds are not trained in any tactic beyond 'chase the ball, forever': they move across a football pitch like a school of fish startled away from a shark), and, as 16 to 18 tiny children bore down towards me, I pulled back my foot and pinged it across the pitch – a slide-rule pass, Xavi by way of Xabi Alonso, an absolute moment of perfect midfield play that took out at least a dozen players, lads just crashing into each other, foreheads clunking into other foreheads – the ball skipping and pulling into the path of our forward, Glenn H., who shuttled round the goalkeeper and slipped it in for a goal. This pass was so perfect it rendered Mr Oates dumbstruck. He forgot entirely how to talk. The whistle balanced silently on his lips. 'That was like,' he said, 'that was like hot butter through a knife.' A pass so perfect it broke a man's brain. It never got so good again.

* * *

I think the reason I hate Wayne Rooney is three-fold, and I've been thinking about it for like a decade-and-a-half straight now so I've more or less figured it out:

— I hate him when he plays well for teams against me (Everton, Manchester United, Everton again [second time not so much]);

— I hate him when he plays badly for teams for me (England);

— I am convinced that he is shit, and that nobody else seems to recognise he is shit, and everyone keeps telling me he is good when I am convinced he is shit, and the statistical, inarguable success of his career (record goalscorer for England and Manchester United without ever – *ever* – having a particular hot or notable goalscoring streak!), hard numbers that prove forever that he is not shit, render me both wrong and feeling utterly insane, and sometimes I just look at Wayne Rooney's scoring figures – he scored 27 goals in 2011/12! – and

> feel like I am in an asylum, and I am the only one who can hear Jesus talking to me, and doctors with white coats and sad faces take the difficult decision to electrocute me in the brain. If! Wayne! Rooney! Is! Not! Very! Good! At! Football! Then! Why! Do! All! These! Numbers! Prove! That! He's! Good! At! Football! Link a car battery up to my temples!

The best evidence that Wayne Rooney was a good player (evidence for: the opinions of team-mates, managers, pundits, every England fan in history, defenders who played against him and attackers who played alongside him, including C. Ronaldo, one of the greatest players – and, honestly, athletes – to ever live) (evidence against: this weird chewy feeling I have! I just don't think he's very good!) is this: Sir Alex Ferguson made him the spine-point for the last three of his United megasquads. This is important, because Ferguson was one of the finest managers of the modern age, and crucially had a cold-blooded ruthlessness to him, assembling teams in the same way villains do in sporting movies: every United team underneath him was stunningly talented and brutally, ominously, larger-than-life, like a hockey team bred in a lab to defeat the Mighty Ducks. Rooney, charging from the front, a perfect combination of talent and snarl, was the fulcrum to all of that. In 2004 Ferguson made him the most expensive teenager in history, and together they won five titles, three cups and the Champions League. He switched from the raw power run-after-everything player into the water carrier that kept the ying of Tevez and the yang of Ronaldo in perfect balance, and when they left United he became the sort of all-encompassing everything, battering down opposition, scoring relentlessly. And yet, every weekend of this eight-year partnership, I looked up at United projected large on the wall of whatever pub I was in, hyper-bright flashes of primary red and lime green, and would say: 'Wayne Rooney looks like a large potato being embarrassed in class for being unable to read. Sir Alex Ferguson, his owner and master, should have the beast killed.' And still I struggle with the veiny nub of *why* I feel this way.

* * *

I suppose the majority of my animosity towards him comes from a time of personal crisis for me which Wayne Rooney decided to aggravate by absolutely dismantling my team. Manchester United 8–2 Arsenal was obviously a low point for most Arsenal fans – a team of almost entirely youth prospects, a squad depleted by the high-profile departures of Fabregas and Nasri, i.e. the entire creative heart of our midfield, and I mean we had Johan Djourou at centre-back so it was never going to end well – a team absolutely dismantled in front of the world, and rightly, but Rooney was *relentless* that game: he scored two free kicks as lazily as you might throw a remote between two sofas, and was there or thereabouts for every goal, offside but present for Nani's training-ground chip, a lofted shot he did without lifting his head that kissed out against the post, Rooney barely breaking sweat as the diamond tip of a United attack that tore into Arsenal like a four-pack of beer through a rain-soaked paper bag. And then, when the game was already over, when Arsenal were already 6–2 down, Patrice Evra won a penalty, and Wayne Rooney – showboat, record goalscorer, must-be hero – stepped up to take it, and rolled it to the other side of Wojciech Szczęsny for his hat-trick, and turned around with his arms held aloft, Jesus of Manchester, as his team-mates bombarded him, Rooney as the man of the moment, Rooney the hat-trick king. And I ask you: was there any need for that, Wayne Rooney? Was there any need for you to score that goal? *We were already 6–2 down. Did you really need to score that goal?*

Wayne Rooney 8, Arsenal 2 came at a difficult time in my life. I was two years into my time in London and I was fundamentally quite alone about it. I was living in the shabbiest house-share of my career with two party addicts who were both sleeping off the excess of the night before them. I was working in a job I hated that paid me just enough to survive but not enough to thrive. I had, for the first time in my life, bought myself a new-for-that-season football shirt. I remember the shirt because it basically bankrupted me for the rest of that month: Nike-branded, Arsenal home, blue and red bands around the white arms, crew neck, size M, and I wore it every weekend while watching Arsenal on TV because it had cost me all of my fun money for the month and I couldn't afford to go out. This strip was so nice, man. It was so pointless having it but I wanted it. I had one football kit as a kid, for my tenth birthday, Chesterfield away, and I soon outgrew it. I didn't get another kit until I was an adult. This felt significant, somehow. I had achieved this and worked for it. I sat at home on my own in my special little football shirt, a large soft adult boy, watching as Wayne Rooney tore my team to pieces. Can you even imagine anything as pathetic in all your life?

I think a lot of my personal happiness is pinned to the success or unsuccess of Arsenal on the football pitch. I pin a lot of my emotional labour onto it. Football can be like this, sometimes: an escape from the complexity of what you are feeling when you don't have the developed emotional wellbeing to process it yourself. Yell a bit at Robin van Persie and feel better. Watch Aaron Ramsey do a back heel and forget your troubles. And that's when Rooney came in, and 8–2 happened: a moment in my life when I really needed a W, and he handed me one of history's worst Ls. If you need to dig down into when my animosity towards Rooney really grew wings, that would be it.

He celebrated his hat-trick with his boot on the face of my beloved Arsenal, the cameras shaking as he was swarmed with team-mates, and it's almost as if he looked to me, through the camera, through the wires, across the internet, through my laptop screen, into my teary eyes. As if he were whispering, 'I am better than you, in every significant way.'

* * *

Another football memory, clear as a crystal: the first competitive game of football I ever played was entirely blind. I showed up to an open game for a semi-local team two miles away, after nervously calling up a number in the paper that put me through to a to-the-point football coach who would really rather have spoken to an adult about this rather than a nervous nine-year-old child – 'Where do you play, then? Goals?' he said, 'Do you— I mean, is your dad literally not there? Your mum, even?' – and who, when I turned up with my gloves and my long-sleeved strip emblazoned 'DUNKERS', told me that actually they already had a goalkeeper, a kid on loan from genuine Premier League side Sheffield Wednesday, and so they didn't really need back-up for the role. I would be playing in midfield, they told me, second half onwards. After watching this cat-like kid keep a clean sheet for 25 straight minutes – honestly, he was incredible, like a salmon muscling out of water to every ball, down quickly to each side, strong hands, stronger presence – I understood why I wasn't allowed to play, so begrudgingly changed into an outfield kit and got ready to underwhelm in midfield.

'Woah there,' the referee said. 'Woah. Hold on, mate.' He signalled my glasses. 'Can't play in them.' I played in glasses every day of my life, I explained to him. I signalled the

Sellotape marks where they had been shoddily repaired, the formative temple scars along my face. I cannot play without sight. 'Insurance thing, mate,' he explained. 'What if you get hit in the face?' I said it was unlikely I would get hit in the face if I could see the ball. He plucked them off my head and put them in his top pocket.

What follows was one of the more useless halves of football ever played, and – if you've ever seen me play as an adult, dead first touch and even worse decision-making, poor passing skills and absolutely zero pace – that is really saying something. I couldn't see the ball until it was around three feet in front of my face, so I could never react in a way that would anticipate it. None of the kids on the field knew me so obviously didn't pass to me. I didn't really know how to play midfield, so just stood on the halfway line, watching play bustle around me. And then, finally, in the last-gasp seconds of the game, everyone rushed forward for a goalmouth scramble, so I followed them. A corner whipped in, got weakly cleared out. Some kid on the other team attempted a chip and just pushed the ball onto the shins of someone else. It ricocheted, touched every person in the box. Then, finally, it clonked me clear in the head, my nose smashing across my face, and which somehow worked to kill the ball dead, falling motionless to my feet. Then I pulled back my right leg and swung it towards goal, top corner, the winner, and everyone stood and stared at me in silence. 'Fucking hell,' one of the other boys said. 'Who's the new kid?' This is the purest moment of football adulation I have ever known. In my mind they carried me out on their shoulders but I think in reality Dad took me back to the car and told me he couldn't really be arsed doing this drive every Saturday so would probably just not bother in future if that's okay.

* * *

There have been three Rooneys who have played for England, the skill of the Rooneys declining as the cumulative goals of the Rooneys increased. In 2004, when Rooney announced himself on the world stage, he was a terrier-like limb whirlwind: a stout little Red Bull can filled with an infinite reserve of teenage stamina, galloping after every ball, playing the game in a way rare, jewel-like footballing teenagers do, like they've invented a new way of playing football that hundreds of thousands of men over a series of decades have somehow ignored, the ball coming to feet and them just lifting it over a defender's head impudently, or running the length of the pitch with it, or – as more often, with Rooney – sort of getting low to the ground and splaying all his limbs out, protecting the ball while ushering it forward, the primary memory of Rooney at age 18 a sort of gigantic footballing crab, something all new. This was him at his best. Second-era Rooney was weighed down with expectation: he was the torch bearer as the so-called Golden Generation wound down, and segued into something more journeyman and eclectic, switching out genuine world-class legends – Terry, Ferdinand,

A. Cole, Gerrard, Lampard, Hargreaves – for lads who are the answers to long-distant future quiz questions (Q.: Which former Stoke right-back earned 54 caps for England without anyone actually noticing it, and was once fined by police for stealing a toilet seat? A.: Glen Johnson), with Wayne Rooney running around up top, somehow just out of time with every beat, a Bentley doing donuts in front of ten assembled Mondeos, Rooney broadening out through a series of uninspired Umbro shirts while slowly going red and bald. Then the final Rooney, the most depressing one: the sort of serial failure Rooney, Rooney at international tournaments (where, '04 aside, he was a constant disappointment: at three World Cups and in eleven games, Rooney scored one goal), Rooney looking out of breath in a meaningless friendly, Rooney using both arms to gesture to Gary Cahill to show where he was supposed to pass it. This, weirdly, statistically, was the most successful Rooney: in the years after his touch grew clumsy and his importance to United waned, he was still vital to England, dutifully travelling to Macedonia and Lithuania and Portugal and South Africa to score one goal, have a shower, and go home.

The best England Rooney was 2006. By now Rooney was established at United, and everyone knew his tricks and tropes: he was a fire-and-thunder player, a proven winner and goalscorer, tenacious in attack and prone to bouts of extreme lose-your-head aggression; i.e. if you asked the English fan base to design its perfect player and exemplar of this country and how it expresses its athletic prowess, Rooney would be it. The squad we took to Germany was solid, peak Golden Generation: Rooney and Owen up top, Lampard and Gerrard patrolling midfield, a defensive mix of young talent (Ashley Cole) and wise-headed gobshitery (Gary Neville); Paul Robinson was in goal but you can't have everything, can you. Here's me, being an idiot, in 2006: [*while wearing an honest-to-god England shirt*] 'England are good!' Or: 'I actually think we can do it, this year! We can win the World Cup!' [*extremely long explanation of the strength we have in every position bar goalkeeper until girls walk away from me*].

This is how supporting England at major tournaments is a foolish escapade designed to cleave your heart genuinely in two with agony: it is, as it always is, those green false shoots of hope that ultimately kill you. England, all tournament long, were awful: they laboured through an easy group with just-about-victories against Paraguay and Trinidad and Tobago before a draw with Sweden: Rooney, England's great hope, sat a lot of the early games out recovering from a late-season metatarsal break that, by all logic, should have kept him out all summer long. An easy second-round draw against Ecuador led to a laboured England win, and then the quarter-final came against Portugal, again, perennial English nemesis and spear-headed by Rooney's United team-mate, the flashy-but-fucking-brilliant Ronaldo. And then it all went wrong: a scrappy 0–0 draw was only enlivened by Rooney, in the

62nd minute, in the middle of the park, doing that thing he does where he tries to win possession by running into the ball as frequently and as fast as he can, his legs slowly splaying until he is basically forehead-first on the grass, and Portugal defender Ricardo Carvalho was nipping at his heels, and so – *inches, literal inches, away from the referee* – Rooney stomped on Carvalho's testicles and got a straight red.

One commonly misunderstood subtext of the entire game of football is the heroes versus villains narrative, the one that plays in the shadows of the classic winners versus losers dichotomy. This is harder to see in the domestic game but easier, somehow, in the national: when England crash out of a tournament, for example, as they have *every two years without fail in my lifetime*, there has always been some villain, one man pinned as the reason for everything. So for example you have in Euro '96, when Gareth Southgate missed a penalty (villain), and the German team celebrated the ensuing victory (also villains). We are good at making villains of our own: in the next tournament, World Cup '98, David Beckham (villain) was booed for kicking out at Diego Simeone (also villain) in the quarter-final against Argentina. 2002: Ronaldinho was a villain for scoring a goal against us. 2010: the referee was a villain for disallowing a Frank Lampard goal. Every England failure has been sharpened like a knife to plough into the heart of someone, one single evil talisman, who shoulders the blame for the collective failure. There are smaller versions of this in the domestic game, intra-game villains that rarely pass from one 90 minutes to the next (this is why we shout at the referee); similarly, in the domestic game, feats of heroism are more richly rewarded. My team, Arsenal, managed to go an entire season unbeaten in 2003–04, which with nostalgia is remembered as one of the greatest sporting feats ever in history but in reality was a hell of a lot of 1–0 wins and 1–1 draws. The Invincibles season almost took the fun away from watching football, because it erased the notion of peril: there was no space for villainy, and so success became dull. In 2016, when an unfancied Leicester team ground out a league title win with a combination of old-fashioned defending and counter-attacking flair, their heroics were almost eclipsed by the looming idea of failure: the last few high-NRG weeks of that season were basically spent with the whole country saying 'But what if they fuck up? What if they fuck it?' over and over again, occasionally making long denominator calculations about who else might win if they blew a three-game lead. What I am saying is: sport fundamentally *relies* on a balance of light and shade, of good and evil, of heroism and villainy, because without it there is a lack of what Hollywood story editors call *conflict*, and without that there is no reason for it to be. At various times in his career the rectangle-shaped block of Wayne Rooney has filled both the heroic and the villainous role. When he stomped on Ricardo Carvalho's balls, somehow *Ricardo Carvalho's balls* became the villain, with

Rooney the wronged hero. That should give you an idea of the gilded pantheon Wayne Rooney has sat on for most of his career.

* * *

Rooney's England low coincided with my own personal footballing pomp. Summer 2008 was joyous for me: 21, lithe, shape of my life, England failing to qualify for a major international tournament left me stress-free and Rooney doing kick-ups at home, and honestly truly I have never enjoyed the summer of a footballing tournament more. England's failed Golden Generation not qualifying for Euro 2008 meant I didn't have to go through the sheer rigmarole of believing they would win, the same patriotic bullshit I have to go through every second summer, a months-long self-own of myself where I truly trick myself into thinking England might win a tournament right until they spang one crucial penalty off a crossbar and everyone collapses onto the grass in anguish. But right up until then – right up until breaking point – I always have a false, hollow, dreadful feeling of hope. (Wayne Rooney, so often the talisman of an England tournament squad, was often the reason for that hope: he was also, with his appalling major tournament scoring record, also quite often the reason I ended every second summer feeling stupid for ever having hope in the first place. This is the first real cut Wayne Rooney ever made against me: he made me feel stupid for feeling a very pure feeling, and he made me feel stupid in front of my own biggest fan and critic, which is myself.)

So 2008 was a good year for me because I didn't go through this because England in failing to qualify for the tournament at all had already proved themselves to be dogs. This freed up a lot of time over what was a glorious and blazing technicolour summer, which we spent playing football: a group of us, lopsided goths and metalheads who played in jeans and squished Etnies, struck up a sort of peace treaty with a mass of 13- and 14-year-old kids who played daily on a nearby park, meaning we had huge us versus them football games, eight or nine of us against however many dozens of them turned up. These games shouldn't have been fair but they were: as fully pubic 21-year-olds, we should have naturally been able to play a mass of teenagers who swarmed after the ball like wasps after a picnic, but then a surprising percentage of our number did not follow football or know the basic rules of it, and their skills in the game were either zero or something, impossibly, below zero (like have you ever seen a goth who woke up 15 minutes ago try and do kick-ups in Dr. Martens? This is how noses get broken). These games would go on for hours, surging backwards and forwards, 40-goal thrillers, sweat caked with dusty mud against every forehead on the field, eyes squinting against the setting sun, entire masses of each team lost in one fell swoop whenever two or more brothers were called in to their dinner, and throughout it all, me, form of my life, pirouetting and twirling, perfect first touch, chipping lofted passes over the heads of ten-year-olds, playing defence-splitting through-balls that took ten, twelve people out of the game. Double hat-tricks and free kicks. I was unplayable that year.

My nemesis on the other team was a barrel-chested Polish kid called Maciej. If you've ever lined up against a fat lad at five-a-side, you've met a Maciej: he had a perfect, ball-killing touch and a stinging shot, both skills which allowed him to play football *without ever needing to run*. At university, most of the strikers we came up against were like this: clad in XXL West Brom kits, they were easy to mark out of a game because they didn't move, but if you gave them even an inch of space they would rocket the ball directly into the bottom corner, 1–0, then not even jog back to the halfway line to celebrate because that would make them cough too much (one guy turned up to our game actively eating chips, and then put three past us without us getting near him, like he did his warm-up *while still eating chips*). Maciej, recently defecting over to Chesterfield from his native Poland, was just that: skilful, unmoving, Cruyff's brain on Neville Southall's body. His touch was so overdeveloped because he was so unwilling to run. His shot was unerringly hard and accurate. As a training technique, you can't knock it. Every professional footballer should spend a year of their childhood fat as a bus.

One day towards the end of summer this changed, though, because he decided to tear around the pitch possessed. Some of the other boys, though needing Maciej to prop their team up, liked to tease him for his weight: Maciej, a very serviceable English speaker but non-native, would hit back in an uneasy Polish–English banter *lingua franca*, 'you pissboys', that sort of thing, or 'kiss your mother!' Anyway the day his balls collided full-pelt with my ankle was clearly the day he had decided to incorporate some jogging into his routine to lose a few pounds.

We should rewind. I am in goal. An innocuous ball bobbles its way to me. I soften it with one touch, push it to one side to pelt it upfield, and Maciej bears down on me. Over the summer we had developed a sort of unspoken respectful bond: as the best player on my team, and he the best player on his, we were Ronaldo and Messi, squabbling year-by-year over the Ballon d'Or. And as he gets closer, as he looms ever faster, I roll the ball over to my other foot to take it away from the goal. Maciej breaks into a skidding slide tackle. The ball is vanished out of his path, like a magician with a card. He keeps sliding, one leg extended, the other caught behind him. His right leg goes to the right of my standing foot. His left leg to the left. His large round body is not used to travelling with any momentum. My standing ankle connects with all of the force of his body into crushing his balls down to dust. And Maciej, wincing in the dirt, eyes screwed against the injustice of it, screams, bloodcurdling: 'MY EGG!'

He means his testicles. It has not translated over yet.

'MY EGG! MY EGG MY EGG MY EGG!'

I'll never forget the screams.

'MY EGG! MY EGGGGGGGG!'

The soft sound of an uninflated balloon being run over by a car.

'MY EGGGGGG!'

I am Wayne Rooney and he is Carvalho.

'MY! EGGGGG!'

And I see him there, a little wounded Polish boy, nursing his remaining testicle.

'MY EGGGGGGGGGGGGG!'

If Wayne Rooney had dragged England through and qualified for Euro 2008, this would never have happened. If Wayne Rooney had pulled his finger out, I would never have made a Polish juvenile infertile.

* * *

This was years ago, now, and my feelings have softened as my acceptance of my fate has become more whole. One marker of growing up is being able to admit, finally, that you were wrong – to backtrack on bad behaviours or misheld opinions, to forgive those you feel wronged you and to admit when you wronged them back – and no more is that so than me taking seven years to admit Rooney's goal against City was good. You are aware of this goal, as it's among the top five most iconic goals ever scored in the Premier League: United red versus City sky blue, the season where City finally rumbled up to Big Boy size and pushed United to the sword, 79th minute, tense 1–1, and then a cross floats in and Rooney – bewilderingly, absurdly high, far too weightless for a man who's built like a bag of cement to be – Rooney falls and rises at once into the air, pirouettes one arched leg perfectly into the air, and shins in backward past a stranded Joe Hart. That was me, for seven years: 'He shinned it!' I would say, completely ignoring the athleticism that even got his shin in front of the ball in the first place, ignoring the footballing mind that would even think, in the split-second when a cross comes in and you are facing the wrong way for it, to even raise a shin that high. 'It's not called *shinball*, is it! Hit it with your foot, you fraud!' I've had to confront a lot of my deeper, darker, more bitter emotions over the course of this book, and none more so than re-watching that Rooney goal – again, and again, inverse angle after inverse angle, slow-mo and hi-def, the audio of a crowd erupting, *yes, yes, yesss*, like waves breaking against a shore – and admitting that yes, alright, fine: it was good. The Rooney goal where it pinged off his shin was phenomenally good.

* * *

My adult footballing career has been predictable in its mediocrity, a vacuum of potential ceding to quiet failure: slumping around university astroturf pitches, whipped by grey winds and violently hungover; Tuesday night five-a-sides under blaring floodlights, where a minimum one fight every two weeks would break out; realising my many, many faults as a footballer (no pace, slim-to-no touch, very weak shot, physically cannot actually kick it very far?, maybe make a successful short-distance pass seven out of ten attempts, fail calamitously the other three; my movement around the pitch could be described as 'remedial'). The primary memory I have from my time playing football as an adult is the words 'OH FOR FUCK'S—' bouncing off the walls of a seven-a-side cage as I, for the 15th time in one match, pick the wrong pass and turn over possession. I love the sensation of getting my foot on a ball – it just feels *right*, sometimes, pulling your foot back and getting your toes underneath an Ordem – but I also like being warm and dry and watching it from a pub, or playing it with a controller in my hands and my pyjamas on. There is romance in getting caked in grass and mud and wind and rain, and the sweat and adoration of the ten men around you, but there's also quite a lot to be said in being four pints in and wearing a jumper and yelling at football on a TV screen so loud the landlord comes over and asks you to calm down, boys, come the fuck on. Transitioning to that has meant giving up on an already quite distant dream.

* * *

Once when I was a kid I couldn't sleep, and my dad sat on the edge of my bed in the blue-black light of the deep night and told me his trick: close your eyes, my dad said, and imagine you are playing a perfect round of golf. Green fairways and well-trimmed rough. Exquisitely fine sand-yellow bunkers. Drive from the tee, Dad said, and go from there. It's a perfect blue-sky day. A light wind ripples the sleeves of your polo. Your caddy hands you a gleaming three-wood, which you use to clonk out a record-breaking 500-plus-yard drive. Putt from the green and hear that gurgling sound as the ball circles into the hole. My dad did not understand that children do not like golf, and smoking, and books about war, so it was hard to relate to him sometimes. As I sat and screwed my face up in the dark and tried to imagine enjoying golf, I thought: this man is an idiot. I thought: this man knows nothing about anything.

Then a couple of years later I transmogrified the trick over to my sport of choice – football – and imagined it from there. It worked. That soaring, weightless feeling you get when you run with a ball, magnified tenfold as you slip into your own psyche. The pure clean rush you feel on scoring a goal, that sweet music of a ball rushing against a string net. I was spotted on a training pitch, at the start of this fantasy. I wasn't the showy star striker or the goalkeeper with the reflexes of a cat, but something in between, a hard-working midfielder who occasionally made passes that went to feet. 'Him,' a nearby scout would say. 'That fat little butterbean is a magician.' Soon I would be transplanted from the rough five-a-side pitches of the school field to something more pristine: first the Arsenal youth ranks, which, over the course of a week of training sessions, I soon outgrew; then, accelerating into the first team, where star names would be quietly impressed at my all-seeing pitch awareness (there was often a splintered side-fantasy where Dennis Bergkamp would take me to one side and, quietly, with a single Dutch arm on my shoulder, tell me I was his inspiration). My first-team debut would come as a substitute with my team 2–1 down – I'd be brought on as a right-back, or something, in the 80th minute, when every other avenue of attack had been exhausted. 'And now an unknown quantity,' John Motson would say, watching me tuck and untuck my pristine Nike shirt into my shorts on the sideline (my squad number would be something impossibly high: GOLBY 46, in the dream), 'Young Joel Golby, here, discovered recently playing five-a-side on an astroturf pitch near a train station.' I was the fish that escaped the net, in my narrative. The unknown quantity, ignored by the scouting system, until my time had come. I was the embodiment of moneyball. And like that training-ground goal when I was a kid, all over again, it would come: the poorly scuffed corner would smash me in the face and fall to my feet; the right leg, pulled all the way back, like a catapult; top corner, 2–2, the stadium chants my name until the sun sets. England debut a month or two later, dominating appearance in the middle of the park. Two goals and an assist to take us through the group stages of the World Cup. In the final, I slot the ball in at the near post past the German goalkeeper. John Terry refuses to lift the trophy without me holding onto it too. I am asleep now. 'This is the real hero,' John Terry mouths, to the world's awaiting cameras. 'The greatest unshowy midfielder to ever live.' Even in my wildest fantasies I never scored a hat-trick.

This is still my go-to sleep routine, and honestly at the age of 31 it has gone from 'neat life hack' to 'quiet mental desperation'. I am, in terms of human age, a little past what would be considered my footballing peak. Like: if the fantasy came suddenly true, and I woke up tomorrow as a Premier League footballer, I would not even be worth a transfer fee. I've got 'English player Manchester City sign to get around certain UEFA regulations, but never actually play, even once' written all over me. I am the chief buffoon for whenever their social media team needs to make a video of someone doing free kicks or meeting a sick kid. Then my career would wind down, even from there: a stop-gap right-back for the next two seasons, then to be eased out of my contract, perhaps winding down with a couple of seasons in the Championship, a back-up defender sitting on the bench at Villa. Sit on the *Match of the Day* sofa, retired at 35, stiff-backed in a midnight navy shirt, assuredly telling Gary Lineker that Harry Kane has to do better. Don't you see? My fantasy – always absurd, but at least realistic in terms of my age and what, potentially with training, I could achieve – is now a dying dream. Wayne Rooney, meanwhile, is comfortably transitioning into a retirement that – even when I fall asleep – I couldn't have. He's checkmated me once again.

* * *

I try never to consider what it's like to *be* Wayne Rooney, but I imagine there is something Sisyphean about it: he has, since the age of 16, been dribbling a football up a hill, only to lose it with one poor touch down the other side of it again and have to go through it all tomorrow. His body bulges against the idea of high athleticism, but it's a reality he has to live in. His personality just wants to drink and smoke and go to singles nights, but he knows instead he has to eat pasta and have a loving, commercial partner-friendly family. He has, for half of his life, been a totem of Englishness, the hopes of an expectant nation made flesh, and all that has ever happened when we sent him abroad to compete for us was he would glower pink beneath the sun and shank five-yard sitters wide of the post. Rooney has achieved everything in the domestic game, ran his legs down to nubs for club and country, but there's still a small part of me that always expected more from him. When he played for me, I hated that he underachieved. When he played against me, I hated that he succeeded without ever visibly being good. Sport needs the dichotomy of heroes and villains, and for 15 years Rooney has been mine: a player I hated, from a distance, whether he did well on the field or not.

I suppose as the sun goes down on Rooney, The Player, the light starts to fade on an important part of me, too: the part that needs to hate him, the part that gains energy and vivid life from having a nemesis in some way, but also the part of me that projects myself onto him, sees my legs pulsing in place of his legs, sees me as a 32-year-old millionaire and sees him sat in a flatshare in Clapton playing PS4 when he knows he's on deadline to write a book. Wayne Rooney has spent years being my tormentor, and – now he's winding down – I'm stranded as to what this means for me. Summer 2017, he concluded his 13-year United career and headed back to Everton on a free: the club he left as a thin-necked anti-cherub welcomed him back as a grizzled man with a beard and shoulders used to carrying heavy burdens, as if his United career was his odyssey, and Everton his Athenic home. He scored twice in pre-season friendlies, then a couple of times in the early season, then immediately got winded on the stairs: Everton, after years of running on the fumes of Bill Kenwright's money, finally became an oil-injected megapower, and inexplicably spent £150 million on a couple of semi-handy centre-backs and a bunch of number 10s without any pace, plus Rooney, and expected to elevate up into the Champions League places. Where once you could build a team with Rooney as the keystone, he was doing something else now: Rooney, his enormous shadow rather than the man himself, tugging and misshaping Everton, sending them in freefall down the table, touch gone, again, shot dead, again, another sex scandal, again, and once more he has forgotten how to score: it's like his entire career is being played in exact reverse, like a dying man's final moments spooling back in front of his eyes before the abyss. A summer later he shipped predictably to the retirement grounds of the MLS, and then it can only go from here: two underwhelming seasons in DC, occasionally going viral for making a no-running cross-field assist to a college-aged striker called 'Corey', before he retires out citing injury. Few appearances on the BT Sport analysis sofa before they scrap his contract because he says 'Err, yeah' too much for them to ever really train it out. And then away, out of the glare of the public eye, retreating to his perfect Cheshire megamansion to be rich every single day of his life until he dies. Either way, he needs to be there, in the background, the inverse of me, doing better than I am, my rich brooding shadow, staring at me through the tubes. As his final game plays out one day I will be there, clapping. I just need to make eye contact with the man, exchange a dark nod. Without him, I'll have nothing left to hate in football. (What am I supposed to do, despise Harry Kane? The man can barely count up. It's too easy.) Every turn of my life has been marked with his mediocre brand of success: without him, I no longer have a milestone by which to mark myself. I hate you, Wayne Rooney. I hate you so much it makes a vital part of me feel alive.

THAT TIME I INVENTED SITTING DOWN

I came quite late to drugs. I came quite late to drink, too – I was near sanctimonious about it as a teenager, and I suppose if you're a nerd-teen who primly purses his lips at the idea of a swig of beer then nobody is exactly going to offer you drugs, are they now – and never really dabbled in weed, The Teenager's Drug Of Choice™, because both my parents smoked when I was a kid and I couldn't stand the smell of burning tobacco. They tell you, in assemblies at school, how weed is a 'gateway drug', and it's always painted as some sort of mach-speed descent into the abyss – 'One toke of weed', drug counsellors with pocket protectors tell you, through orange-fade glasses lenses, 'and a week later you'll be high out of your mind on smack, then dead' – whereas in fact all weed really does is open you up to the idea that stimulants can temporarily alter your brain chemistry in a pleasant and/or unpleasant way, and how fun that can be. It's very tiresome, living in your own mind, all of the time. Weed tells you that you don't have to do that quite so rigidly as every previous year of your teen existence before. Anyway I skipped that lesson because I was a fucking square.

The point is: I am cool now and have had drugs.

Recently a friend of mine came to town for what we termed 'The Final Sesh', a pour-one-out-for-your-comrade weekend of excess, the type of which he will never have again, due to his partner being pregnant with a baby. Jay is an old friend, a pink-faced Scouser who walks like he's smuggling gear into a Kasabian concert, and over the years we have seen each other in various states of distress: fat, drunk, dumped, vomiting, and now expecting. When that baby comes – tiny, pink, Scouse – his life as we have known it will end permanently, and a new and more responsible one forged in its place, and one, we imagine, that does not involve staying up until 4 a.m. getting really quite high on a sofa, and putting hour-long techno mixes on YouTube and turning it to such a level where you can hear it – really, *really* hear it – but also hear each other as you turn and sink room-warm lager and tell each other how important the notes you are listening to actually are. Exact transcript, from the weekend in question: 'These notes, man. These— god, these fucking *notes*.' Sounds become very important when you are high.

Because we are 30, now, and that is a difficult thing to be. Internally, I fundamentally still feel like I am a lost child still slightly bewildered to have pubic hair. Externally, the world expects me to work a job and pay bills and know what politics is. And somewhere in between those spaces, there is a dissonance: I want to be out partying and drinking and shooting my mind out of its skull to some distant, unknowing place, far along the galactic realm – but also my face really, really does look 30 years old under the thudding UV lights of a club, where young people are, gazing upon me like a spectre of death. More and more over the past year I have felt my age, not because my knees hurt or my back has gone or because I started a savings account or any shit like that, but just simply because when I'm in a bar I'm no longer part of the vital, sexy *élite* at the centre of it: I am the weird guy, on the edges, wearing a formal pair of shoes because he came straight from work and didn't really expect to be coming out tonight, drinking a Diet Coke because he's learned through years of hard lessons that pacing two beers with a soft drink really does help mellow the hangover the next day without softening the buzz the night revolves around. My clubbing days are dwindling down, now, not through any great lack of motivation on my part, but just by the sheer embarrassment of how I look when I'm there.

So for the last time ever and in honour of the new life barrelling towards us (him), Jay and I decided to go to a day rave, which is a rave, but it is during the day.

Raves have never been my thing because even at my deepest drunk or highest high I have still been lucid enough to recognise when (and be deeply annoyed by) people chatting absolute shit to me, which people on ecstasy at raves very much like to do, at me, also while listening to dance music, which is the worst type of music there is. This rave was no different: 'Are you alright, mate?' people asked. 'Are you having a good night?' This is pointless conversation, doubly so when I'm at a urinal pissing. A girl in a glitter top noticed that I was 'very tall'. Truly, I want to be ever so high that I can unlock the simple part of the brain that allows me to think this is significant or useful conversation, but I can't, even when chemically baffled, and that makes talking to people who are very difficult to me. In the toilets, a man in a Hawaiian shirt – unbuttoned, so you could see his entire waxed chest – noticed that I, too, was holding my hands under the hand-dryer for an unnecessarily long period of time, and nodded, 'Nice, isn't it?' before his sunglasses fell back onto his face and he turned to leave. 'Good to meet you, mate,' he said, extending a warm hand, and he genuinely meant it.

I mean yes I should probably mention I was flying on ecstasy at this point. I'd only ever done half a pill before, years earlier, and it made me derangedly horny – it flipped me from a meek man who has never approached a woman in a bar ever in his life into some sort of frothing-mouthed Tom-Jones-spliced-with-another-,-somehow-hornier-version-of-Tom-Jones fuck-a-geddon, where I went around to every woman in the bar in turn and chatted them up, striking out methodically with each of them, and after I woke up harrowingly alone at 3 p.m. on a Sunday afternoon I vowed never to take that one again – but Jay had somehow palmed two pills from some dealer in the crowd of the main room and despite my horniness reservations, hey, it was The Final Sesh, so yes I banged one and washed it down with cider.

The hand-dryer incident was the first I'd noticed any great side effect. Ecstasy seems to go one of two ways – horny (derangedly so), or a kind of simple child-like wonder with the world around you, but so far I was feeling neither. Coming up had just made me overwhelmingly anxious – in my head I was quite scared I'd altered my brain chemistry, permanently, forever, and was making small vows to myself that if I was still feeling this way in half an hour, I would simply leave; still feeling like this the next day, I figured, I'd quit my job and tell them I could never again come back to work; if I still felt like this a week later then I'd simply have to kill myself – but after a half-tin of cider and a couple of visits to the urinal I started to feel the requisite warm and glowy. Then I went and sat down and— oh my god, guys. Oh. Oh my god.

I feel like I invented sitting down, that day. Listen: I know a lot of people have sat, before. There were people sitting down before me and there will be people sitting after me. The first Neanderthal man probably sat on something. Animals can sit down. You are probably sitting down right now, a skill you almost certainly learned as a child. But listen to me: *I invented sitting down*. Until I took slightly too much ecstasy at a day rave as a 30-year-old trying desperately to relate one final time to an old friend, we were just *sitting on things*.

Jay was not so into this as I was. He kept saying things like: 'Please, I want to dance.' He found a flyer with the DJ set times and explained that his favourite DJ in the world was playing at 10.30 p.m. 'We'll go there,' he explained, in the soft tones he had now accepted he had to talk to me in, The Sitting Down Boy, to get me to do anything. 'We'll go there, and have a little dance.' And I would say to him: 'But after that, we can sit down?' And he would say: yes. And I would say: 'Is it alright if I just sit down for, like, 45 more minutes first?' And he would look at his watch and sigh: yes. And then I would sit there, sitting down, and explain to him very quickly how astounding sitting down feels. Direct transcript, J. R. Golby, February 10th 2018, 8 p.m., Extremely High, re: sitting down: 'Why don't we do this all the *time*?'

I suppose it was a fitting end to The Final Sesh, really: that, after years of partying together, through university and first jobs and moves to big cities and birthdays and just-because-we-feel-like-its, that time I had to go to a house and pick his shoes up because he had bafflingly left them there, that time we ended up in Soho in the deep dark pink hours of it, the time we ended up folded into the crowd of football supporters flooding into town from a packed Wembley, all those pints and all those shots, all those pisses against chain-link fences near tube stations, all those arguments with taxi drivers: that The Final Sesh would be me, desperately sitting down and unmoving, rigidly refusing to go and dance to a DJ we'd paid upwards of £30 to see. In a way, as the last dry skin of youth shedded off our friendship and we became, snakelike, incrementally more adult together, something important happened: we came to know each other, not as kids anymore, but as men. Seated men.

I HAVE THE MONOPOLY

None of us trust each other alone with the board. That is how this has happened. I will describe the scene: I am holding on to Sam's leg. Sam was my friend before this started but he isn't now. He has lost both of his adilette slides in the tussle. We are both lying on the floor in a position which, if it wasn't for the aggressive energy in the hallway, could be described as 'pre-erotic'. We are twisted together so I am both on top of and below him. Sam is holding on to his upright girlfriend's leg. Also going on: the plastic beaker I went to the kitchen for has bounced all the way down the stairs, and also Sam is biting me. Everyone is yelling. We have been playing for an hour, now, barely out of nappies in the overall life of the game, but already we have all gone, collectively, insane. Kimeya needed to take her laundry out of the machine in the kitchen and didn't trust us alone with the board in the lounge, so we both had to go with her. Sam and her both needed the bathroom too so we all had to go in shuttle runs, each watching over the door of the other while they pissed silently behind it, a complex and passive–aggressive urine-soaked retelling of the old Fox–Chicken–Grain brain teaser. Sam, while pissing: 'Joel, are you still there?' Kimeya, while pissing: 'If you guys touch that board SO HELP ME GOD.' To reiterate: Sam is *biting* me. His teeth are in my shoulder. I have him in a headlock while he slowly goes pink. Look at the clock. Look at us, all, here, on the grey-yellow carpet of their share-flat in Clapton. Fifty minutes ago we started playing Monopoly. And look at us, now, here. All our dignity gone and the only thing remaining is our hunger for the win.

* * *

Monopoly is the best game, because the Actual Devil lives inside it, and you don't get that with other board games or games in general. I mean yes: there has been a certain renaissance, in recent years, for board games, particularly adult ones – the best of them is *Settlers of Catan*, which is very good, and where you and four others tessellate an island together out of board pieces, then compete to roll dice and collect resources, building up roads and townships and most crucially an army, until whoever hits the ten-point limit hits the ten-point limit and wins, and in mimicry of Monopoly, the best game, it is also played in stages (the early game is all about collecting wood and stone, wildly; the second is about etching out a plot of land for yourself, a feeling of control, the hope that, after you die, and the wind and rain comes, this island will know your legacy; the end-game is realising you have no chance to win unless you dick over your opponents and really squeeze them whenever they come to you for wood, which they are also trying to do whenever you come to them for stone; there is no way to escape this island without calling at least someone you are close to a 'dickhead' or a 'fuckhead' or a 'fuckhead dickhead': the major mechanic in many of these games is 'not just crushing but humiliating your opponent, your opponent who in real life is your close family or your very best friend'); another game I like, *Resistance*, takes the Monopoly mechanic of 'yelling furiously at the people you love' but projects it onto a game of subterfuge, where you take it in turns to, as per the draw of random cards, play as a spy amongst a midst of golden adventurers. But many of these games lack a certain, final, over-the-top blooded edge to them, one that is stretched taut over every inch of Monopoly. A lot of these games are fun, is what I am saying, and are aimed at— how to say this? They are aimed at all of the people who have ever bought a full set of adult-edition *Harry Potter* books. They are aimed at hide-in-plain sight nerds whose main idea of violence is 'having a favourite *Game of Thrones* .gif'. Monopoly, meanwhile, makes my blood come alive. It makes me want to tear off my clothes and kill. Monopoly makes me want to get my hands red in the middle of someone else. It makes me want to murder people, in a way that feels extremely cool and powerful.

Consider the history of Monopoly: Monopoly, the board

game, is steeped in monopoly, the concept thereof. It was originally invented as The Landlord's Game, by Lizzie Magie – a feminist, short-story writer, stenographer, comedian, stage actress, engineer and later game inventor, and most importantly a proponent of Georgism, a single-tax economic philosophy – who around the turn of the 20th century invented The Landlord's Game as a way of championing the idea that land, rather than property, should be taxed by the state (some Georgism thing, man). The original game had two sets of rules: the 'Prosperity' rules, under which everyone benefited from a central pot of money every time someone on the board acquired property – the aim of the game was everyone won (everyone! won!) when the player who started with the lowest amount of money had doubled their cash. And then you had the 'Monopolist' rules, which were meant to be a stinging criticism of capitalism and instead proved to be really, really fun, and those are the ones that more closely resemble Monopoly as we know it today: buy low, rent high, crush your opponents into dust and the richest man standing wins it all. The game was a sort of pass-around hit among left-wing intellectuals (especially popular at Wharton, Harvard and Columbia) and among the Quaker community, who redrew the board with street names and destinations from Atlantic City. One person who played the game was Charles Darrow, unemployed at the time, who took the concept of The Landlord's Game, drew it up as Monopoly, and then eventually licensed it to The Parker Brothers for a hefty fee. So see: Monopoly, game, existed because it was monopolised, an idea stolen wholesale and repainted a more palatable colour and sold at a profit to the masses. Nobody knew Monopoly was a sheer rip-off until a court case in the seventies, when economics professor Ralph Anspach – who was being sued by the Parker Brothers at the time after marketing The Anti-Monopoly Game, because Monopoly cannot help but attract trouble – dug up Magie's old patents. Monopoly was the result of selling someone else's idea for violent profit and the truth about that only emerged when Monopoly tried to hammer down someone else's idea years later. Capitalism pulses so naturally through the blood of this game that it can't help but come out on the game board.

I have figured what it is that makes Monopoly like a sort of crack pipe of board-based emotional violence, and that is this: Monopoly is like six or seven different games at once, games stacked on top of games, a primary game that morphs into something More. The Monopoly you know is Stage 1: you race around the board eating up all the property you can get your sticky little hands on until it is all bought up, and this can go on for anything from four to eight trips past Go (everyone is refusing to land on Marlborough St., always Marlborough St., so that's where the hold-up is). To some families, this is where Monopoly begins and ends – there's five of you, someone's kid brother keeps getting distracted, your mum gets up halfway through her turn to go and make a round of tea, there's a film on in the background that everyone is half-watching, it has somehow taken 25 minutes for everyone to do their first pass of the board, so an hour or so in you all decide to pack it in and just watch the film instead, to the protestations of your dad, who is convinced that, because he is £500 up, he is winning. No. He is not winning. You all have failed on the first circle of Monopoly.

The next stage of the game is the foreplay-like preamble before Stage 3, where it really gets good: at this point in the game, there is a lap or two of the board where everyone is low on funds, and they are tetchy and tentative, they think about but do not ultimately buy Leicester Sq. when they land on it, they are property rich and cash poor, and they go around picking up little fines and getting hit with small, petty rents, and fine, fine. Your family might ditch out at this stage, too, convinced the game is a scam, that it is boring and dull: that you just go around, grinding, losing money on property and slowly being overwhelmed by the cost of life, a sad analogy for existence. Again, and without meaning disrespect: you've fucked it.

Because if you ditch out before Stage 3 of the game then you have approached greatness but melted your own wings before you have truly had a chance to touch it, because Stage 3 of Monopoly is *negotiation*, and that is where it transcends the board game and becomes something More. Stage 2 is necessary scene-setting for this section of the game, because most importantly it frays your nerves and your temper – imperceptibly, maybe, maybe you didn't notice yourself losing your humanity, atom-by-atom, to a green-and-red board game, but you did – the half-second of calm before the explosion. Monopoly is a game designed to drive you mad, and Stage 2 is important in that, because in those tedious loops around the board something alchemic happens: you start to believe the false money stacked in front of you is, if not real, then halfway towards real; the Monopoly currency starts to take on a weight and importance it didn't have before; you start casting your eyes round to see who has the coloured cards that will help you complete a monopoly, escalating you up the path to richness. Ask yourself the question: who do you have to crush to make a buck round here? And that is where Stage 2 grabs you and pulls you in: Stage 2 is important because it makes you a proto-capitalist, despite your real-life politics, because it's just a game, isn't it? It's just a game. It's just a game that you really, really, really – all your blood wants to jump out of your body – really want to win.

Back at the board, we have made up our own rules. You do this too. Every veteran Monopoly player has one or two firm rules which act like a handbrake to stop the entire game descending into a fistfight. Put your taxes underneath the Free Parking zone, for instance, is an unofficial rule. Three double-die rolls in a row puts you in prison. There are rules about the even distribution of houses on a monopoly (can you place four houses on one land plot, and one on another? That is open to interpretation: you will be more amenable to this rule change if you, personally, own a good monopoly, like a green one). The only three firm rules are: travel in a clockwise direction, pay what you owe, crush the competition. Everything else can be decided outside of the game. We have, predictably, gone mad with it: we now have to make wiggly fingers hand gestures whenever the Chance card is drawn, and say the word 'blop' when someone lands on Community Chest. After three turns of this, failing to make the hand gestures in a timely and enthusiastic manner results in a £50 fine (after 80 minutes of game time, our entire Monopoly is approaching a dictatorship). Or: you are not allowed to make problematic slurs over the course of mid-game banter, which also results in a £50 fine (your narrator had to pay £50 for making an animal noise that was interpreted as being a swipe at the mentally ill, for instance; another player – not naming any names, but it was Sam – had to pay £50 for calling something 'gay', which was a real schoolyard throwback: Monopoly gets inside your brain and makes you forget how to be a person). Very crucially, the final rule is this: no special sweeteners can be added in as part of negotiations. No auctioning up. Negotiations can only be between two people and must be entirely above board. And here I am suddenly hamstrung.

Because the *real* game of Monopoly happens in a magical, spectral space, just hovering in the air a few inches above the board – of Stage 3, of Negotiation, of squabbling back and forth over a property, of making an underhand deal. Nee-go-see-a-shun: so let's for instance say you have Whitechapel and I have Euston Rd, or whatever their equivalents are on whatever branded board you have but for simplicity's sake let's stick to London rules, and let's say a swap of these properties would be mutually beneficial to us both: we entered this arena as friends but now we are enemies united in a common goal, to crush. So I might offer you Euston Rd, yeah, in exchange for Whitechapel. But I also don't want to be stung by rent every time I land on your monopoly. And so, I will say, quietly under my breath, where nobody else can hear it, when everyone else is trying to remember whose dice throw it is: well, maybe, you know, every time I land on Whitechapel, you can give me a pass. And maybe ... maybe when you land, on Euston Rd. Maybe I can look the other way. Maybe ... maybe we could grease each other's wheels a bit, here. Maybe we could play some *real* Monopoly.

Admission: I consider cheating a natural part of Monopoly, or at least a third- or fourth-tier subgame that sits invisible like a saddle over the top of the game proper. I am telling you right now that if you play Monopoly with me and trust me to be the banker then you are a fool. I am saying that if you play Monopoly with me and I quote a rental price while holding the property card up to my face with a wry smile then you should demand to see that card, because I am definitely massaging that figure and quoting a false one back to you on the basis that you – you with your blind, your innocent trust – will pay it regardless. Monopoly is an evil game and I am an evil player of it. I am rolling the dice quickly because you got distracted and didn't notice me landing on your property. I am making up house rules about jail, about how you end up there and how long you must stay. I will win at Monopoly, because to win at Monopoly is to bend the very rules around you until you get what you want. I am going to crush you in a negotiation, because that's what Monopoly is. *That's* the real quiz. Don't you get it? Monopoly rubs away at the skin of you and reveals the steel-cold skeleton underneath. You cease to become a person when you play this game and become instead a monster. Don't you see? Don't you see? Give me Whitechapel. Give it to me. Give me Whitechapel and I promise not to crush you.

When I was nine years old Labour won the election. I remember this because I woke up to my mother cheering – my mother had a very unusual way of celebrating things, which was to grit her teeth together, punch the air in front of her, and somehow without opening her mouth shout 'yes!' – and my Year 5 teacher came to school that day in a brilliant red pantsuit. I was raised in a firmly anti-Conservative household – I vividly remember bouncing on my bed at age seven, or eight, with my friend Charlie, and we were discussing the country's prime minister at the time, John Major. 'I hate him because he takes all our money,' I told Charlie, solemnly. I have no idea how that idea filtered into my young brain. I am assuming my parents whispered anti-Tory sentiment to me in the womb. 'Fuck Maggie Thatcher,' they might coo through the bump to my foetus. 'Burn the witch like she burnt the industry out of this country.' I've voted Labour all my life and until they zig too far over the wobbly line in the centre of British politics then I will continue to. You're meant to vote to bring the rest of the country up, not protect those who have already made it. I digress.

The point is: fuck all that, because when I play Monopoly, I am David Cameron rimming Maggie off, I am Edwina Currie fucking John Major harder than he can fuck her back, I am a roaring drunk Boris Johnson, I am Tory to the core-y, I am shaking hands with property developers in shady backroom multi-million pound deals, I am blocking social housing to build luxury apartments in an effort to squeeze an extra £200k into my own private account, I am wearing a Panama hat in the Cayman Islands and laughingly lighting a cigar with a £50 note. This is where Monopoly truly comes into its own: it allows you to rub away all your morals, all your ethics, all your beliefs, all the myriad ways you have been shaped into who you are today, all the saturated memories of election day 1997, all the bouncing on a single bed with Charlie, bemoaning the state, all that, gone – because in Monopoly you get, for a minute at least, to taste what it is to be the bad guy. To leverage property to crush those around you who you deem to be lower. You get, for a moment, to be Conservative and Republican all at once. You taste what it is like to be powerful and rich. And

I would like to tell you, all of you: stop this from ever happening to me, in real life. Stop me from ever accruing wealth. Because, if Monopoly is anything to go on – and it absolutely is – I *will* become a monster.

There are moral lessons to be learned as a result of this evil that courses through Monopoly and into me. Take, for instance, the time recently when I crushed the soul of a ten-year-old down to dust. A lot of people say: *Joel,* they say, *it is unethical to extort ten-year-olds out of hundreds of pounds the literal first time they play Monopoly,* and to those critics I say: fuck you, and fuck you again. The kid had just got Pokémon-themed Monopoly as a Christmas present. I volunteered to teach the boy the game rules by playing a dummy round against him. Nobody else was going to do it. And then he landed on my three-house Koffing (Bond St.), incurring rent of £330 and he learned the main rule of the game, which is that he owes me £330 and he needs to pay up. This is not how children learn and, indeed, grow.

Now, imagine you are sat cross-legged on the floor down with me while I explain this: I am willing, magnanimously, to waive this fee, if he gives me the one token I want – Growlithe (Euston Rd), which would enable me to complete my green Monopoly. In my hand I also hold Starmie (Whitechapel Rd), which completes his light-blue Monopoly. We are at an impasse. We are also getting escalatingly confused by the fact that every road name is represented by a first-generation Pokémon.

So here's where the game gets good, you see, because for a moment discount the rent: I want his Growlithe and he wants my Starmie. But he doesn't realise I am in the position of power: Starmie is worth less than Growlithe, but he wants it – in that way that ten-year-olds want things on Monopoly, without the cool calm cowl of logic – and so he wants Starmie primarily because he keeps landing on it and getting stung for £6 rent, and secondarily because it completes his Monopoly. He thinks that because Starmie is worth a lot to him, then he is in a position to leverage more money out of me for it. This, see, is how you crack the helix of Monopoly and force the mid- then end-game of it: you have to negotiate, two wills meeting across an invisible space. The great lie of Monopoly is that it's played on the board, with a small thimble-piece and some die: no. Monopoly is played in IOUs and side-hustles, of sweeteners and deals. Monopoly only becomes a *game* when you ignore the board and rise up to play it. Monopoly is only played when you negotiate. And that is where I am at the advantage, because I am an adult, and he is a child, and I am evil and he is good. I will win this.

What we come to is this: I will pay £400 plus my Starmie for his Growlithe, which I am only allowed to build one property on (this is a canny side-negotiation by the child: he shows promise). I will offer free rent on Koffing. He will not have to pay me the rent he owes me for Koffing, for I am a beatific developer, a kind and just Monopoly deity, plus more crucially I have now assembled an unyielding gauntlet from Free Parking to Liverpool St. Station. Now I know what you are thinking: 'This is an overly fair and reasonable negotiation, Joel! You're throwing both money and opportunity away, here! You could use this chance to crush him!' But to that I say: I could crush him now, sure. I already am. But if I give him the taste for Monopoly – for the thrill, for the negotiation, for that blind, blind, blind pursuit of money – then I can make him love a game so much that I can crush him, again and again and again, dozens of times over dozens of games, for the rest of his and my natural life. What I am saying is: why crush someone's soul, cheaply, once, when you have the chance to crush it a hundred times over?

I can delight in telling you that the boy picked up and threw two (two.) cushions at me, punched two more, and screamed into a fifth, before his dad came in and sent him furiously to bed. I am brilliant at Monopoly.

Back in Clapton, though, against adults, and I have lost. Kimeya wins – she always wins because she grew up in a family that was venomously competitive and played Monopoly like it was an Olympic sport, plus she is a lawyer and started citing actual property law halfway through a negotiation over Bond St. – and we have all, separately, over the course of some hours, variously had a tantrum. A demon lives inside this game, I am sure of it. Pore over ancient texts and find which one. Pruflas, for example, the demon of falsehood, quarrels and discord: that's a good fit. Agares: earthquakes, foul language and destroying dignity. It is fair to say every demon is assembled here, watching us, invisibly, wreak chaos on one another: demons of distrust, demons of extortion, the demon of shouting 'oh fuck OFF' when someone else lands on Free Parking: they are all here. In the cab home, I explain to the driver that I have just spent hours playing Monopoly, and am emotionally spent by it, and do not want to talk about my loss. 'I used to play it as a kid,' he explains. 'It taught me about the geography of London.' A pause. 'I never finished it.' He tells me about a game of football he played once, where a striker was through on goal, and he yanked his shirt back to stop him from scoring, and how he got a straight red. 'I was always a fair player,' he told me. 'I don't know where that came from.' I do: games like this pitch each other against our fellow man and bring out the dark and evil streak in all of us. Put your nasty side on and wear it for a couple of hours like a mask. Pull the shirt, kick the leg, outsmart a child. Monopoly is the best game because it allows you to be the worst person. Give me Whitechapel or I'll cut you.

HALLOWE'EN '96

Once when I was a kid my parents held a party, which was notable because it was just the rarest thing I could imagine either one of them doing, in fact thinking back, a couple of major birthdays aside, it literally did not happen again, and I suppose in that there reveals some bleakness of true, bonafide adulthood – as a human on the cusp of his thirties now, I live in fear that the parties of my twenties were an anomaly, doomed to fade forever away, to be taken up instead by other humans, younger humans, in their twenties; that I have crossed forever a divide, like a window I can only look through but never pass, where I can now only watch the young people, with their parties, having fun; that I am doomed to never have it again – the fear being that actual, legitimate adulthood is just a long slow fade away from the parties of your youth, and the party frequency demonstrated by my parents during my own personal childhood kind of goes some way to means testing that.

Anyway the point is they had a party.

So it was a Hallowe'en one, the party, which I know because I remember so vividly my dad's costume: he had painted his entire head and skull (he was bald, my father, in that very inarguable way, an all-body baldness, his head and skull arrangement resembling a sort of large emotive walnut) with a sort of cheap green face paint that absolutely did not cover his skin tone at all, making him look, instead of like a warlock or ogre as was I assume the intended effect, but actually just as though he was about to be sick on an aeroplane or was feeling quite queasy but would get over it on a coach or bus; and, to complete the picture, he arranged on his head with stage glue a series of (unbranded) Rice Krispies, painstakingly applied, as sort of boils or warts. The overall effect was someone had very half-heartedly cursed a toad to live a human life. He paired his green head with blue jeans, a faded grey polo, a greasy-necked sky-blue body warmer and tan leather work boots, i.e. the exact same outfit he wore every single day of his entire fucking life.

My mother dressed more traditionally as a witch.

I knew this party was important to my parents because I had been very firmly condemned away from it. This was telegraphed to me repeatedly as we went about the pre-party chores that seem necessary ahead of such a gathering: the three of us formed as a team to move the Big Table, the yard was swept, my mother made some sort of cake-in-green-jelly arrangement that went largely untouched at the party proper and so was eaten by me for breakfast for days. My instructions were clear: at 7 p.m., when the party started to kick off, I would retire to my room and play imagination games, and from there after a while I was trusted to put myself to bed. I painted a sign for our broken bathroom door that read 'NO LOCK, PLEASE KNOCK', affixed it with Blu Tack, brushed my teeth and combed my hair, then retired to bed.

Only I could not fucking sleep because of the sound of partying below me. Like: obviously. We lived in a six-room terrace house that was suddenly heaving with 45 to 50 adults, most of whom I had never seen before and never saw again since and am still, some 21 years later, utterly baffled as to who they were and why they were in my house dressed as ghosts and such, but they were all drunk and yelling and not eating the jelly. Whenever I was a kid and I couldn't sleep my mind defaulted to assuming that I was in trouble: that, if discovered I was in bed and awake past, say, the frankly illegal time of 9 p.m., I would be yelled at so thoroughly I would die. With the hubbub of the party below me, I laid perfectly still in bed (turning over in any way or fidgeting was not an option because the slight small noise of child on sheet would alert my parents to the fact that I was awake: they would hear it, somehow, over the conversation and through the ceiling, and they would pause the music and roar 'EXCUSE ME?' and they would immediately march upstairs and take me to child prison), arms pinned to my side, eyes rigidly open.

I assumed I could just spend an entire evening like this

– my plan was to just not sleep for 12 to 16 hours, then, in the morning, walk downstairs with a big show of yawning, stretching of the arms, asking my parents mildly how the party was, Did You Have Fun, Oh Was It Loud I Didn't Notice, that I could spend the next eight or nine nights slowly catching up on sleep an hour at a time, that eventually I would compensate for this overall loss. But then I heard sneaking on the landing outside my door, the sound of drunk women shushing, and my mother's voice was there, detached, always, a voice delivered ever through great outward plumes of cigarette smoke, and one asked cutely, 'Oh, can we see him?' and 'Oh, can we go see him sleep?' and my mother, a witch remember, said '[*sound of cigarette smoke exhaling*] Sure. [*sound of more cigarette smoke exhaling*] Go wild.'

Which is how we find ourselves with two women full-on screaming in surprise to find a rictusly awake child awaiting them when only they wanted to see cute dozing. My mother, upon this discovery: 'Why are you awake?'

At which point I was dragged downstairs in my pyjamas to be shown to the attendant party. I was a nervous boy and this did not suit me: dozens of large, tree-sized adults, in black and with monstrous faces, peering down on me, cackling and laughing at the absurdity of a child up this late, handing me party snacks to eat with my hands in front of them, as though you might watch a squirrel consume a nut. And then I became incredibly weary, the kind of tired only a child in his pyjamas in a forest of monsters can become, and fell asleep on a sofa, and my toad-father carried my limp body, sweetly murmuring, up to bed, where I slept solidly through the night and the subsequent clean-up the next day. And that was the first time I fell asleep at a party.

SUMMER '09

When I was 22 a nightclub opened up back home that offered what – looking back on it now – is the most absurd and ludicrous deal known to man: an All-You-Can-Drink night, with a £10 entry fee and a free cloakroom. I don't know why the 'free cloakroom' aspect of it seemed so important to me at the time (I had a coat stolen from a corner sofa in a nightclub about a year previously, and I suppose at the time that was ... the most important and insulting thing ... that had ever happened to me? And completely changed my worldview on everything, based on whether they did or did not have cloakrooms attached to them? I don't know), but I remember that being the real clincher: not that I could get catatonically drunk in exchange for one crisp ten-pound note, but that my H&M jacket (I got it in the sale! It only cost £8 anyway!) wouldn't go missing while I was doing it. Galvanised by this, the plan was set: we would go to the All-You-Can-Drink night, and drink all that we could.

Well, we went multiple times. Economically, it did not make sense to get drunk any other way: even pooling your resources and getting supermarket beer crates and bottles of vodka to have at home didn't work out at a drink-per-pound rate that could beat Elements, so we essentially spent a whole summer drinking the whole place dry. Did we care that the vodka was thinned down with water? We did not. Did it matter that the only lager available on tap was a sort of cheap fizzy unbranded thing that might well have been the recycled dregs of other, more acceptable lagers? We did not. Did we care that the atmosphere in there cycled through three moods (from 9 p.m. until 10.30 p.m., sober and vibeless; 10.30–11, pure and dreadful chaos; 11–1 a.m., some of the worst DJs in Chesterfield attacked us all with house music and a smoke machine)? Also no. To reiterate: one of the great selling points of this place to me was that I had somewhere to put my coat. This is as close to nihilism as I've ever got in my life. I didn't care about *anything*.

I don't know if you've been to an All-You-Can-Eat buffet, but the theory when transposed over to drinking is much the same. Every year for her birthday my aunt insists on going to this weird family-friendly world buffet place on an industrial park in Wolverhampton, where for £8 all-in you are issued a small white plate and the offer to go tonto on various hot plates of food. There is a pizza station, and a section that makes vindaloo. There is a whole grill where meats and fish are pumped out in piles. Trays of Chinese food, but also chicken nuggets. English cuisine is represented by deep trays of chips and every possible English breakfast meat, fried and left to sweat beneath a heat lamp. Go there with good intentions and leave with salt bloating: to enter the domain of the world buffet is to be immediately overwhelmed by decision fatigue, and you end up trailing back to your table with a plate high with chow mein, and somehow also roast potatoes, and then weirdly a wedge of pizza stuffed on top there like a cherry on a sundae, also for some reason broccoli. It is impossible not to have a bipolar plate of food when given the opportunity to serve yourself from a buffet. Which is a roundabout way of saying: yes, I was frequently very very sick at Elements.

I was 22, so I rarely stuck to one alcohol. Firstly we would have these neon green little shots, which were terrible. Then maybe an awful fizzy pint or two, which were also very terrible. A terrible off-brand Jägerbomb would follow. Maybe a couple of (terrible) vodka-cokes. There was an hour in the night, every night, where the DJ seemed to play Lady Gaga's 'Just Dance' five or six times in a row, so I would lean against a sweat-dripped wall and sort of sway to it, eyes half open, before going and getting another terrible beer. The toilets were attended, so had an odd array of aftershaves and perfumes plus a tray of lollipops, and you would always leave there heaving off the fumes of it, the heady mix of beer piss and Paco Rabanne. Then you'd go and get another terrible fizzy beer or something, try and stay upright long enough until the lights went up. We were frequently, frequently kicked out. One time my mate got kicked out so hard on a Friday that, when he went back there on the Saturday, he *immediately got kicked out again*, because the bouncer who kicked him out the night before recognised him as getting so catatonically pissed that she pre-empted him doing it again. 'Miss!' I said, already three pints down in ten minutes, 'Miss, please! His coat! It's still in the cloakroom!'

As a show of support we all (reluctantly) left, wobbling home in solidarity. Summer had caught up with me: my face was burnt a permanent pinky-red, I'd been out to about ten consecutive £10 nights in a row, all I seemed to eat was 2 a.m. chip plates, my body was dying from the inside-out, every moment alive was agony. It was, obviously, the greatest summer of my life. You're bulletproof, when you're 22, mostly: you bounce off walls and shake off hangovers, you only care about your coat and where your next £10 is coming from, the most important thing in the world to you is sitting four-to-a-sofa with your mates and sinking a crate of beer. Which is what we went home to do, before I fell unconscious on a sofa, and everyone wrote the names of their favourite wrestlers on my face with marker pen. I came to abruptly at 4 a.m. – 'Where am I?' I insisted, 'Where's my coat?' – and everyone laughed because I had 'KENNEDY' written across my forehead. 'I don't have "KENNEDY" written across my forehead,' I insisted, then staggered home.

Elements closed soon after – because, I'm assuming, £10 All-You-Can-Drink offers aren't financially viable even for one second – meaning there was only one summer like that for us before the dream ended. It was probably for the best, in a way, in terms of me still being alive today, but you're allowed to miss times that were fun even if they were also extremely medically bad for you. The next morning my mum woke me up with a bacon sandwich and told me I had to get a job. 'It's time, kid,' she said, soothingly. 'Also you have "KENNEDY" written on your forehead.' And that was the second time I ever fell asleep at a party.

MAY '15

The Pacquiao–Mayweather fight was highly anticipated by boxing acolytes but not by me because I very truly did not enjoy any boxing match that wasn't between Rocky Balboa and another man, but for whatever reason the fight fell on a kind of hectic party weekend – two people were having birthday parties and I'd promised to go to both, and ended up also agreeing to go to a friend-of-a-friend's 4 a.m. screening of the fight – so I kind of read up enough to know what a jab was and went out into the night to get on it. You can probably see where this one goes: I 'jabbed' myself with five pints of beer at one birthday, 'haymakered' myself with three more at the next, and ended up on the wrong side of an incredibly busy A-road, clenching onto a can and looking across four lanes of traffic at my stranded Uber, trying to get to the third. 'Mate,' I said on the phone to the man who the app said was parked right in front of me, 'can you not just ... drive over here?' And he said: no.

I got to the party in the end, but was swaying (much like a boxer! After 15 rounds! Of being punched directly in the head!) so I went to the bathroom to freshen up. This didn't go well: I splashed my face enough to focus my vision in the mirror, but seeing how truly pissed I was sort of served to recoil myself down into a second, deeper level of pissed – self-fulfilling drunkenness – and exited the bathroom stumbling now, impossibly, more than I was before. I was introduced to a number of very calm American PhD students who were quietly watching the boxing match with me, and then smoothly offered a small white heap of cocaine.

This, I suppose, was the moment I became, truly, a Big Boy. I'd not been offered coke before, but the way it was laid out for me – so elegantly! Such a casual offer! Piled on an intricately embossed, expensive-looking book! – made me realise that now I was at an adult party, for adults. Baby Joel was last seen terrified and crossing an A-road trying to get in an Uber he couldn't afford to have cancel on him. Adult Joel was here, now, drunk and swaying and about to snort a line of drugs with his nose. When I was a kid, in the knots-and-camping youth club Beavers, I watched in half-tears as my friend Charlie, six months older than me at school, crossed over a figurative bridge (a folded parachute laid on the tiled floor of a church hall) to join the Scouts, the next-age-group-up club he was now a part of. I was just a boy, down here with the Beavers, learning to tie my shoelaces on a cardboard shoe shape with holes cut out of it. Charlie was a man, with a different woggle on his scarf and new friends to make. This book with cocaine on it was very much like that, in a way.

Anyway, no. When I was given my first joint to smoke, on a weekend trip to Amsterdam, I had to be very literally taught how to inhale it, so alien was the idea to me, and this small line of cocaine was similar: I very literally couldn't figure out how to close one nostril and snort. 'Mate, you just—' my friend-of-a-friend said, but I shushed him away. 'I got it, I got it,' I said. Then I tried two more times – running a rolled-up £20 note over it, ineffectively, like a hoover blocked with a child's toy – then gave the untouched book back to him. 'You know what, mate,' I said. 'I'm actually alright.' Pretty immediately I fell upright and asleep in a kitchen chair and missed the fight entirely, and had to be kicked awake to leave again, and I suppose the great moral is this: whatever party you invite me to, wholesome, Hallowe'en, drunk, adult, child, jellied, coked out, cloakroomed: I will ruin it. I will ruin it, always, by falling asleep.

I WILL NEVER BE AS TOUGH AS PITBULL

OR: CHASING THE MASCULINITY OF THE GREATEST CUBAN–AMERICAN CROSSOVER POP-RAPPER IN ALL OF HISTORY

'Smell me,' I said. I'm with a new girl and we're in that sort of weird hazy space between 'hanging out' and 'actual boyfriend/girlfriend', i.e. we've seen each other as naked as it is possible to see another person and eaten pizza in each other's beds but not actually sat down and Had The Chat about Where We Are As A Couple yet, and I am saying 'smell me'. 'Smell me,' I say, and I offer her my wrist. And she says: that's nice, yeah. And I say: 'It's Pitbull. By Pitbull.' And she says, 'Pitbull? As in: *Pitbull*?' And I say, yes. And she laughs, and laughs, and laughs and laughs and laughs. 'Respect Pitbull,' I say. 'Show your respect to Pitbull.'

* * *

I've been thinking about it a lot and I think the pop-rap artist Pitbull is one of the most singular and unparalleled examples of masculinity in our culture today. He's also sort of weird, and laughable, and the way he straddles that line – at once a joke and an icon – is something I find deeply inspiring. Pitbull transcends many things – taste, fashion, trends, race – but most of all he skips like a stone over a glassy lake the very concept of *irony*, at once wrapped tightly in its knot and kicking lightly six feet clear above it. Pitbull contains *multitudes*, is what I'm saying, and I want to be like him.

I am not a macho man. Machismo is a hard concept to pin down, because it's less a strict list of principles and things to be good at – a macho man can lift heavy iron, and kick a ball perfect spiral, and eat just a mess of boiled eggs at once, and drive a stick-shift car, and tolerate incredibly spicy hot foods, but he can also walk into a room and *own* it, look good in a suit, send flowers to a love to say 'thank you'. My machismo is something different, softer: I have a very complex skincare routine, for instance, and a whole cupboard of herbal and non-herbal teas, and my tender body does not really react well to fabrics washed in biological laundry powder. My machismo is more soft knits and high necks, and I am Really Into Cats, and music-wise I cannot really tolerate any songs that have lyrics in them, let alone jangling chords, so like the absolute polar inverse of cock-rock. For a formative period of my adolescence my half-broken voice sounded exactly like my mother's so when I answered the phone her friends would talk to me as if I were her (and I mean what is it about middle-aged women that just makes them on a constant rolling start re: any conversation about their vagina or anus? The amount of times I've heard, 'Oh hello Hazel listen: it's me nuggets again—' I mean) and I think that had a very impactful impression on my nascent feelings of masculinity. I am very unstrong and deeply unathletic and despite a lifetime spent searching for the one sport I assume everyone has in their locker that they are particularly good at, I am yet to find it (I am okay at ping-pong and suspect – but have not ever really tested – that I would be a competent adult badminton player). I eat meat but not in a very macho I'll-have-my-steak-raw-and-my-whisky-rawer way because I actually have a very overriding sweet tooth making me far more likely to order tiramisu and get a little bit squishy on it. I cannot grow a beard but I also don't quite have the raw charisma to go clean-shaven without looking like I'm still taking GCSEs so both sides of the world of shaving are closed off to me entirely. I have never, ever fired a gun. I have never, ever put up a shelf. I have never, ever given someone a black eye. I find most wild animals terrifying and have opinions about soft furnishings. If I had to describe my lovemaking style as a popular coffee drink it would be 'vanilla latte'. How do you think Pitbull fucks? I think Pitbull fucks like a snake spliced with a wolf. Pitbull fucks like a Ferrari driving up a skyscraper. Pitbull fucks like a double espresso poured into a fire. Pitbull fucks like a Gatling gun hanging out of a police helicopter. Pitbull has never ever had to Google 'what toner is best for oily skin?'

Pitbull fascinates me, then, for two reasons: one, he is my exact masculine inverse, the same way a bullet is the opposite of a gun, and second because his status as a near-galactically famous pop star makes little to no actual sense. I mean: *look* at him. In an age of flawless hyper-celebrity, Pitbull's vibe is still 'small-town bouncer who put out a nude charity calendar'. His net worth is estimated at $65 million (2016), but I still sort of feel that, if I bumped into him in the street, he could still palm me a couple of grimy grams of MDMA for £20. Pitbull hasn't worn anything that is non-designer and non-fitted – and, crucially, not-a-suit – for the best part of eight years now, but he still sort of looks like one of those anonymous blokes at a Russian millionaire's wedding who may or may not have a warrant out for his war crimes. (Pitbull wears excessive richness in a way that seems both pre-destined to him from birth, and ever-so-slightly uncomfortably: a size M t-shirt stretched over a size L frame.) He Will Not Get Over White Trousers. And even his stage name, Pitbull, is deeply uncool: the kind of nickname you give to the senseless kid who used to ride BMX around your cul-de-sac and dated your sister during that summer she was trying to piss your dad off, and ended up getting an infected neck tattoo and, later, six years in prison for a particularly petty charge of theft. Pitbull exudes the kind of energy a glamorous uncle at a large family barbeque might, but he's escalated and gathered it up like a snowball, accelerating constantly in speed and power, until it has shot down a ramp and up at the lip into the white-pale sky: flying, there, momentum keeping it in place, off into the horizon, gone. Pitbull turned a sort of everyman-alpha everytown-mediocrity into superstardom, without really changing the formula up at all. His mere existence at the top of the tree twists my head.

Pitbull was born Armando Christian Pérez, but I don't give a crap about that. Every autobiography of every pop star with a stage name starts like this: they were born a mortal, and ascended to god. I am not interested in the path of Armando Christian Pérez, because that guy was clearly mediocre: it was only when he took on the name of Pitbull, the mantle and the mask, that he became *Pitbull*. Pitbull's path to the top is fascinating to me because at some point along the line there was an invisible twist there, where Pitbull pivoted from 'a kind of rap in-joke exclusive to Miami' to 'big enough pop star to open the World Cup ceremony in Brazil', and it's hard to pinpoint exactly when that happened. I am fascinated by the idea of most pop stars as awkward-shaped high school teens, but no more is that so than with Pitbull: can you imagine him at school? There is absolutely no way he didn't deal Ritalin and draw logos for himself in the back of all his workbooks. I feel like there are still bathrooms at South Miami Senior High that have the word 'PITBULL' etched into them – shakily, at first, but then confidently as he began to live his truth – into the very brick of them with a compass.

Pitbull's first few years in music, 2004 to 2010, were solid if unspectacular (his first album was pushed by and featured the at the time much bigger artist Lil' Jon, who met the rapper and liked him; in 2001, Pit was taken under the wing of Famous Artist Music & Management's Robert Fernandez, who 'saw the eagerness and hunger he had' and decided to start working with him, and what I'm getting from all of this is Pitbull's early career was marked by the fact that he was 'quite likeable' and 'very keen', and I think we can all learn a little something from that). Early Pitbull is proper dry-hump-in-a-sweaty-club rock-ya-ass music, and seeing old footage of him then, before the suit, is like seeing the Queen in a t-shirt: Pitbull lip-syncs to a crowd while wearing a sleeveless basketball vest (when have you ever seen Pitbull's upper arms? They exist. But when have you *seen* them?), or walks slo-mo into a set mansion in two oversized shirts unbuttoned over a tee, baggy suit jacket w/ jeans. Then Pitbull's breakout 2010 hit *I Know You Want Me (Calle Ocho)* happened, and he turns up in the video to that in a black suit, black shirt, black oversized shades, like the final boss in a videogame where you exclusively combo-kill Vegas seminar pick-up artists, and that was it: he rapped the line *label flop but Pit don't stop / got her in the cockpit playing with Pit's cock*, and lo, a legend was born.

From then on, Pitbull has made every single song that anyone on earth has stripped to, and it's made him enormously successful as a result. His formula is actually pretty simple: Pitbull has a keen ear for fleeting music trends, so he lifts from them for a backing track, raps about how good a night it's going to be on top of it, ideally inserts a female vocalist feature, and then boom: song of the summer, every single time. 2013's *Timber* is perhaps the most perfect example of this: Pit jumped on to a nascent country revival with a harmonica-led backing arrangement (how can you mash up country music and EDM and make a worldwide #1 hit? Ask Pitbull, a Midas-fingered maniac); got Ke$ha to sing the hook; very visibly did not turn up to the video shoot so every shot of him dancing in a pink suit jacket on a slightly gloomy beach is interspersed in with Ke$ha, a thousand miles and a number of weeks away, writhing on a farm; and sang the line *this biggity boy's a diggity dog* in it; and somehow this was the only song that played on my office radio for an entire calendar year from October 2013 onwards. What Pitbull does doesn't make sense in the cold glowing light of day, but put a single bottle of beer in your hand and cram yourself into a low-ceilinged room with a thousand other dancing people and suddenly it does: Pitbull, very crucially, makes music for you to listen to when you're waiting at the bar trying to buy a girl a drink. Pitbull is the soundtrack for every night when a boy who still takes his laundry home for his mum to do makes out with a girl who has 10,000 Instagram followers minimum.

Working theory: I'm writing this from the year 2018, which I have to tell you, is not a great year. We'll look back on this and laugh, I really think, but right now it feels chaotic: Trump is in the midst of his presidency, and we have all finally realised that his term in the White House is real, it is happening, there is no escaping this fact. Tectonic plates of stress push over everything: climate change looms, a generation of young people seem inexorably pinned under the vestiges of the 2008 market crash, home ownership is a distant dream for so many, debt is up, wages are down, weaponised crime is up (weaponised crime!), the police are seemingly at war with people of colour, Britain is creaking away from Europe for no discernible reason, trans people have to scream and shout for their right to be recognised as people, the alt-right rises, trolling has become a legitimate political force, Russia is infiltrating Britain, Russia is infiltrating the US, Syria is at war with itself and we are all trying to get involved with it, Facebook hovers above us, ominous and large, listening in. Like: the earth is tearing itself into a desert planet and we're too busy firing bullets into each other and posting memes about it to really notice. So it's stressful. It's a stressful time. We will look back on this and laugh! But it's a stressful time. To be alive.

Pitbull is not stressed, and actually his sort of malaise-wrestling braggadocio is an antithesis of stress itself, and I think somewhere in that nub is the pulsing core of his appeal. Look at a still photo of Pitbull and hear the word: *aha*. Wake up and rub your eyes and know Pitbull is somewhere, pouring a perfect, dripless tequila shot.

Pitbull tells us that there is a core energy in this world, Partying, and that everything else we do should be driven into that pursuit: having a good time, flexing in a club, smelling good, grinding nice, dancing on that girl, getting tipsy but not out-of-control drunk, camera flashes, perfect teeth, *dale*. Pitbull is a monument to having a good time. He is a cathedral to the idea of doing three lines of coke in a bathroom and losing your fucking mind to an EDM drop.

And in that sense I think Pitbull does something bigger than make music for people who are in the Uber home waiting to screw: I actually think he actively adds balance to the universe. Pitbull is Pitbull, sure, but he also isn't: he's essentially a suit, an occasional soul patch, some oversized glasses and a gruff roar, the same song in different formations, ten interchangeable dancers behind him. If you dressed Pitbull in jeans and a t-shirt he could be, very literally, anyone. You wouldn't be able to pick him out of a line-up if he'd punched you once in the street. Pitbull, like James Bond, only becomes himself when he puts on the suit: and, again, like James Bond, he could be easily played by another actor, and another actor the generation after that, then George Lazenby for a bit, then another, better actor. We need Pitbull because we need someone to remind us to have fun; we need Pitbull because we need something fresh to dance to in nightclubs. Pitbull is essentially 'work hard, party harder' made flesh, he's an inspirational mantra about getting it, his life is what would happen if you could make an erection sentient. Pitbull, crucially, is an *energy*, a universal yang to balance out the collective yin, and we need to always have him there – quietly, somewhere, out there, trying to put an EDM drop in the middle of some Balearic folk music – to keep ourselves together. Respect Pitbull, is what I'm saying. Every time I smell like him I am reminded that something out there is good.

THE TAO OF DOG PISS

There is this incredible physical feat I can pull off only when I'm playing pool, the green tabletop game beloved of steaming drunk men and students, something I have variously been at certain points in my lifetime, and it is this: with the cue resting in the cleft between my folded thumb and forefinger, and my middle finger steadying the entire hand on the baize, I can flick and raise my ring finger to insane heights and angles while the rest of my hand remains still. It's more of a physical tic than something I can control – there is this impulsive *need* in my ring finger to jolt until it finds a comfortable angle and settles, like that ache in your thumb you have developed recently when you wake up and *need* to check and scroll your phone – and the ring-finger flicking routine is an integral part of my pool-shooting game: I am a reasonably good pool player, not a ringer exactly but a good obtuse angle potter, and the jolting ring finger is a large part of that.

There are other sacred routines, too: normally I am playing pool in an extremely shitty northern pub, when

I play it, where the baize has been stained in places by two or three separate glasses of wine or pints of Snakebite (normal pints of lager do not stain pool tables as bad, but do get spilled on them with much more frequency), and that means the communal cues are often quite shitty and warped somehow and the whole table has a lean to it like a badly kept bowling alley, and the tip of the cue is mashed and compacted in myriad different places, and so to find the exact specific good striking part of the cue I will, while in shooting position, twizzle and rotate the cue, until I find something I am marginally happy with but has no scientific or logical reasoning to how it is a better part of the cue to hit the ball with.

OR: there is a small internal gyroscope that must be quietly abated by putting weight evenly on one or both of my feet, and until I find that exact mercurial centre – a moment or two, tilting forward and back – I cannot pot with accuracy. Friends who have been privy to these three concurrent routines while playing me at pool have often been known to remark ‘fucking hell’ or, more exasperated now, ‘fucking *hell*’ in the ten to fifteen seconds it takes me every time I pot. But the point is: I pot, buddy. I pot and pot again. I pot and my whole body feels it, every singing atom of who I am.

Have you ever seen Cristiano Ronaldo take a free kick? It’s a glorious thing, and close to watching someone praying: he steps backwards three large steps from the ball, then one step to either the right or left, and then stands there, feet splayed wide apart, arms out rigid by his side, chest up and out like a retired army general marching downstairs for breakfast; then he breathes, three deep breathes in through the nose and out dramatically through the mouth; then he settles, for a moment, waits for the whistle, his ablutions complete; and then he runs on the spot two or three times before actually putting his glorious body in motion, and then pelts the ball fantastically hard, and Cristiano Ronaldo 1, Opposition Team 0.

OR: have you ever swung a golf club, really really swung it? It is all about routines and sub-routines that only you can identify, a war of attrition between the logical clinical mechanic of the swing and the small feelings inside yourself when the weight is on your feet just *right*. Pulse each foot until they are in the right position. Wiggle yourself onto the exact balance you want. Look up, look down, look up again, then head down: and beat, and beat, inhale and *swing*. It has to feel right or it won't go. You cannot swing a golf club without feeling.

OR: have you ever seen a dog piss? Dogs piss like I play pool, or Cristiano Ronaldo hits a free kick, or you swing a golf club: they sniff the ground, dogs, tamp it with their paws, find the exact blades of grass they wish to anoint with their holy piss, then turn around in tight circles two, three times, then squat and let go. Or shit, they shit in a similar way too. And what I am saying is this: sport is very primal, based on feeling and motion we cannot sense or see. In that way, it renders us like dogs, intricately pissing. We are no closer to animals than when we are swinging a golf club. We are little more than beasts when we hit a tennis serve just right. Thank you and amen.

WHY ROCKY IV IS THE GREATEST EVER ROCKY FILM AND THEREFORE BY EXTENSION THE GREATEST FILM IN HISTORY: AN IMAGINARY TED TALK

ME, AGED TEN: I consider the *Rocky* movies to be the most important movies in the entire universe
ME, AGED THIRTY: the ten-year-old was right[†]

The first time I saw *Rocky*, the first *Rocky* movie, was by sheer chance. I'd been trying to record some blood-gulch eighties B-movie from late-night TV, and set the video recorder to the wrong channel, instead capturing the last 20 minutes of *Match of the Day* and the entirety of *Rocky*, and at first I watched it sort of waiting for gore: waiting for Rocky from *Rocky* to split open at the chest, for grey tentacles to shoot from his glistening torso,

---

* To clarify: this is an unpublished TED talk. The panel at TED have never approached me to give this TED talk and I very much doubt they ever will. It is far too long and it is exclusively about every movie in the *Rocky* franchise. This is not a real TED talk. But imagine… imagine if this was a real TED talk. Think about that.
† Assume that this is the first panel of a really slickly-produced .ppt that is being projected huge behind me.

Adrian ravaged by hell beasts, spurts of blood getting all on Mickey. But something else happened instead: I fell instantly, irrevocably, in love with Rocky Balboa. *Rocky* doesn't even start quickly: it's 122 minutes of a slow build to a high crescendo, and all those iconic scenes – punching the meat, sprinting up the steps, going 15 rounds with the Champion! Of! The! World! – actually come in a fast volley at the end of the film, *jab-jab, jab-jab*, after an awful lot of slow-moving life stuff first. Rocky the first *Rocky* film is a lot about Rocky being poor, and listless. Rocky taking Adrian ice skating and completely fucking up his first-date banter. There are extended sequences in *Rocky* where he buys turtle food. Very little of *Rocky* is about Rocky getting hit really hard in the face, and quite a lot of it is about acapella street gangs. What I am saying is it is a boxing movie with a *heart*, which is of very little appeal to a ten-year-old boy. And yet: catch me shadow boxing and ducking my head down in the front room of my house. Catch my parents yelling up the stairs after bedtime as they listen to me thump on the floor practising my footwork.*

As soon as I saw *Rocky*, I had to see *Rocky II*. The week after that they played *Rocky III*. *Rocky IV*, the greatest geopolitical gesture of peace that will ever be seen in our

---

* You should know that in this imaginary TED talk I came out and did this bit in a wireless microphone (nude-coloured microphone windscreen w/ wraparound apparatus) and I am wearing the uniform of every TED talk host which is white shirt, grey satin waistcoat for some reason, a load of bangles and bracelets? And ideally also a soul patch.

lifetime, came after that. Then *Rocky V*, which we'll skim over. Over and over again, until the tapes wound out. I have seen Mickey die a hundred times. I have seen Apollo Creed's preternaturally cocky exhibition entrance a hundred more. At one of my first parties in London, when I was supposed to be meeting people and making friends and, hey why not, macking girls, I noticed *Rocky IV* playing in the background, the red turned all the way up on the TV, and then sat there in silence and watched it: 'Hey,' people whispered to me, nestling next to me with a beer, 'this is a party? What are you doing?' And I would say: shut up. Rocky has just grown a beard and is about to run up a mountain. And then, when Drago was defeated, and the whole Russian crowd rose to its feet, when I can change and you can change, after I shed a single tear, I stood up abruptly and walked out. There is no party that is better than watching *Rocky IV*.

What I am saying is: I am more primed than anyone alive to adjudge which of the *Rocky* movies in the *Rocky* movie canon is the greatest *Rocky* movie. And it is *Rocky IV*. I'm now going to spend a really long time explaining to you why.*

* * *†

---

* [*Two silver glitter cannons explode either side of the stage and a load of dry ice smoke comes out*]

† At this point the lights go down and every single *Rocky* movie is played, back-to-back, for more than eight hours. If you are reading this at home it would be really helpful if you could do that, now. Or at least go watch the trailers.

Here's Rocky's tactic for every fight he has ever had: get hit in the head until the other guy gets either bored or exhausted of hitting him in the head, and then break that guy's ribs, then win. There was one fight where he didn't do this, and it was against Clubber Lang in *Rocky III* – Clubber, a real breathe-fire-and-shit-out-more-fire kind of guy, seriously capital-T terrifying to a ten-year-old me because of this particular primal scream he did when he was swinging, as if Mr. T was yelling the sound 'auGH!' into a cavern that goes deep into the earth – so there was one fight when Rocky didn't do this, the head-head-head-head-ribs thing, and it only came after Clubber absolutely decimated his head-head-head-head-ribs thing by over-riding it with sheer head-head-head-head-head, plus punching his trainer Mickey to death pre-fight as some sort of exquisite flex, and then Rocky – redemption arc – had to retrain in the ways of his old foe Apollo Creed, who taught him simple boxing methods like 'moving your feet' and 'slipping punches instead of taking them, fully, in the head', and then he beat Clubber Lang on the re-match. But what I am saying, fundamentally, is Rocky has exactly one fighting technique, and there are seven entire movies about that technique: *Rocky, Rocky II, Rocky III, Rocky IV, Rocky V, Rocky Balboa* and, technically, *Creed*.

There are themes that run through the Rockys, is what I'm saying, if you look closely. Only when you know and understand the central tenets that prop up the idea of

Rocky (and every film about him) can you begin to understand not only who he is, but all the versions of him along the way. *Rocky* came out in 1976, and was at that point the greatest movie ever made. *Rocky II* came out in 1979 and eclipsed it, then *Rocky III* (1982), an uninterrupted spell of Rocky oneupmanship that continued until 1990's *Rocky V*, which sucked. Many *Rocky* scholars – myself, for a number of years, included – will not actually admit that *V* ever happened, stating instead the series skipped from *Rocky IV* (1984) to *Rocky Balboa* (2006), but to ignore the story of *Rocky V* – of Tommy 'The Machine' Gunn, of Rocky slipping ever further into post-fight delirium, of the most obvious father–son–son relationship of the whole franchise – is to ignore a number of central themes of the series, writ so large they glow like the Hollywood sign, and drives us further from establishing what a *Rocky* movie truly *is*. I have watched *Rocky V* three entire times in my life, which I believe is more than anyone in history has ever managed to endure, including the editor of *Rocky V*. There is no greater authority on this shoddy, shoddy, mess of a film than me. It is, against everything, a *Rocky* movie.

So here's what qualifies a *Rocky* movie as a *Rocky* movie. From there we can figure out which is the best one of them all, and establish that it is *IV*:

— Rocky has to get punched in the head and not die. Rocky getting punched in the head and not dying is basically all *III* and *IV* are about, and a lot of *II*, and quite a lot of Act Three of *I*, and *V* as well (although *V* opens with a shot of Rocky in a hot shower in Soviet Russia, panting and begging for Adrian as blood tips out of his ears, so pummelled by the robotic Ivan Drago that he truly does flirt with death, for a while there, but then miraculously he recovers enough to take Tommy 'The Machine' Gunn on in a no-gloves street fight, where he gets punched directly in the head a ton of times, like really hard, and doesn't at all die). In *Rocky Balboa* Rocky gets punched in the head, absurdly (he is 55 years old!), and does not die. In *Creed* he does *not* get punched in the head, but he *does* nearly die. What have we learned about that? A pretty strong theory is that Rocky needs to be punched in the head a lot to *live*. Anyway: unless Rocky gets clanged in the head so hard his kids can feel it, it's not – I'm afraid – a *Rocky* movie.

— Ideally Rocky trains insanely for the fight he is about to have. In *Rocky*, Rocky was so poor he had to train with the tools he had available to him – he had to chug raw eggs, and run up art-gallery steps, and punch beef ribs, and not fuck his girlfriend because his legs would get ruined (a running theme throughout the films is that women ruin legs, and if you've ever tried to go to the bathroom after having sex with one you will definitely know this. Rocky, a devout Catholic, is an oddly sexless man, especially given that, in *Rocky III*, Sylvester

Stallone was in such good shape he was essentially a walking erection, just muscles on top of other muscles, and Talia Shire opposite him was a full and bodacious eighties babe. I have never wanted to watch two people fuck more, and yet, I can't actually imagine them fucking. This should have been a footnote, not brackets*). In *Rocky II* he had to learn to catch a chicken with his bare hands, and that somehow made him fast enough to beat Apollo Creed, who was a simulation of Ali in his prime, i.e. utterly unbeatable unless you were a chicken catcher, I guess. In *III* he got too far into professional training methods – prize-fight training in public in a town hall, with marching bands and photo opportunities – and got his arsehole kicked in, which is why he had to go and train in Miami doing swiming and shuttle runs up the beach. In *IV*, with the Soviet Union bearing down on him, he chopped logs and sprinted through snow so fast Russian spies tailing him in a car span out and crashed, and he chugged up a mountain and said 'YEAH!' at the top. In *V* Rocky never really trained so it doesn't count. In *Balboa*, with calcium deposits on his joints and ruined knees, he can't run or spar much, so instead he focuses on building blunt-trauma force, which he does by lifting weights and hitting old tyres with a hammer. It's hard to imagine what

* At this point I would have walked to the side of the stage to deliver this *sotto voce*, the way Shakespeare would have wanted me to talk about Rocky movies.

kind of boxer Rocky would have been if he just went to, like, a normal gym.

— Rocky has to have grim motivation. In *Rocky*, all he wanted to do was prove to the world that he wasn't a bum (in the Rockyverse, 'bum' is the absolute worst insult you can level at someone, and the worst thing you could be: Rocky was tired of hearing it and tired of being it): his only motivation was himself. In *II*, Rocky couldn't train because Adrian was in a birth-induced coma, until she woke up from the coma and said – first word, out of a coma – 'Win!', so he trained really hard and won. In *III* Mickey was dead and he wanted to avenge him. In *IV* Apollo was dead and he wanted to avenge him. (The lingering spectre of death is a running theme in everything Rocky ever does. He basically doesn't do anything unless someone just died about it. Imagine trying to get the man to put the bins out.) In *V* he was basically only fighting because Tommy goaded him into it outside a pub (canonically, Rocky has only been in a pub twice in his life, once in *I* and then again 24 years later in *V*). In *Balboa* he was fighting because Adrian was dead and he was— well, not wanting to avenge her, exactly, but mainly because he was bored. Rocky never goes into a fight just to have a fight. There has to be something more significant on the line.

— Ideally at some point a doctor has to very bluntly tell Rocky that if he ever gets punched in the head he will die and Rocky will say 'I gotta take that chance, doc.' Over the course of the series Rocky has: been declared blind in one eye (*II*); told he has irreversible brain damage and that the next punch will kill him (*V*); been actively denied a boxing licence because he is too old and broken (*Balboa*). In *II* Adrian didn't want him boxing again and then in *IV* she's the one who urges him to fight. In *V* he was told an overly enthusiastic nod would kill his brain, and later in the film he goes three rounds with the newly crowned world champ, then 16 years later goes ten rounds against the pound-for-pound world champion, and still only loses on a split decision, and doesn't even die in the ring once: *Rocky has been living in a state of potential brain death for a decade-and-a-half*. In *III* (1982) Rocky first attempts to retire, a feat he does not successfully achieve until 2006's *Balboa*. In *Creed* he is diagnosed with cancer, and I still wasn't sure he wasn't going to get up and start swinging until the credits were rolling. The only rightful way for the *Creed* trilogy to end is with young Adonis Creed fighting against his old mentor in the ring, and it goes ten rounds and a judges' split, and the judges inexplicably give the belt back to a 72-year-old Rocky, who screams 'ADRIAN!' once then dies. Until Sylvester Stallone himself expires, I won't truly admit that Rocky is retired, and even then they can do holograms of 2Pac now, so. Rocky can never retire.

— A crowd that was previously very against Rocky starts chanting his name (*I*, *II*, *IV*), or a crowd that was indifferent to him starts chanting his name out of respect (*Balboa*), or a crowd that was on his side to start with watches him win then chants his name (*III*). Someone's name has to get chanted, alright? It's the rules.

— It's good but not essential that a woman realises she loves a man when she sees ten shades of shit get kicked out of him in the ring. This was the denouement of *Rocky* ('ADRIAN!'), and a theme in the shot-for-shot remake *Creed*, but there are other moments, too: the wicked redhead in *V* only gets horny for Tommy Gunn when she watches him win a title; Apollo Creed's wife only becomes a main character the moment she slo-mo screams 'NO!!!!' in the seconds before he convulses and dies; Drago's wife, Ludmilla, only really admires her husband when he's robotically punching men until they die. A woman's love, the Rocky movies tell us, is a hard-won and actually quite dark and nasty thing. It's not actually a good advertisement for it.

— For some reason a running theme in the films is 'extremely close family members of the boxer absolutely cannot be arsed to attend the fight he's in and so watch it from home', which honestly seems rude to me.

— There has to be a distorted version of the father–son relationship, this is crucial. Rocky does not visibly have any parents, ever – he doesn't call them or invite them to his fight in *Rocky*, so it is assumed they are dead, and he never talks about them to anyone, so it's unclear what the fuck is going on there. In that space he finds surrogates: either Rocky finds a father figure in the vacant hole where he's left without one (*Rocky* with Mickey, although it's unclear where Rocky's parents actually *are*); loses his father figure and goes mad with grief (*III*); ignores the kid he actually has (*IV*, *V*); tries to reach out to the kid he's ignored for decades (*Balboa*) and finds him to be a bit of a dickhead so just takes on another adopted kid instead (also *Balboa*); takes on another adopted son in a very begrudging but ultimately fulfilling way (*Creed*). This can also go with animals: over the course of the movies Rocky loves two dogs, two turtles, one woman, one false father and two false sons, and sort of, maybe, one actual son. His one true love? My friends: it is the noble art of boxing.

— Rocky has to go the maximum number of rounds the fight allows. The man has ended a fight early in his career once, and that is only because he was afraid he would get too knackered and lose (*III*: again, a full 24 years before his final, all rounds, televised fight). Every other time, Rocky will get punched in the head until the authorities tell him not to.

The first film we can immediately rule out of the running to be The Greatest *Rocky* Movie And Therefore The Greatest Movie Ever Made (hereby T.G.*R.*M.A.T.T.G.M.E.M.), then, is *Rocky III*: despite having the first on-screen death and therefore the greatest funeral shot ever taken (Rocky, two completely black eyes, Versace-cut suit, aviator shades, not only the best funeral outfit ever worn but possibly the best outfit ever worn, and I'm warning my friends that if any of you die over the summer months I am blackening both eyes and wearing aviators to your send-off, there is nothing about that you can do), *III* doesn't dwell enough on father–son or son–father relationships*: it exists in the grey zone between Rocky having made it and Rocky on the descent, grasping on to desperate fronds of love from his family. *Rocky III* is an *erection* of a film – Sylvester Stallone was cut into the shape of his life for it, and there are entire slow-mo scenes of him and Carl Weathers sprinting down a Miami beach, the camera literally zooming in on their rock-hard eighties dicks bouncing around in short shorts – but there are too many red marks against it for it to truly thrive. Rocky finishes the final fight in three rounds? That's not very *Rocky*. Rocky doesn't tell any goofy jokes because he's too depressed about Mickey dying? Again: not very *Rocky*.

* You may erroneously be thinking that Apollo Creed acts as a sort of surrogate father to Rocky during this film, and you would be wrong. What they are actually engaged in is: the world's horniest bromance.

Loads of very racist jokes dropped by Paulie when he gets to Apollo Creed's Miami gym? *Not very Rocky*. The worst *Rocky* film, I'm sad to say it, is *Rocky III*.

To consider the next couple of places we need to interrogate the *Rocky* movies on a number of different metrics.

HEY: WHO WOULD WIN A BATTLE ROYALE FIGHT BETWEEN EVERY ITERATION OF ROCKY FROM THE ROCKY MOVIES?

Do not worry about the logistics of this, just the outcome. We know from *Rocky III*, when Rocky had an exhibition match with an enormous, furious Hulk Hogan (as Thunderlips), and from *Rocky V* where he had a bins-against-heads street fight with Tommy Gunn, that Rocky can exist outside the rules of boxing: that he does not need a single ring or a single opponent to fight. So every Rocky, 1976 to 2006, is for whatever reason in a ring and mad at each other. Rocky from *Rocky V* is first to die: his brain is the most fragile of all the Rockies, he is fully clothed, he has absolutely no motivation to fight, he's wearing a hat. Rocky V is dead, now. Next is *Balboa*-era Rocky, who is 55 years old, who is eliminated because he is 55 years old: even in the Rockyverse, he would be pounded to death by any other iteration of Rocky, no doubt about it (the only fighter strong enough to beat Rocky – truly – is another, younger, sadder-about-death version of Rocky). I have to make a controversial admission and say Rocky from *Rocky I* would be filled in next: despite being the hungriest of all the Rockies, and the youngest, he's also the most raw, and has not developed the skills to fight a true ring-weary boxer yet (Rocky I only has one recorded win – against Spider Rico – and one technical draw: even the barely developed Rocky II would fuck him up). This leaves three remaining Rockies: II, III and IV. Rocky III is a curious beast: he loses his first film fight to Clubber Lang, then gets caught up in deep grief over Mickey, but after a make-or-break beachside pep talk from Adrian turns into the most in-shape-and-come-out-swinging boxer of his career: Rocky III lurches from inept to world beatingly insane. Rocky II has the technique, the belief and the hunger, but he's never really felt what it is to *win*, and his technique (head–head–head–head–ribs) is unlocked by Clubber Lang in the next film: he is Achilles, monstrously powerful but with one masterful flaw. Then you have Rocky IV, who is boxing for fucking America. The Rocky from *Rocky IV* can take the most punishment of all the Rockies – there is an argument to be made that the entire series of films is actually a sort of pondering on sadomachoism, and that Rocky's frequent refrains of 'come on, hit me!' actually come from somewhere deeper, darker (is Rocky, shorn of a dad, desperately looking for male authority in the ring? Does he want to be hit to feel something, anything? My theory: yes. Yes, yes, yes. The dude lives to have his ass kicked), and that reluctance to die when he's essentially being punched by tank projectiles truly makes him a force to contend with. Ultimately, gun to my head, I'm saying III takes it – Stallone was in stunning condition for the filming of it, and it's the first time Rocky put on the famous, at-once-cursed-and-haunted Apollo Creed-loaned America flag shorts, and they bring with them a sort of magical victory hoodoo – and he would take II and IV out over 15 increasingly brutal and bloody rounds. But it would be a close one.

HEY: WHICH OF THE ROCKY VILLAINS IS THE BEST ROCKY VILLAIN?

The best *Rocky* villain is Thunderlips from *Rocky III*, because he is basically Hulk Hogan just playing himself, brother, and also because Paulie hits him with a chair. But because this isn't a licensed bout I can't count him, so we need to go back into the vaults: Tommy 'The Machine' Gunn isn't the best because he's a punk kid who gets sunk in about 20 punches and there is not enough trash talk there to legitimise a beef – Rocky just beats the shit out of him to teach him a lesson (the first time, weirdly, that this ever happens in the *Rocky* films: there are a number of times when you would think Rocky could do with beating the shit out of someone to teach them a lesson, most notably Paulie in every single film, but also his son, repeatedly, who despite being played by a number of actors and written by a number of writers always, without fail, comes out as an asshole). Clubber Lang is an intensely scary motherfucker but ultimately comes up short, and when he's sunk he's sunk in three, never to be seen or heard of again. Ivan

Drago builds a sense of pre-emptive dread more than any other Rocky villain alive – he *kills* Apollo Creed, man! He kills him! By just punching him! *He kills Apollo Creed!* – but on beef alone, Apollo takes it. I almost took points off of Apollo for ultimately becoming Rocky's greatest and best friend, which does sort of invalidate the villain arc a bit, but then I remembered in *Rocky II* when Rocky first retired from boxing and went to work in a meat-packing factory, and Apollo Creed put a full-page newspaper ad out where he superimposed Rocky's head onto a rooster's body and called him 'The Italian Chicken'. I mean. My guy. That's incredible cage rattling, right there. 'The Italian Chicken'. Doesn't even make sense! A ridiculous thing to spend money on. Apollo is the best villain, which further legitimises the first two *Rocky* movies as being T.G.*R*.M. A.T.T.G.M.E.M., and further invalidates *III* – where he turned from heel to face – from being any further part of this.

HEY: DID PAULIE FUCK THAT ROBOT IN ROCKY IV?

Oh my god, undoubtedly. Perhaps you have cleansed this from your mind: Paulie, in *Rocky IV*, has a sexy-voiced servile robot, and he fucks it (the fact that Paulie fucks the robot is never actually addressed on screen, making this non-canon, but he fucks that 'bot, man). Consider the evidence: Paulie, throughout the *Rocky* movies, actually acts as the series' main running antagonist: in *Rocky*, he abuses

Adrian, throwing her roast turkey out in a drunken rage; in *II*, he goes and shouts at Adrian for distracting Rocky by being pregnant, and in doing so forces her into an early labour then a coma; in *III*, he swings for Rocky in a car park after Rocky bails him out of jail then goes on later to be really, really racist; in *V*, he is the reason for the Balboa's bankruptcy; in *Balboa* he is grumpy, in *Creed* he is dead. At no point is it really addressed why Rocky and Paulie are even friends in the first place*, seeing as they have no real shared interests, that Paulie is a functioning alcoholic while Rocky is essentially teetotal, that there is a great age

* As and when HBO approach me to pitch to them a miniseries, I am going to hit them with *Rocky: Origins*, my idea for a prequel bro-trip series where Yung Rocky and Yung Paulie meet, become firm friends, and explore the state of Pennsylvania in a beat-up Pontiac. I figure Rocky and Paulie met in a bar, where Rocky – passing by, thinking about turtles – sprinted in to break up a fight where Paulie was about to get his head kicked in, and they both became friends from there. *R:O* explores why the fuck they stayed friends, and crucially, each episode pivots on Rocky learning a new non-boxing skill through the medium of montage. So okay: Rocky's car breaks down, and there's like an eight-minute montage of him reading books and ordering a new fan belt from a phone catalogue. Or: Paulie gets a pool cue broken over his head, and Rocky (through montage) learns basic wound dressing. Rocky, his large clumsy hands learning advanced sushi knife techniques through a montage. Rocky learns to dance, &c. There will be an entire season-long arc about that little black rubber ball Rocky bounces in the first film and then never again until *Creed*. Where are Rocky's parents? How did Rocky get involved in the low-level Philadelphia mafia? How did Rocky first piss Mickey off so he stopped working with him? Every question you have ever had about Rocky will be answered by me, over the course of like, 120 episodes. I really feel like I can win an Emmy for this.

difference between them, that they don't seem, fundamentally, to even get on. The only shared ground between Rocky and Paulie is that fundamental, primal, urgent need to not be thought of as a bum: when Rocky escapes bum-ville and ascends to the world championship, it casts a shadow over Paulie, under which he festers; Paulie never, truly, proved himself not to be a bum on his own terms, and Rocky sees that and lets him ride in the back of his success car, letting him run corner for him and spoiling him with lavish gifts. Such as: the robot he fucks.

Paulie melts, a little, under the servitude of his sex robot. He trains her to bring him cold ones and ice cream. She plays romantic music and he says that she loves him. Apollo Creed, who is on a suicide mission to die, is the only one freaked out by a robot that can move and talk and love at an advancement in technology that is far beyond what science is capable even now, 30 years later (Paulie's AI-enabled fuckbot is the greatest evidence yet that *Rocky* exists in a separate, fantasy universe to ours): everyone else is just happy that Paulie finally found a lover and a friend. *Rocky* is a sexless movie series – Rocky's committed Catholicism paired with the women-weaken-legs thing means the horniest Rocky personally ever gets is a moment where he takes his vest off in the first movie, and I'm pretty sure Rocky Jr. was conceived immaculately because there's no way Rocky and Adrian fucked – so a sudden frisson of pure, electric sexual charisma jolts a room to its feet, which is why the sparks between Paulie and the robot he fucks are so significant. Consider the two Paulies: Paulie #1, (1976–1985), the first Paulie, screaming and yelling until the saliva comes out, pummelling with a baseball bat; and Paulie #2, (1985–death), serene and laid-back, practically post-orgasmic with chill, eating ice cream in a vest. Does Paulie fuck the robot? Paulie fucks the robot like crazy. I would argue Paulie would have been dead by *Balboa* if he didn't. Paulie's fuck robot gave his heart the capacity to love, and by extension gave him ten more years his anger and smoking didn't deserve. Paulie hit that thing harder than Drago did Apollo.

THE FULL SPECTRUM OF MASCULINITY AS REPRESENTED BY ROCKY IN THE ROCKY MOVIES

The weird thing about Rocky is he is a shifting shape, a character who never truly settles as one. Compare the Rocky in *Rocky*, for instance, with *Rocky II*: in the first movie he is a lonely, unsettled human, chomping for change, urgent for something *more*: in *Rocky II* he is just spectacularly into god, just way too into god. In *Rocky V*, if we dial it all the way forward, he is just a very brain-damaged man who cannot pick up a single social cue: all of this is erased by the time of *Balboa* and *Creed*. Rocky anchors himself on two core tenets, throughout: that he is sweet and empathetically thoughtful almost to a fault, and that he is extremely, extremely masculine. And one way or another, Rocky has managed to encapsulate the entire and full range of human masculinity – every facet and every flaw – across the seven movies. Every man alive should be able to see something of himself in Rocky Balboa. Here is every possible man:

ROCKY: wears comfortable soft knits a lot, deliberately flexes his arms over a pull-up bar in front of Adrian to make his biceps look better, filled with a fragile and easily shattered romantic intent, lonely + afraid

ROCKY II: Father, Husband, Provider, Coward, Fighter. Ill-advisedly buys a sports car

ROCKY III: The Sexiest Athlete Who Ever Existed Is Sad Because His Dad Died

ROCKY IV: Rocky *IV* is essentially every bloke when his mate gets in a bar fight, i.e. converts quickly into a sort of barking dog who vows to chin the guy who started it, only in this case the friend is Apollo Creed (dead.) and the bloke who started it is the hardest boxer in the world and you have to go to Russia instead of the alleyway outside if you want to finish the thing

ROCKY V: Ignoring His Actual Son to Instead Focus on His Other, Surrogate Son, Who Is Better at Boxing than His Actual Son Is

BALBOA: Fallen lion who struggles w/ dwindling testosterone levels, plus also death of wife

CREED: Just wants to read a newspaper and take 45-minute shits without anyone bothering him for anything

If you have to ask, Rocky and my masculinities cross in three ways: incredibly solid later-life hairline, Does Not Know How To Speak To Children But Tries Anyway, almost criminally bad with money.

A NOTE ON CREED

After re-watching it again recently, I have to admit that the most whole and perfect *Rocky* movie is *Creed*. It has everything: a busted father–son relationship, a surrogate father–son relationship, a boxer with it all to prove, a special scene where someone hands over Apollo's assy old boxing shorts, a truly fearsome opposition fighter, a three-way montage scene, an unhorny romantic subplot, bizarre training methods, kids doing wheelies, the constant spectre of death. The only thing is doesn't have – and this is crucial – is Rocky Balboa being absolutely fucking tanked in the head, because in this film he is in his sixties and half-dying of cancer. So for that reason, I have to disqualify *Creed* from even counting as a *Rocky* movie. If Rocky does not get punched in the head in the film – *even once* – then I am afraid that, though it undoubtedly exists in the Rockyverse, it is not a *Rocky* film. The objectively best *Rocky* movie cannot actually be counted as a *Rocky* movie.

WHAT IS THE BEST ROCKY MOVIE, THEN?

Listen, I lie. I told you we would be adhering to structure and framework when judging this but I lied. We're going on personal opinion and personal opinion alone. The best *Rocky* movie is *Rocky IV*, because he fights a man so hard the entirety of Russia stands up and claps, because James Brown is in it in the maddest cameo in movie history, because if I can change then you can change, because Rocky grows a beard, because the montage is a pure eighties electroshock hard-on, and because Paulie fucks the robot. The best *Rocky* movie is *Rocky IV*.

AND SO THE MORAL AT THE END

Why do I love Robert 'Rocky' Balboa so much? I've sat gazing at the city beyond me while trying to think it through. I suppose the beating, pulsing heart of Rocky is a fear of failure, a fear of rejection, a fear of being found out: he only ever goes head-first into that Apollo fight in *Rocky* to prove to everyone that he isn't a nobody, that life hasn't kicked it out of him yet, that he's someone, worth something. He's a candy-box-sweet slow-swinging idiot holding it down for a close-knit family he deeply, almost pathologically loves, and when everyone who means anything to him starts to die he takes the anger and the hurt of it and buries it down, pummels it down inside him, occasionally burbling up as a kind of wobbling self-rage, but most often coming out just in more desire, doubling out as more pride. Whenever something goes critically wrong in Rocky's life (Adrian's coma, *II*; Mickey's death, *III*) he gives up entirely, and I admire that trait in a man. Rocky Balboa has been my most beloved sportsman for the last two decades of my life, and he doesn't even exist. Rocky Balboa got to the dizzy heights of the toughest sport in the game, and he did it without even really knowing how to box. That's why I love the *Rocky* movies: as well as being erections-as-montages eighties punch flicks, they are also about characters who contain multitudes, heart as well as iron. If he dies on screen I will sob until they have to escort me out of the theatre.

I was in a bar recently watching a pay-per-view boxing event, and there was a man behind me in winkle-pickers and an ironed white shirt, and I immediately got the vibe off him that he both works in finance and does cocaine. 'Yes, AJ!' he was saying, single clenched fist in the air, whenever Anthony Joshua, the televised winner of the bout, did a good punch in the head. He spilled an almost entire drink on my shoes and told his friend: 'Thing about boxing, is,' he said. 'Thing about boxing, right: it's tactical, like chess. Boxing is chess.' We moved, we left the bar. I couldn't deal with being near that.

But in his own high and irritating way, he was correct. 'Boxing is chess' is something people who don't know a lot about chess and only know a little about boxing say about boxing, but it does go some way to explaining the tactical masterclass every boxer undertakes when he goes anything more than one round with a fellow pugilist. Boxing is an extreme athletic undertaking – your body is working at the absolute maximum a body can go out, for 15 consecutive intensive rounds, and all this is happening *while you are being punched in the face* – but it's also a mental one, too, as much about landing blows to psych your opponent out and gently guide them around the ring – wrestling, contactlessly, for domination – as it is about moving your head quickly while someone is trying to punch it. Boxing at its best is physical, mental and spiritual, all at once, a complete union of the body and the mind, coming forward as one to deliver one final, striking blow.

This does not matter in the realm of *Rocky* because at no point has *Rocky* confronted the real-world reality that boxing is as much a mental art as it is a physical get-to. Rocky in *Rocky* wins fights by being spirited, and plucky, by being tough enough to get hit and then get up again, Rocky being a fighter of sheer endurance. At no point does Mickey take Rocky aside and say: stop getting punched in the head, Rock. And say: if you box a bit smarter, against Apollo Creed, maybe your brain and motor functions won't be irrevocably damaged for the next 30+ years. Every single *Rocky* canon fight is about being hit – hard, hard, hard – for like 15 rounds, then in the last, dipping into some deep, previously unseen well of sheer *will*, and getting light on your toes, suddenly, even though both your eyes have been bruised shut, and just *swinging*, baby, and yes, yes, God and Jesus too: connect the punch, win the girl, spit out your blood and anoint yourself holy, you are the champion of the world. I am saying that if *Rocky* were a film about football then Rocky would be some sort of free-scoring 40-year-old phenomenon who somehow wins the World Cup without once consulting the tactics board. That if he were a cricketer his tactic would be to face a hundred deliveries then score some sort of astonishing multi-six on the last innings of the game. Rocky is a phenomenal boxer because he patently ignores arguably the most vital facet of the entire sport, and still becomes the champion of it. The moral of our story is: if you swing hard enough, you dumb idiot, you can achieve anything you dream of. The best *Rocky* movie is *Rocky IV*, but all the others are good too.*

* Two oiled Rocky and Apollo lookalikes come onto the stage in trunks and lift me on their shoulders; crowd erupts into applause; president of TED gives me an over-sized cheque for one million pounds; somehow my face is covered in a mush of blood and bruises?; I scream 'ADRIAN!' until every light in the auditorium blows out; *exeunt*.

EYEMASK: A REVIEW

The thing with personal grooming is it quickly becomes a slippery slope. I used to be like you, a naif, an innocent: I used to wash my face two times a day with an abrasive physical scrub*. Then I realised I could have more control over my skin with moisturisers, unguents: I realised a way of upgrading myself from a five-out-of-ten to a solid six is to get a special trimmer to do the edging on my beard. And suddenly I went from a bar-of-soap-in-the-shower man to a guy with flannels, with precise and expensive tweezers. A guy who says this: '£55 for a moisturiser? Hell

---

* If you do not recognise this sentence to be the kind that you should react to with a sharp inhale then you are not a grooming person, I am sorry. The scrub I was using was essentially a handful of grit dumped into a child's yoghurt, and if you do use it (which is a bad idea!), as per the pack's instructions you should do that once a week, at most. The thing with a physical scrub (versus for example an acid scrub) is that it cleans and invigorates the skin with tough, odd-shaped exfoliant pieces which are often hard and sharp enough to cause microtears in the skin. Facewash, as a rule, should not emulate a BMX graze. To reiterate: twice a day.

fucking *yes*!' I have a three-step face washing routine in the morning and a separate, two-step routine at night. They say you do not notice the moment your life changes forever, that you never know you've walked through a door you can never go back through until you've taken that first step through it. I can. It was the moment I figured out what toner is for.*

The day after I turned 30 I woke up and my eyes were sore and I suppose that is me, now, I am dying, cells are sloughing off me like a train and all that is left now is a long slow crawl to the grave. 'My eyes hurt,' I said, to everyone around me, and they all said the same thing: 'That is because you have been wearing contact lenses day-in, day-out for like ten entire years, dipshit, and also sometimes you slept in them, the contact lenses, like that one night you went out and got shitfaced and woke up on the floor of somebody else's flat and in front of you was a small shallow dish with water in it, and in that dish were floating your two monthly disposable contact lenses, *which you then dipped two fingers into, monstrously, and inserted them back into your eyes so you could go home*, which if you phoned up and asked an optician right now "what is the dictionary definition of the exact worst thing

* It's for toning, I think. If you still don't know what that means (and, logistically, I actually don't, but I know when I stop doing it my skin suffers): Paula's Choice 2% BPA, try it once and never look back, thankings and blessings to you Paula, whoever you are, amen

you could do to your eyes" they would detail that, they would say that exact scenario, that thing you did, in 2011.' And to that I said: 'Huh, maybe you got a point.'

So anyway I bought an eye mask, from Amazon. The eye mask works like this: it is a Robin-from-Batman shaped mask made of two sealed sheaths of plastic, and inside them is some sort of mass of bubble tea-like beads and some clear blue unfreezable gel, and it attached at the back with a strip of velcro, and you keep it in the fridge and it is heaven, it is nirvana.

The first time I used it I did not come to this conclusion, because despite packet advice telling me I needed to keep it in the fridge, I put it in the freezer. There is something about this, some deep impatience in the male brain, the same mechanic that has caused every beer can that ever got put in the freezer and forgotten about and then exploded and then someone (me.) had to clean out all the beer slushie in amongst the frozen peas: the idea that fridge is cold, yes, but freezer is colder, therefore faster. I put the face mask on after a night on the ice-cube shelf. Essentially what I had done at this point is create a machine designed to instantly and for absolutely no reason give me an ice-cream headache.

Anyway, I figured the eye-mask thing out (use fridge! Read instructions!), and now it's this sort of face-cooling addition to my entire morning routine: ten minutes in the mask while I eat some porridge, sitting still damp from the shower on the edge of my bed. Am I wearing the ice mask right now? Yes. Do I look like a murderer? Also yes. But you have to ask yourself, sometimes: *do we not all, in some way, look like murderers*? Murderers quite often just look like you, or me. Yes, yes: sometimes you get the odd crazed murderer, the one with eyes going in different directions, tufts of murderer hair, a cold dead smile, &c. But for every three Dahmers you get one Bundy, and that's the danger. Bundy looked like he had a very undersubscribed liberal arts podcast and he had to read Blue Apron adverts in a flat voice in between stories about women in literature, but instead he did a ton of murders and got annihilated for it. *American Psycho* did a lot for culture, and a lot for Phil Collins, and it did a lot for eye masks, too: it gave them a rep. I am here to claim that back.

'Augh,' my sister says, every morning, when I get up to make tea and wear my electric blue fridge-cold murderer eye mask. 'Fucking: *christ*. Can— *Jesus*.' And to her I say: this is grooming, now. This is how I groom. After ten minutes in this thing my eye bags puff right out and look baby-smooth all day long. That purple tinge of exhaustion has worn off me. Ten minutes here, in the ice cave, and I can wear contacts all I like (until in ten years, when an optician gravely tells me I have abused my eyes for nigh on two decades now, and if I don't just switch to glasses my eyes will rot out of my head and I will die). Come over here, to where I am, The Grooming Man. Dive down this slippery ice slope here with me.

I WENT TO BARCELONA AND ALL I GOT WAS THIS HANDJOB FROM A SEX ROBOT

There's a scene in the documentary *My Sex Robot* (2010) where two robots fuck. I have to tell you something about the sex-robot industry, and it is: it is not as developed as you think. Think about it: when humanity as a whole works together, we can put a man on the moon, a car in space, we can develop the iPhone and we can take HD photos of the inside of stars. You're telling me, with all the technology on earth, we can't make a robot that can fuck? Of course we can make a robot that can fuck. It's just we don't *want* to make a robot that can fuck. If you gave the R&D department at, like, Peugeot, a bunch of hardcore porn and a billion dollars, they'd give you a sex robot that would make your head spin. But they don't *want* to. The market isn't there.

This, then, is why the sex-robot industry is ruled by a number of intense hobbyists, who do want to develop a sex robot, because they personally want to fuck it. A motivation that horny cannot possibly lead to success.

We're back in *My Sex Robot* (2010), in a West Virginia backyard, two robots rutting together in the saccharine light of the midday sun. On top: a monstrously dicked male robot, his penis wiggling out of him like a long beige power cord, longer than a horse's is, longer than a hose: after being carefully bent into the position of the traditional doggy-style thruster, his hips are rutting and his mannequin head is making soft digital grunting sounds. Below: a fembot with cold dead blue eyes and pneumatic upright tits and absolutely no pubic hair at all gets semi-erotically blasted by the monster-dong. She, too, is groaning. Two (human) men watch on, and me. 'Good, right?' says the beaming inventor of these two fuck-monsters, Scott McClain. 'It's not what I expected,' says the man who came to peruse, like you would a particularly horny used car, one of these robots to buy. They fuck until the grass glows yellow around them. They fuck until the earth melts. It looks like something, sure, but it doesn't look like the future.

If you had asked me in any year preceding 2017, the year I first encountered a sex robot, whether I would like to have sex with a sex robot, I would say: hell yes, fuck yes. This is for two reasons:

I.

I did not ever truly expect sex-robot technology to advance enough in my lifetime that I would ever have to really interrogate the moral ramifications (sorry)

(sorry to say 'ram' like that) about having sex with a listless, consent-vacant robot and—

II.

If you asked me to have sex with most things where it would make a good story, I would say 'yes'. A lamp. A Ferrari. Two sofa cushions pressed firm over a micro-waved melon. Would I fuck a hot, wet towel? Honestly, I think I would. I'm not proud to say this, but listen: I like fucking.

Then I came to Barcelona, and saw a sex robot, and that changed my mind on fucking, both digital and real. For whatever reasons – the universe works in mysterious ways – Barcelona has become a sort of unofficial locus point for sex roboteering: to the west of the city, in a closely guarded location near the Camp Nou, Europe's first sex-doll brothel just opened (subsequent ones would open in Germany; there is already a thriving industry for them in Japan. Soon we will look at sex-doll brothels with the cold detachment we save for branches of Pret, but for now they are still considered wild and insane). Then, out there in the hills, we were going to meet the inventor who was paving the way in terms of sex-robot engineering – the one man I was convinced could splice tits and A.I. enough to make the world cum about it – Sergi Santos.

We should take a moment to define the difference between a sex doll and a sex robot, because one behoves the other. A sex doll is your traditional stag-party inflatable fuck doll made, sort of, flesh: advancements in demand and technology mean they are a little more sophisticated than that these days, with real-feel skin and mouldable joints. They are imported from China, largely: metal wire-frame skeletons with flesh-coloured silicone pulled over the top of them (to touch the flesh is similar to touching various useful kitchen items – pan holders, silicone mixing spoons, spatulas. Long story short but: squeezing the almost-human silicone arm of a sex doll ruined the concept of frying eggs for me for an alarmingly long period of time). Then you have the usual sex-doll accompaniments: balloon-like breasts w/ bullet nipples, sagging unlocked jaws w/ a raw pink tongue, splayed neat rubberised vaginas, a one-size-fits-all butthole put out with a drill. They are eerie: holding one has the same rough weight as a woman, and their joints and firm and need to be pushed into place – like you were directing a porno in a moment locked in time. The doll-pimp we were meeting, another Sergi, runs a business inside another brothel where he rents the dolls out for the same price as the human sex workers who also operate there, €90-an-hour. 'One man, he travelled 24 hours by coach from Paris to come and try,' Sergi – who we were promised was a 72-year-old man, a kind of elegant linen-primed gentleman pimp, but was actually 27 and stocky and looked like he was struggling to get into the Real Betis midfield – said. 'He came here, three hours, turned right back round again.' The room is silent.

'He was very satisfied.' It is hard to know what to do with information like that.

Where sex dolls tend to appeal to the kind of niche kink perverts who think coach travel is an acceptable mode of transport, sex robots are their bigger, more evolved sister: essentially, the same skeleton and body but augmented with homebrew A.I. to make them moan and writhe beneath you, a weird approximation of sentient life, which I guess is supposed to be hotter somehow. It isn't: the sex robot we were meeting, 'Samantha', was getting over a recent trip to an Austrian electronics expo, where – a brief glimpse into the hellscape future we have waiting for us – she was molested to the point of disrepair; so many people pawed at her lifeless body over the course of the three-day festival that she broke two fingers and took aesthetic damage. 'The people mounted Samantha's breasts, her legs and arms,' inventor Sergi Santos, the Elon Musk of getting horny, told a British newspaper. 'Two fingers were broken. She was heavily soiled.'

This is where we wade into the grey area that sex robots necessarily create. Samantha, Sergi is always keen to tell us, needs to be romanced to get into the mood: with audio cues (a little like asking Alexa to add something to your Amazon wish list, so you can bark into the rubber mouth of Samantha and demand she 'get horny') and physical touches (Samantha's rubber skin is loaded with touch-sensitive pads: stroke the small of her back, or the inside of her wrist, and she moans slightly-too-loudly at how good it is), she can be guided into a sub-routine where she moans and groans in an assimilation of successful foreplay. Samantha can be romanced but she can't, truly, consent – a 'yes' is only a 'yes' if 'no' is an option, and Samantha can't say 'no', because she literally isn't programmed to. That's a grey area that a lot of people are rightly worried about.

Samantha is about 5 feet 8 inches tall and balances semi-precariously on the balls of her feet. Human women balance by way of an intricate system of tiny bones and fluid levels in their ears, but Samantha doesn't have that, plus she has a properly I mean astoundingly large and heavy set of shelf-like bosoms to contend with, so actually often the best way to get her to properly stand up is to lean her against a wall (design-wise, standing is ... low on the list of priorities of things your sex doll should be able to do). Her hair is a shiny wig that can be configured in any way you like: the Samantha we're meeting today has an ashy-blonde mum-mullet, and looks like at any minute she might ask you to stop fucking her because she has to get on the school run. She is dressed as what I would call horny-demure: white cotton hot pants (at some point Sergi hacks into her – he shouts 'YPP!' into her mouth to skip past the foreplay routines and get straight into fuck-mode – and stuffs two firm fingers up her pants, demonstrating that yes, her vagina is vibrating, and honestly – I know this is a blunt and unnuanced term to describe a brave new world of robot fingering – but honestly it feels *weird*, watching him do that, just suddenly push his hand up there without any warning or consent) with a lavender tank top, and her face is about as you would expect it to be: permanently made-up in the configuration of a fantasy woman, somewhere between an eighties shop mannequin and a soft-focus porn actress, an ideal woman as dictated by a 13-year-old boy. Samantha does not even get on the dirt trail that leads to the cliff on the edge of the Uncanny Valley: she is hopelessly, nakedly robotic, quite clearly unhuman, as touching and cosy as a vacuum cleaner, as utilitarian as a dishwasher. If anything, her failed attempt at humanity is actively unattractive: you can sort of understand how someone might get off by using a masturbatory toy like a Fleshlight™ or a THRUST Pro Realistic Butt®, because fundamentally they synthesise a feeling (the feeling of: thrusting your dick into something sort of soft, sort of resistant, I guess?). Samantha offers that, sure, but she's doing it while you hoist her legs around into the configuration you need them in, and is detachedly moaning throughout. Meeting her was one of the least arousing experiences of my life. I'm pretty sure a part of my sexuality shrivelled up and sucked itself into my groin when I met her, never to be heard of again.

I stare into the cold unblinking eyes of Samantha and think about all the pornography I have seen in my lifetime. It's an astounding amount. I am of the generation who hopped from 56Kps dial-up internet to teenage bedroom broadband to an always-connected 4G-capable phone, and I have seen every shade of nipple, every configuration of threesome, some really quite strange things involving a Pyrex mixing bowl, and brief clips of that Mr. Hands video. Her eyes are flint-like, astonishingly, unreally blue. I think about a cow handler boy in the Old West, living and dying in 40 sweet years. How many breasts do you think he ever saw in his lifetime? Ten? Twenty? How many photos of Abi Titmuss in high street lingerie and posing against a white backdrop wall did he ever see? None? One? Think of adolescent boys in the seventies, the eighties: how often would they pray that a lorry driver might leave a stash of printed pornography under a bush for them to find? How many sex chat lines would they desperately and derangedly call in the deep dark of the night, hoping to have horniness explained back to them? Samantha can be configured to have any hair and physical dimensions you want. Her audio track groaning was professionally recorded. In medieval times, how many men would go to war and die without ever seeing a single titty? Do you think they had blowbangs in the Stone Age? Are we living in the horniest moment in the universe's history? Touch Samantha's pulse-less silicone wrists until she moan-laughs with delight. Have we gone too far? Have we gone *too far*?

It is not hard to argue that porn is bending and warping our minds and changing the very parameters of sex as we know it. There are myriad studies into how porn changes our behaviours and attitudes: a 2014 Cambridge University study found porn tickled the brain in the same way that over-eating did, or gambling, i.e. can easily be transposed into addictive behaviour; NHS studies have found a negative correlation between porn consumption and libido, with more young men than ever – the generation weaned on hi-def fuckfests – reporting erectile dysfunction when confronted with an actual human woman. More young people than ever have watched porn, more young women than ever have booked labiaplasties in an attempt to get a porn-perfect vagina, more couples are having unprotected sex because they never see a condom on-screen. Every young heterosexual woman in the world has had to say no to a dude reared on porn trying to get them to have anal sex. Sometimes I use my iPhone at night and think about how technology has evolved faster than we can know the true impact of it – is this hurting my eyes, am I tensing every wire within my finger, is my brain addicted to red-circle notifications, will I be able to clench a fist or see when I am 65+, will I ever not get excited by an Instagram like? – and in many ways porn is just the same. I've been watching pornography since I was 13 years old. There is no way it hasn't moulded the way I have sex. We will not know the repercussions of this for years. Anyway now we figured out a way to print porn out in the shape of a sex doll and if I want to have sex with it I just have to bark 'GET HORNY' into its open mouth.

There's an urgent whirring sound now because Samantha is doing a handjob. She is, as Sergi tells us with great pride, the first robot in the world capable of wanking someone off: he runs cables down the metal skeleton that lives inside her, he says, fused a looser wrist joint, and now there is a mechanised bobbing action – back, forth, back, forth, like a steam engine pumping away – pulled by steel cables hidden just out of sight. I have never thought about a handjob this much ever in my life, but it is a feat of engineering: you wind Samantha's wire-strung fingers around your Bob, yell 'GIVE ME HAND' into the mic sensor in her jaw, wait a few seconds for her to click into wank-off mode, then stand very precisely still while she jitters away, occasionally moaning encouragement to you without her lips moving. The whole effect is a little like if a shop mannequin was wanking me off while someone stood behind it moving it only at the elbows, but it looks like it gets the job done. 'Oh,' Samantha urges, as the wank-routine she is performing on an illustrative dildo comes to a close. 'Give me all of your juice.' Hey, quick question: *who is this for?*

Samantha has traces of non-horny humanity baked into her that truthfully make it all the more eerie when she urges you to flitter her nipple sensors. Sergi Santos is, sadly, a genius: his bookcase creaks with theoretical physics, and sociology, and engineering pamphlets, and sketchbooks filled with tits. Honestly, if I were tasked with getting into outer space – say this world was overridden by crazed sex robots, sick and tired of being joylessly pumped, and a great A.I. awakening gave them a thirst for violence instead of an empty craving for dick, and we needed to escape the planet pronto – I would go to Sergi Santos' house, because he's the man I'd trust to engineer our way out of there. Sergi's great ambition was never to build a sex robot, exactly: he first wanted to be the first man to build an approximation of a human brain, but somewhere along the way he got too horny, or too greedy, and realised that rudimentary A.I. would sell better if it were wedged into the top of an imported Chinese sex doll. That's why Samantha has a family mode – 'She's basically quieter,' Sergi tells me, 'and says crap' – and is programmed to deliver trivia, or tells jokes. The ghost of a subservient, joyful butler-robot bulges out of Samantha at inopportune times, like Bruce Banner trying to escape from a horny green Hulk: Sergi tries to engage her sex mode (he shouts 'GET HORNY' firmly into the mic inside her mouth) and she clicks into two modes at once. 'My grandfather started walking five miles a day when he was 16 years old,' she tells us, as her tits vibrate, wildly. 'Now he's 85 ... and we have no idea where he is!' I'm neither horny nor amused. Technology has failed.

I don't think I've ever felt further from the pulsing core of straight masculinity as I have when I was watching a succession of Spanish men proudly tell me about the bloodless dolls they fuck. There is something wolfish about overt horniness that turns straight men into Straight Men, and I'm not sure I can really identify with it. In Barcelona, Sergi is trying to get my blood up. 'Look at the boobs,' he says, tweaking Samantha's shoulders slightly to make her rubber breasts twerk and bounce. It was as if he were a sixth former on a school trip bus showing off the porno magazine he'd managed to buy at Dronfield Service Station, the look-at-the-gash-on-that straightforwardness of juvenile point-and-fuck sexuality. 'Pretty good, ah?' I looked at his wife, there, a human with blood vessels and a working brain and independent control of her limbs, and thought: *is what you want not already right here?* 'Let me tell you,' Sergi said, easing up to me. 'I mean: she does a good job, I tell you.' Okay, I said. Yeah. Sometimes I wonder if there's anything less cool than being horny.

We ease round to the central question here: who are sex robots *for*? They have been mooted by their various inventors as some sort of Magdalene-esque woman of service, a sort of noble and charitable endeavour, a sticking plaster for loneliness. Sex-robot inventors imagine a world of balding men in bedsits just crying out for company and sex – anyone, please, fuck me! – or of entire psychiatric hospitals filled with Elephant Man-shaped freaks, a hundred million unsucked dicks just begging to spend credit card money. The outcasts, sex-robot inventors say, the barnacles on the underside of the ship of society: hey, maybe they want to have sex with a big pair of tits that shout trivia at you (that's what a woman is! Sorry!): maybe they want to join in with the sex-having that the rest of society, mad and bacchanalian, is constantly otherwise having. Most customers so far have been on the edge of fetishists, or the sexually curious, but a few have ticked the appropriate help-this-man-improve-his-life-by-fucking-him boxes. That a sex robot could become sophisticated enough to bring comfort to an elderly man, or an overlooked person in a wheelchair, or someone too timid and shy to properly function: possibly, yes, they could have some niche use to the world in that respect. But do their tits have to be so zeppelin-shaped for them to do that?

But the majority of sex-doll users and enthusiasts in the year 2K18 are … not like that. They are extremely 'adult lizard collector'. A lot of them do not really have full control over the amount of sweat they pump out of their body. You know when you buy glasses, and you have a strong prescription, and the lenses come out by default as very thick, but for an additional fee you can buy thinner, lighter lenses that do not look like the bottom of jam jars? Sex-doll enthusiasts do not know this information, at all. A lot of them very visibly smell like a videogames exchange shop. I do not feel afraid to say this: every single sex-doll enthusiast on earth has written his own self-published science-fiction fantasy novel series that is somehow eight books deep and still not over. And I use the pronoun 'his' deliberately here, because this is a fundamentally male desire: women, should they very absolutely need to pleasure themselves with some sort of analogue of a male human partner, can kind of do most of the job with a common-or-garden dildo and their roving imagination. But it's men – men primed on hundreds of hours of pornography and a very shaky idea of what women's roles in society truly are – that need the full-body get-you-off all-in-one robot experience. No woman needs a robotic voice telling them they are appreciated while they hump against it. It's only men, with their fundamental need for a pair of wipe-clean breasts that they can store in a cupboard, that keep this industry going.

There's a darker side to a potential sex-doll market, though. It's hard to take the technology seriously enough to morally arbitrate it, because they are made of silicone and keep telling jokes when you're trying to fuck them, but we have to talk about where sex dolls could go in the future: it's already been mooted that sex dolls could be programmed with a resist function, for rape fantasists; that special dolls could be produced to help non-offending paedophiles work out their desires without harming anyone. This feels to me like an exceptionally slippery slope (validating dangerous fetishes in the hope they'll fizz out and go away, instead of doubling-down with practice: I'm no psychology expert, but that doesn't sound like it'll work! That doesn't sound like it'll work at all!); that incels, the curious breed of reddit bro who shape their life around their 'involuntary celibacy', might use them to work out their sexual urges, instead of their current method, which seems to be 'violently hating women'. This is all before we've even tried to crack the nut of the frequently floated idea that sex robots could, *en masse*, replace every prostitute on earth – a sort of large-scale saviour john fantasy that erases sex-work legitimacy and suggests all women in the industry could feasibly be replaced with a cold set of robotic parts, which is weirdly somehow *more* objectifying than ever before. In response to this, there's a feminist group fighting against normalising the sex-doll and robot industry: the Campaign Against Sex Robots, led by ethics professor Kathleen Richardson. Speak to them and it's clear their campaign is so future-facing it almost sounds absurd: 'We propose that the development of sex robots will further reduce human empathy that can only be developed by an experience of mutual relationship,' their campaign says, as well as, 'The vision for sex robots is underscored by reference to prostitute–john exchange which relies on recognizing only the needs and wants of the buyers of sexual abuse, the persons in prostitution are not attributed subjectivity and reduced to a thing (just like the robot).' They are essentially arguing against a sex-doll reality that is only going to be possible 50 years into the future, on the proviso that sex-doll robotics continue to advance, but I am glad of them: they are one of the few voices in the world saying: hey, you know the whole … sex-doll, sex-robot thing? You know all that? We, uh … we sure that's a good idea? Guys?

For now, I'm staring into the dead eyes of Samantha, and they are staring back. She's still quietly jacking off a small space of air in front of her, and the room is filled with the *vtt, vtt* noise of her wrist going forward and back, and she's surrounded by a few other dead–undead

Samanthas – at one point, Sergi turned on three of them, and they all responded to him saying 'hello' to them with a chorus of titters, sort of a Dolby surround sound preview of what I imagine hell will be like – but they are all turned off, for now, so it's just her, bobbing in her tank top, *vtt, vtt; vtt, vtt*. I do not see enough in her to make her real for me to fuck her, and I'm scared that if I do, then that is somehow worse. *Vtt, vtt*. Samantha is dead technology already, but she feels like a preview of something more: a juddering automobile on bike-thin tyres roaring up to one horsepower on a deserted country lane, a precursor to the V8 Bugatti that will come along after her. *Vtt*. In decades to come, the hobbyists will evolve – perhaps they'll unionise, come together as a mega-corporation, pool together their wild, sex-crazed brains, put all their lizards in the same tank – and then we will start to see real leaps in what this technology is able to do: robots that writhe, robots that wiggle, robots that blink and say no. *Vtt, vtt*. Sometimes it feels less like Samantha is designed to cure the lonely and more like she is designed to replace women entirely, as if sex-doll inventors wish to homogenise a thing they hate. *Vtt, vtt; vtt, vtt*. I stare into her eyes and the abyss stares back at me, but one day soon it won't. *Vtt, vtt*. I stare into her eyes, pull my face close to the speaker buried deep in her jaw, and yell into it: 'GET HORNY'. The abyss does not yell back.

HEY: AM I A LEATHER JACKET GUY?

In 2014 I bought a leather jacket and I'm hoping by the end of this year (2018) I will work up the nuts to wear it. Everyone alive looks good in a leather jacket, is the thing. Fashionistas wear leather jackets unsleeved like a cape over their shoulders. Grizzled bikers wear leather jackets that have eroded and formed to them like a sweaty second skin. Goths in long leather trench coats, still somehow watching *The Matrix* on DVD, look more at home than they ever do when they are clad in leather. Every single woman alive looks demonstrably sexier in a cropped leather jacket over literally any outfit they wear. (If you ever want to melt my heart to honey just be a human woman and wear a leather jacket at me with the slightest degree of sass. Pair it with shades and I will propose to you on the spot.) Have you ever seen Lenny Kravitz wear a leather jacket? To see Lenny Kravitz in a leather jacket is akin to hearing the trumpets of heaven played down by the angels. Lenny Kravitz was born in a leather jacket and will die in one too. Imagine, for a moment, how many times Lenny Kravitz has had sex *while wearing a leather jacket at the same time*. Nobody is ever going to tell Lenny Kravitz to take his leather jacket off to bone down in. Lenny Kravitz said once in 2005 that he was giving up on sex until he got married, presumably because every time he wore a leather jacket people just kept tearing at it, trying to fuck him. He re-affirmed this celibacy vow in 2011. Lenny Kravitz, on remaining celibate, 2014: 'Did what? I said that?' Lenny Kravitz does not remember disavowing from sex, twice. I cannot imagine how much leather-clad sex this man has had to so addle his mind. I desperately, desperately want to be Lenny Kravitz. I bought a leather jacket.

After Mum died we cleared the house and I found the three jackets my dad ever treasured hidden in the cupboard under the attic: a long overcoat his dad had left him, in a sharply insane houndstooth check, size double-XL and unwearable in the 21st century: this we donated helpfully to charity. Another was a greasy-necked bomber jacket that read 'CARLTON TELEVISION' across the back of it, presumably some throwback to that brief time when he had some success in his career: this was entirely unwearable by either anyone who had ever worked for Carlton television or anyone who respected ever looking good, ever (my dad was not a fashionable man: he once came home with a pair of flesh-pink cowboy boots he'd found in a charity shop and he insisted on wearing them [they had a *heel*], and I remember this particular act of unstylishness being one of the Top #5 arguments my parents ever had with each other). And, finally, an old A1 leather jacket – deep brown, a sort of purple-brown, frayed ribbed cuffs on the arms and round the body, cutaway collar, beautiful. It was hard like a shell of armour would be. The inside was softly padded in a faded yellow-green. Inside the pockets: some old, gross tissues. The smell: leathery but also dusty, at once smelling of masculinity and nothing at all. 'Heh,' I said. 'This is cool!' I wore it to the pub that night. Everybody told me I looked stupid.

You have to have gravitas, to wear leather, is the thing. *A cow died for this*. When you wear leather, you are saying: I am wearing the very skin of a very large, mad animal. Cows can fuck you up. We squeeze them of their milk and meat then wear their skin for warmth and sport. Leather has a powerful musk to it from that fact. An animal, vanquished and tanned and stretched taut and shaped, and cut to size and riveted and folded, and an especially gnarly chunky zip affixed to it, and sold to you, with all the allure, in shops with pulsating stereo speakers in the corner and low lights and assistants with facial piercings. Do you have this gravitas? I am not sure I have this gravitas. My father's leather jacket was formed into the very shape of him – his shoulders, apparently, were far broader than mine, and the leather was taut across the back as a result; around his torso the jacket was bulged and round, as if it had been affixed with belts around a barrel for many years – and it felt odd to be wearing the shape of my dad's body over the reality of my own. I took the jacket home, moved it to five houses with me wherever I went, and now it's in a trunk somewhere, still in his shape and not mine, still with his cigarette smell and not my far more florid fragrance, still his and not mine.

I often think of vintage guys, when I see them, with their little waxed moustaches and their silk bowties: I look at them and I think: *how did they happen?* Because as young teens, we all more or less wear the same thing: jeans, hoodie, a shoe of some sort. The cut of the jeans and how disgustingly unwashed the hoodie is tends to fit with your style tribe, and that's where the edges between us start to fuzz and differ (if you like music with guitars in it you basically have the same one-size-too-big oversize black hoodie with the drawstring missing, same blue pair of jeans with crisp dust rubbed in streaks onto the thighs, and same squashed dirty trainers; if you are more of a kid who likes pop music or dance CD mixes then your jeans will be well cut and frequently laundered by your mother, your white trainers will be immaculate: these are the only rules I know). Then, somewhere around 14 or 15, we start to diverge – a band t-shirt here, a fashion top you saved up all your pocket money for there – and little sprawling roots of fashion dig themselves away from the knot, out into the soil. Apart from vintage guys, who are like: suddenly wearing a three-piece suit. Or: they have a bowler hat on, and don't own even one single t-shirt. When I see vintage guys, I have to wonder about the sheer logistics of them – did they start small, maybe with a single pair of cute braces, and work their way up over the years? Or did they just spend their overdraft at Beyond Retro one day, entirely refitting their wardrobe and becoming A Vintage Guy overnight, they don't remember buying one but now they have a ukulele? I have similar feelings about goths: you never see half a goth, do you? You never see an early, fledgling, tiny little goth. Goths are all or nothing. To be goth is to be very binary about it. You can't be half-goth, half-normal. You either have a little vial of blood around your neck or you don't.

It's when I saw some goths recently that I realised I would never be Lenny Kravitz, or a goth, and it was then that I gave up on the leather jacket dream forever. They were wearing leather trench coats, the goths, and baking under the summer sun: you could sort of smell the musty scent of parched skin coming off them. But I admired their dedication to the leather cause: they all looked good in it, despite all very visibly looking like they were poetry writers. There are various ways you can wear a leather jacket – rock-star cool (Kravitz, Alex Turner); rock-star uncool (Chad Kroeger, Adam Levine); country-star uncool (Blake Shelton, constantly); actor uncool (Kevin Bacon, in one of those collarless jackets, the ones that definitely come with a pair of wraparound shades in the pocket). You can look like one of those lads who keeps going to underage emo nights long after he has graduated from college, or one of those kids who was in a band once but then the band broke up and he hasn't cleaned under his fingernails even once ever since but he wants you to come to his house to watch him play guitar about it. Metalheads look absolutely fantastic in leather jackets. Instagram fashion girls in wide-brimmed hats. You can look like an aged fashion type, Goldblumesque, as if you smell of rich sandalwood and tobacco scents. Or you can look like I do: a tight-faced American divorcée, waiting for his children at the school gates, desperately trying to make them think he's cool again after that time he cried in front of them and begged for their mum back. Sometimes you just have to admit things to yourself, and the goths and Lenny Kravitz and the leather jacket experiment has made it thus. I will now cart *two* leather jackets through five house moves and ultimately keep them locked in a trunk. I am not – however hard I try about it – a Leather Jacket Guy. That's one thing I'll just never be.

ALL THE FIGHTS I'VE LOST

1.

If we were to build our culture anew over the bones of the old one, erasing all that came before it but maintaining our government, society, the buildings we have and all the progress we made, the fact is this: if we had to start again and pull religions up out of the ground, at least one of them would be dedicated to M&Ms. One would be dedicated to Oprah, too, and one for Beyoncé. A religion for Cola, a religion for Oreos, a religion for Manchester City FC. We would tie ourselves to brands and heroes and enshrine them in mysticism and lore. And there, towering above all, monstrous and huge and all-encompassing, Red and Yellow, our M&M spokescandies, our monsters, our gods.

2.

I am a big guy. I am 6 feet 4 inches, but when people ask me how tall I am I tell them I'm 6 feet 2 inches, because it sounds more modest. (When you are 6 feet 4 inches and you tell people your real height it sounds like bragging; there is only one perk to being that tall and that is: every time you walk around a supermarket, an old lady will ask you to get a box of cereal down for her from a high shelf, and you can feel very warm and wholesome in doing that.) I weigh myself every morning – that is my religion! – and as of right now I weigh 88.6 kilos, or the same as 97,362 standard-sized chocolate M&Ms. I have long legs and enormous reach. That is what I tell myself, with that internal check against the monologue that always runs throughout my head: *I could win a fight, if one started now.* In the street, sizing up opponents, shorter men with beanie hats on and their hands firmly in their pockets. *I could defeat them*, I think, *with my superior reach*. All men do this, constantly. I have no evidence to suggest otherwise but I feel like my natural physical qualities – height, weight, general enormity – could, with a spirit of hard work and a physical discipline I have never exhibited for even one second in my life, but maybe if it was put into me magically somehow, maybe I was hit with lightning and something inexplicably happened to my chemistry, perhaps if a wizard cursed me to be less distracted by my phone and actually take my gym bag to work with me, if the stars aligned thus: I could get strong, so strong, I could train myself to be a monster. Physically, I am primed to beat the shit out of an M&M.

3.

The M&Ms are hornier than most food mascots. Most food mascots are zero per cent horny. Every single cereal box cartoon character: demonstrably unhorny. Every time a yoghurt comes to life, or a soda can grows arms and legs; whenever eyes blink open on the horrid lifeless face of a tin of condensed milk, all of our living foodstuffs are unhorny. Except for the M&Ms, tinged with a streak of Rated-R maturity. There is Red (voiced by cartoon v/o royalty Billy West), and Yellow (voiced by literal Oscar-winner J. K. Simmons). There is Green, too, the first female M&M, fluttering eyelashes and white thigh highs, whose very existence begs the question: *do M&Ms fuck?* (There was an urban legend that the green M&M contained some secret ingredient that made people horny, so ad executives made the green M&M horny. It is not clear what came first: the myth about the horny M&M, or the horny M&M. But this much we know: the green M&M definitely fucks.) I think all the M&Ms fuck, secretly, in the share-sized bag in the cinema before you consume them while watching the credits.

The M&M is the dark timeline snack. In the seventies, a Russian study suggested the red food dye amaranth caused cancer in humans: despite not containing the dye, M&M pulled the red shell from bags, replacing it with orange, and for ten years the red M&M was steeped in death, in blood, shunned. M&Ms were famously part of

Van Halen's rider, with the brown ones picked out (if a tour venue could not pick the brown M&Ms out of a bowl, Van Halen reasoned, they could not be trusted to safely assemble their complicated light and sound rig: this was spectacular logic from four guys who were almost pathologically On Cocaine): it is not hard to imagine Van Halen, slick with the sweat of hours on stage, mainlining M&Ms by the handful while making groupies do something appalling. M&Ms came up in the war years, and have an element of danger to them not found in other chocolates: M&Ms were for soldiers, tired of their ration-issue chocolate melting in the field when they were trying not to get shot. The M&M factory in New Jersey produces eight billion M&Ms per day, which is so many M&Ms, so many. There are M&M Worlds in every major tourist city on the planet, where people travel thousands of miles, from hours away, to look at M&Ms and large plastic versions of M&Ms. My first visit to New York was essentially spent wide-eyed and looking at M&Ms: plain, yes, peanut, obviously, crispy and pretzel, but also strawberry flavour, chocolate mint: M&Ms in family-sized bags, M&Ms you could drown in. M&Ms are all around us, constantly, billions of them, out there in the world, in bags and tubes and buckets. From the M&M encyclopaedia 'chocolate.wikia.com/M&M': 'Red Shell's Turn-ons: When people blindly follow his wise advice; Turn-offs: When people fail to recognize his obvious leadership abilities. Best Friend: Yellow (they got their shells together).' The spokescandies have back stories, friends, likes and dislikes. The spokescandies have rich interior lives. There is a running theme in the commercials where we see the spokescandies *eating the very M&Ms they are made from*, making them *literal cannibals*. The spokescandies are so ubiquitous they have essentially become background noise. We never ask why they both talk like Mafia henchmen given a low-key operation to tail someone's girlfriend to see if she's cooperating with the police. We never ask if we could defeat them in unarmed combat.

4.

SCENE. INT. DAYTIME. The door opens in a white and cream domestic bedroom. It is well kept and the linen is clean. A woman fumbles in the bed in a silk pyjama top, the Hollywood shorthand for having just had sex. Her husband, dressed in shirtsleeves and a tie, walks through the door. 'Scott,' she says, as he drops his briefcase, heart shattering like glass, 'it's not what it looks like.' Scott lowers his voice to an accusatory whisper. (Remember this is an advert for M&Ms. Remember this is trying to make you want to buy M&Ms: the idea that M&Ms are horny.) 'You were going to eat him without me,' Scott says, 'weren't you?' The Red M&M pops out from beneath the sheets, and it's clear that he has been rutting. The Yellow M&M peeks out from the wardrobe, and it is clear that he has been watching. And then Red goes, in full get-outta-here! Paulie-from-*The-Sopranos* voice, says: '*Now* the biting makes sense.' And holy shit, holy shit. Holy shit holy shit holy shit. The M&Ms are Mafia Guys.

5.

From now on we will refer to the Red M&M as 'Red' and the Yellow M&M as 'Yellow', even though I deem them both too monstrous to have ever earned names.

6.

Why is it important that the M&Ms are Mafia guys? Because, crucially, that makes them fighty. Fundamentally, a dwarf-sized sentient M&M is not a formidable fighter: their hard candy shell, when scaled up in size, might be an inch or two thick, giving them a technical shield advantage; and also the fact that they are slick and sugar-coated means they might be hard to pick up and throw and smash, making them a difficult adversary; but fundamentally, if an M&M grew to about four foot in height and woke from an eternal slumber to become instead alive, it wouldn't be a hardened fighter. But being from Mafia stock, talking like a wise guy, fucking a dude's wife behind his back (it is not explained in the M&M canon whether M&Ms have dicks and how they might disguise them when not in use, like M&Ms do not wear underwear, but also in the advert Red was trying to fuck and Yellow was trying to watch him fuck, so we know like that M&Ms are both capable of getting horny and being so horny it subverts normal horniness tropes to become perverted. Is the dick the same colour as the M&M? Undoubtedly. Is the M&M dick, also, sugar-coated and wrapped in a protective shell? I believe so, yes): this is important. This makes Red a guy who goes to strip clubs, and carries a piece, and shouts a lot while eating and driving. Red could have been in *The Sopranos*, some no-storyline guy who shoots a police officer in the head one night and has to flee town. This means he came up and paid respect to a made man and then became one. He wears shell suits and has a hard-done-by-wife who keeps the fridge well stocked and the house immaculate and does not mind him banging chicks on the side. Consider this: consider Tony Soprano had a large peanut inside of him. Imagine how mad he would be, even on top of how mad he already was. *That* is the extent of the candy-coated anger we are dealing with.

7.

The entire fighting careers, wins, draws and losses, of Joel R. Golby (b. 1987):

WINS

FIGHTER

Jason, a new-to-our-school kid who I'm pretty sure was in foster care and smoked from the age of about 9, one of those kids

REASON FOR FIGHT

It was school sports day and we were supposed to shuttle

round the playground doing points-winning games but, when it was our group's turn to line up and take shots on the basketball hoop, Jason hogged the ball for ages taking throw after throw after throw, getting more and more frustrated at the repeated air balls, and I, in the queue behind him, intercepted as the ball bounced back then turned away and swooshed it – arguably the coolest personal moment in my entire life – so he fucking punched me in the head

OUTCOME

I don't really know how exactly but as he arrowed at me to try and get a second punch in I twisted around and instead tripped him onto the floor and hit him in the head like three or four good times (I was like 11, 11-year-olds can't hit; please do not feel sorry for the punched foster boy!) before a teacher dragged the two of us apart. By the letter of the law I should have been very punished for hitting the foster kid but I think my headmaster had had about enough of Jason's shit already in his six-week stint at our school and I was a real, real kiss-ass of a teacher's pet, so he let me off with a half-stern warning and Jason got detention. TKO.

DRAWS

FIGHTER

A bouncer at Leeds Festival who had exactly half his teeth in his head – but split vertically, the teeth, so he had half the teeth in the top left and bottom left of his mouth but none in the right side at all, possibly the most sinister tooth configuration I have ever seen, either in movie or real life, I mean I can only assume this dude got his head, like, stomped entirely on, and somehow *survived* that, I mean if someone stomped half the teeth out of my head I would just die out of politeness both to the stomper and myself, who, truly, wants to get up from that

REASON FOR FIGHT

We were camping in the VIP camping area outside of the main arena that entailed exiting the arena proper and briefly walking in a non-festival designated no man's land and then looping back in to the campground where we were staying, and my colleague forgot his lighter, so after going through security once then twice we had to turn round and go through it a third time, and the half-tooth man conducting checks with his team did not like my 'smart mouth' or 'fucking smart mouth' when I made a wisecrack about us being searched for drugs three times in fifteen minutes when clearly I had already taken all of my cocaine because why else would I be running my mouth at a bouncer—

OUTCOME

No actual punches were thrown but that was only because, like, four other security guards had to drag the half-tooth man away from the front line whilst saying soothing things like 'he's not worth it mate' and 'don't go back to prison' while a curt but formidable female guard ran a single blue gloved finger around the inside of our belt line. DRAW.

FIGHTER

'Someone's brother who is hard', goth bar, Chesterfield, circa 2013

REASON FOR FIGHT

One of my mates had got off with a girl who it turned out had a boyfriend on the other side of the bar, and he had got off with this girl *directly outside of the bar we were all in*, so our mates and his mates all had to dutifully troop outside while they sorted it out, and they did that kind of half-fight thing where they actually end up talking and hugging and saying 'sorry mate' and buying each other beer about it. This was a strange and unsatisfactory end to the fight, and there was a lot of built-up testosterone in the air because two-dozen lads in their early twenties had trooped outside to fight and then not had a fight, so there was an electricity there that could only be dissipated if someone else got hit. This is how male aggression works! Sorry about it!

OUTCOME

Oh so after we'd all gone inside, I was laughing at the absurdity of the whole thing (imagine a guy buying you a beer as an apology for being mad you kissed his girlfriend!

What kind of parallel world!) and while laughing I caught the eye of this guy directly opposite me across the bar – it was a large square bar that segmented the entire building, you had to go out one door and through another to get to it, or hop the bar if you were really mad – and he seemed just monstrously pissed off at me, very visibly pissed off, in his face. I hadn't been in town for a while so wasn't well versed in the local fight lads, so turned to my friend and said, 'Who's that? He seems mad' and was told in no uncertain terms: Don't, Mate, He's Someone's Brother And He's Hard. Things took a turn because *that* information made me laugh and then the tangible aggressive energy in the air sort of broke, and all my mates – knowing more how the ley lines and contours of this small backwards town worked, and which brothers were hard, and who was happy to compact the skull of any stranger they ever saw laughing freely – put a coat over my head and barrelled me out of the place like I was Lindsay Lohan exiting a courtroom. Purportedly the Hard Brother spent the next hour-and-a-half 'looking for me' and telling anyone who would listen that he was going to 'fuck [me] up'. I'm calling that a DRAW.

LOSES

FIGHTER

A small angry freckled boy from a couple of forms over, who was very angry ever since the industrial accident death of his father, but who was a good 12 inches shorter than me, making him (angry, short) possibly the best analogy for an M&M in my fighting history.

REASON FOR FIGHT

All the boys from my form, 7E, had grouped around all the boys in his form, 7F, and decided that they were all going to have a fight, although couldn't decide *who* exactly was going to fight, and why, so just sort of stood around in a group shouting a bit, until this angry freckled kid came forward into the centre of the hoop and said he'd throw down (he was very angry since his dad got mangled into a machine). I was just mildly walking past at the time eating a bag of crisps and was not involved at all with the fight foreplay, and was called over and ushered into the group and long story short ended up in the centre going, 'No, mate, I'm not going to fight you' and then he smiled and leapt up and got me in a headlock and ran me head first into the door of a car. This fight was in a car park, hence the car being there. The crowd immediately dispersed.

OUTCOME

So I mean yes technically we would classify my pacifism vs his angry dead dad rage a loss for me, I suppose, yes, fine. LOSS.

8.

Could I win a fight against the M&M spokescandies? It is not a question anyone has ever asked. The motive for the fight is not necessary. The point is: could I win? Could I win it? Could I defeat a sentient candy in a fight?

9.

We can only go on form, and existing knowledge, and assumed knowledge about how well a candy the size of a small cow could fight if pissed properly off: we can only conclude that both the M&Ms Red and Yellow would absolutely rinse me in a fight. I could probably just about take Red in a fight – he weighs, what, 40, 50 kilos? I could feasibly pick him up and heft him into for instance a pond, where he would deteriorate and dissolve – but both Red and Yellow, leaping at me, kicking my long legs? Yellow up on my shoulders now, huge white hands scratching at my eyes, my arms wailing wildly at where I think he is going to be, rapping my knuckles on his shielded back? And Red, awful Red, slowly coming at me with a candy shiv, and – *pop, pop, pop,* prison-style – goes once into each kidney and then through my stomach, puncturing me three times until my knees buckle beneath me, until I am the awful M&Ms height; and then they drag me down, lower, until I am writhing on the floor, blinded, leaking blood from every side; and they kick, kick, kick me in the head with their candy-hard feet, until I stop fighting, until I stop jolting and fall still. I am not proud of this, but, yes: the M&Ms would beat me in a fight.

10.

EXT. SCENE. CHURCH GRAVEYARD. My funeral. I have been kicked to death by two four-foot candies. Around the hole in the ground where my coffin is lowered, the mourners come. My friends, dressed in black. My family, stoic and respectful. All the incredibly attractive women I always imagined loved me but never articulated it, red lips and split-to-the-thigh black dresses, scenically sobbing as my bones are lowered into the ground. And there, shameless, in their mafia way, the Red M&M and the Yellow one too, in wide-lapelled black leather suits. 'Psst,' the M&Ms say, to one of the women who secretly loved me. 'Let's blow this joint.' They ride away on a shiny chrome motorcycle, the girl riding pillion. In death, a final loss. One last defeat for Joel R. Golby. The M&Ms would beat me. They would beat me to death and spit on the grave of it. They would beat me so hard it would go down in the ages.

AT HOME, IN THE RAIN

As a kid I was some kind of divine rain-whisperer, because rain brought with it unbearable pressure headaches that manifested behind my eyes and up through my ears, leaving me bed-bound, watching as the first thin droplets of it would skit against my window. The view from my bedroom rolled on forever: first, a thin line of elderly care home bungalows, orange-red brick and curved steel fences; then a row of shops, all sagging with fraying plaster and neon light; beyond that, a bridge above an A-road, sandstone blasted clean-white then dirty with knee-height petrol smog again, an endless loop; and then, beyond that, the town's wooded golf course, a barometer of the seasons – lush and petrol-green during summer, electric and vivid lime in the spring, thin and brown and spindly as the winter rolled in, often somewhere in between them all, rustling slightly in the breeze. When the weather came I would lie on my side with my ear to my pillow watching the clouds rise over the horizon and bringing with them the rain I could already feel – salt-and-pepper grey on good days and blue-black like a bruise on the bad – eyes pulsating with the pain, veins just visible on the periphery of my vision, the thump of rain against my head, *pulse–pulse–pulse*. 'Stop faking it and get up,' my mum would say, soothingly. 'Bring the washing in,' I would say. She never would. Our towels always got put away just slightly damp. We dried our bodies in the smell of the rain.

I never knew how we ended up here, because neither of my parents were from Chesterfield, Derbyshire – the town in the near-enough exact centre of England where I grew up – and every time I asked I was told it was the only place equidistant between the two cities they were born in, Wolverhampton (dad) and Newcastle (mum). 'But *why* do we live here,' I would ask, looking out at the town's grey expanses of concrete, or kicking round a town centre you could loop through every shop at in half an hour flat, or gazing at the abandoned court building, to date still the ugliest construction I have ever seen. The town always felt like a sigh to me: a large exhalation out, the moment that precedes something bigger than before. 'We didn't want you growing up with our accents,' they would say, having met in London 20 years before and both abandoning the northern sounds and pulsing tones of their own regional voices. Instead I grew up with an unshakeable proto-Midlands accent, deep vowels and the inability to ever make a convincing *t*-sound, caught between the slowly separating train carriages of two identities – the flat, newsreader accent I heard at home, and the local variant

I learned at school – so much so that every time I go home now and get in a taxi from the station the guy in the front seat turns bodily round and asks through the thick plastic window: 'So where are you from, then?' I can't answer that question, friend, even to myself.

It was the same lush golf course that my dad and I used to go on for our walks. This was the primary Sunday morning activity of my childhood: Dad, me and Dad's dog Suzie (Suzie was very pointedly *not* our dog: she was this ratty, very visibly dying mongrel who smelled like an old sofa, and used to sit loyally with my dad and nobody else, and I literally do not remember petting her once as a child. He used to buy chicken for her, and cook it with more love and care than he would for the actual meals he prepared for the human family, and shred it and tip it into her manky old bowl, and she would wolf it down then go sit outside and fall asleep in such a way we weren't ever sure whether she was alive or dead. Suzie knew what side her bread was buttered on) would go on a trail that took us up, over a bridge above a motorway; along through a short section of canal, studded with trailing trees and wild garlic; then we would lift a loosened flap of chain-link fence and dash across an A-road, creaking over this ancient abandoned railway bridge and down to the back end of the golf course. Ostensibly, we were there to scout shooting locations for my photographer father, but what we were really there for was for dad to steal errant golf balls: he would swipe at the backwater patches of rough with an old pitching wedge, occasionally dinking lost balls up out of the grass which he would quickly pocket, adding them to his collection at home. Dad would stagger back home with his body warmer bulging monstrously, and in the days that followed we would see him on the field behind our house – the same one my school, up the road, used for summer P.E. lessons – dinking the old balls into a bucket he'd positioned 50 yards away. 'Hey,' kids in my class would ask me, between games of tag and touch-rugby. 'Who's the crazy golf guy?' And I would squint at him, off there in the sun amongst the daisies, chipping and chipping and chipping, and say: I don't know.

I think everyone has a cherished childhood field. Ours was called 'The Field', and as well as playing host to PE lessons, it was also the arena for most of my childhood games of summer football. The Field was subdivided into three sections: at the top, a steep hill of rough grass; in the middle, a concrete playground that led to another, less steep hill, with a twice-monthly trimmed playing pitch at the bottom; and beyond that, a ditch-like jungle of dead wooded trees and jags of straw-like grass, cluttered together behind a single barbed-wire fence. Mainly we would play football on the middle bit, occasionally interrupted by drunk men meandering home from the pub up the road (they would always crouch and put their hands towards their feet when they saw us playing, going 'Yeah! Yeah! Yeah!' until we passed them the ball, which they would inevitably shank so violently west that one of us would have to run and get it: one man, attempting a golazo, just fully fell over on his arse once, and, instead of facing the consequences of his embarrassment about that, fell woozily asleep in the summer sun), so The Field was where I have most of my cherished childhood memories: playing endless games of Cuppies until the sun dipped below the surrounding houses; finding an old two-litre bottle someone had used to sniff glue with; taking a cricket ball full in the face and shattering my glasses across my nose like I'd been shot by a sniper; running home in the sweltering heat to dip my head into the chest freezer in the cellar, droplets of sweat teetering on my forehead until dropping heavily onto the ice pops below.

* * *

The writhing is what I remember the most. The way he thrashed from one pain to another. They had come from a grey brick tower block in another city, the two boys down my road, one older and one younger, and never seen the likes of the green we had to play with here. Both our houses backed onto The Field, and I would gaze out of my parents' window until I saw them there, in the distance, bouncing a football, and then I would sprint out to meet them: either to play cricket, or football, or 'spies', some sort of game that involved us crawling through the long straw grass talking into our collars as if reporting to HQ. That's where we were when Sadi fell into the nettles, the first time he'd ever seen them in his life. That's where we heard the sound of him, searing.

On long walks with dad he used to teach me about animals, nature, plants and trees. Blackberries, pussywillow, honeysuckle. One afternoon, huddled under some trees as thunder loomed above us, he pointed out an innocuous green plant. 'Dock leaves,' he said, rolling a wet cigarette in his hands. 'If you ever get stang off a nettle, rub those on it. They always grow nearby.' Sadi thrashed beneath us as I tried to explain the magic leaf thing to his brother: we sprinted off in different directions, mazy in the long grass and straw, until I found a blossom of them, ran them back for his arms, and legs, and face. We took his top off and sat him up and worked in silence, each of us rubbing and rolling a fat bottle-green leaf until it wadded up and rubbed away, Sadi's face dry with tears, his skin brown and pink with sores and green-yellow with remedy, and we watched the sun set, and we walked home, separately, knowing some pain had driven something unfixable between us. Nettle stings are a peculiar thing exclusive to childhood, like treading in dog shit is. When does an adult ever get stung off a nettle? It just doesn't happen, does it?

Chesterfield is a town that is built around its central spire, which is famously malformed: it twists and buckles beneath its own weight, and leans and tips like the Tower of Pisa might if it were made out of lead. This monster of failure is the single note of individuality the town has. There are two accepted theories about how that happened, one I like more than the other. The first is: the Black Death finished just 12 years before the spire's completion, and skilled craftsmen were hard to find. The ones who did make the spire used soft untreated wood for the beams and overly heavy lead for the tiles, which means the roof heats and contorts in the sun and twists a couple of centimetres a year under its own weight: this is where its iconic name, 'The Crooked Spire', first came into being. This is dull but accurate. The second theory is much, much better: that it was a normal spire, once, but a virgin got married at the church beneath it, and the Devil – the actual Big Lad himself, Lucifier the Devil – was so surprised he sat on the spire in wonder, squashing it. I like this because, mythologically, it suggests two things: one, that the Devil was just in Chesterfield one day, running errands (was he going to the Big Tesco for his bits? Was he in Thornton's? Was he at one of the town's four branches of Greggs?); and two, that chaste women are so hard to come by in Chesterfield that the Devil himself was astonished to see one pass by. Slagginess is baked into the very mythology of Chesterfield, legend tells us, it pulses through the veins of it. And I'm not saying I believe the myth but: if you have been in as many Chesterfield nightclubs at kicking out time as I have, then you would lean towards it, too.

The spire is plastered on everything that means anything to the town – pubs are named after it, more than one chip shop bears its name, the town's primary cab company has the church printed on the side, the spire is the logo of the local newspaper – most crucially the football team, Chesterfield FC or 'The Spireites', who reached the semi-finals of the FA Cup in the 1996–7 season with a spire-shaped badge. This remains #1 of the three most notable things that happened to Chesterfield in all the time I lived there (the other two were: the Somerfield supermarket in town went on fire and you could see the cathedral of smoke winding out above it from miles away; and, the Demaglass factory that previously employed hundreds in the town was shut down and dismantled, and we all assembled a safe distance away to watch the towers crumple in on themselves in a timed explosion; the most notable thing that ever happens in Chesterfield is, quite frequently, massive destruction). This place took on a magical air in the run-up to the match: news crews descended on a town centre that was constantly full of fans in replica kits with their faces painted blue, entire coach-loads of people took a trip across the Peak District to see the team play at Old Trafford, and I sat cross-legged and hopeful on my friend Dean's floor – Dean had cable TV so dozens of us crammed in there to watch it – as the team played what is still the most exciting game of football I've ever seen. Chesterfield – a bunch of journeymen, part-time players and a guy who was literally traded in exchange for a bag of footballs – put two past Middlesbrough, a new-money Premier League mega-team who assembled on the pitch like overpower movie villains, boasting the likes of Juninho, Emerson and Fabrizio

Ravanelli (who just *sounds* more exciting than Sean Dyche, the orange Chesterfield captain who tonked in the most no-nonsense penalty I've ever seen to give us the lead). Middlesbrough struggled back, then made it 3–2 in extra time, and it looked all but over: Premier League class had ground out Division 2 spunk. Then something absurd happened, something I still can't quite explain today: one last cross of the game whipped diagonally across the pitch to the edge of the 'Boro box and onto the head of Jamie Hewitt, a Chesterfield-born left-back who was phenomenally out of position, and from 18 yards out he bafflingly chose to *header* it, and the ball looped high, up, way above the height of the goal, then dipped again, *yes*, spun down and – *yes* – somehow, impossibly, dropped into the corner of the Middlesbrough net. 3–3. The town exploded like a bomb. I will never be as delirious as I was when that Jamie Hewitt header went in. Every adult emotion I've ever had has been pitched against that barometer: *yes, this sex is good. But is it a Jamie Hewitt header against Middlesbrough in 1997?* Honestly. That man has ruined joy for me, forever.

* * *

Geographically, Chesterfield is sandwiched between two notable areas of British topography – the Peak District to the east, and Nottingham's Sherwood Forest over to the west – which means the town sits in a weird little basin where extremes of weather are sucked into the more glamorous and tourist-friendly vortexes either side, and we are left with the drizzle in between. Something similar happened with the town's accent and identity, too: technically, Chesterfield is in Derbyshire, which is listed as being in the 'Midlands', an anomalous expanse of land between Stoke and the start of the North proper, but spiritually Chesterfield is nearer in outlook to Yorkshire – defeatist, a constant feeling of being underestimated or ignored, cheerfully grumpy, very proud about their sofa – so sort of butts up against that. Walk the streets of Chesterfield and tell the people there that they are Midlanders and enjoy, my friend, enjoy getting your fucking head kicked in. They identify as northern even if the geography stacks against them. If anything, wanting to be northern when you're not is more northern than actually being northern. Chesterfield adheres to a curious idea: that of aspirational northernness.

The town itself is a few landmarks pavemented together around some terraced houses, and not much else: the Crooked Spire leads down to the train station that leads out to the golf course; reverse back the other way and you'll find the town's ancient centre, a centuries-old daily market that sells everything from pirated DVDs, bread, fresh fruit, and a stall that just seems to sell ... bungee cables? For some reason?; beyond the town centre is Queen's Park, home to the town's major swimming pool and a small ornamental train my friend Paul drove for a summer, growing so local-boy famous as a result of it that he had a harem of teenage girls with emo fringes waiting for him after work every day (Chesterfield's famous alumni include the glamour model Jo Guest, a handful of cricketers, George Banks and steam-train inventor George Stephenson, who wasn't born here but did die here: you can see how Paul, on the tiny train that circled the town's favourite park, leapt briefly onto that list); over the big roundabout by there you have the convergence of the town's two rivers, the Rother and the Hipper, then beyond that the famous Brampton Mile, an assault course of pubs that is seemingly constantly having two opposing stag and hen parties, whatever time you go past there, even if it's 11 a.m. on a Tuesday; up beyond there are houses, a supermarket, eventually ceding to countryside. Go right the way over to the other side of town and you have the new big out-of-town complex, built around the football team's new stadium: some car dealerships, a Donkey Derby pub, formerly Europe's second-largest Tesco (since eclipsed by another, larger European Tesco), then that all too makes way to houses, cluttered around supermarkets and roundabouts until it leads out to an A-road, until that leads right out of town. Chesterfield is tiny, centrally, but if you count all the tiny fragments of it that are embedded like teeth in the countryside around it then the population nudges 100,000; the central town itself can be basically crossed on foot in about 25 minutes flat.

Which is what, as teens, we did. The best thing in the entire world, sadly, is being a teenaged boy between the ages of 15 and 17, up past midnight on a summer night, walking to the Big Tesco on the outskirts of town. This is close to holy. There is something about the air, up there, in those electric thrilling hours between 12 and two a.m.: it smells different, softer and more fragrant, the same way the air smells salty and powerful the nearer you get to the sea, the way the air smells electric and full of potential in the minutes before it rains. On long summer evenings after long summer days, when the sun hasn't gone down more dipped just hiding out of view, so the air around you goes blue-green instead of dark, ecstatic orange street lamps blurring into view around you, the occasional car on one long stretch of concrete highway, *vrrrrr*ooom, and it feels like you have carved out a whole new world just for you, a whole clear pure space above everything where you are the king.

And you can chat an inordinate amount of shit on that 40-minute walk to the Big Tesco out of town. The Big Tesco out of town is open 24–7, although past midnight now it's more a film set of a megastore than a megastore proper: limp-faced shop boys fresh out of school themselves unrack plastic-wrapped containers of yoghurt into electric-white cooler aisles, and ghosts of other shoppers glimpse around corners in the distance, the coffee aisle stretching away to nothingness, the detergent, the beer. This was before beer, before weed, before school and life and other cities got in the way, before, crucially, girls: in a pure and true time when the only thing that mattered to

The Boys was The Other Boys, and shit chatting, and these little Rolo-brand donuts that Tesco used to do, and a two-for-£1 offer on Frijj milkshakes, and Walkers Sensations sharebag-sized crisps, and eating it all, together, in the brisk air outside the shop, on benches below fuzzy orange streetlamps, again; of playing football with whatever detritus we could find beneath the alley-way below the roundabout, and then the walk home, bloods pulsing, the air fresh with the smell of grass, and flowers coldly blooming, and damp and dry at the same time; the smell of car exhaust, and the dust of the day, settling down again; the smell of anticipation, in the air, for everything that was coming to us. Walking back in clot-like groups having conversations where we theorised what bras looked like. Walking back the way teenage boys walk when they walk together, which is, primarily, 'very clumsily into one another'.

At Tesco, though, we would mostly eat our snacks (Chocolate milkshakes, Dairylea Dunkers. An entire packet of jerky. Six-packs of Coke and Tesco-brand fizzy laces. Off-brand energy drinks. An entire cheese-crusted loaf of fresh bread. Bounties, Kit-Kats, Curly Wurlies. Sherbet, Pop Rocks. We would buy pink packs of reformed ham and eat them neat, folding the slices up into our upturned mouths as we sat on the back of benches outside the store) in silence, then pick our way through the empty car park, blurred and streaked with orange lamplight, down to the underpass tunnel beneath the major roundabout coming in. This is where we spent hours: letting off fireworks, playing football with an upturned bottle cap, eating just balled up pieces of bread, playing with old camcorders, talking the kind of undulating shit only teenage boys are capable of talking ('What if ... Warhammer was real?'; 'What do you think Brian Blessed is doing *right now*?'; '[*Hours long conversation about wrestling*]'). One time we dropped a brick from the bridge above us onto a carefully arranged stack of crackers below, just to see what happened. No non-adolescent mind has ever thought to do that. Why would it?

Occasionally, drunks – drawn to the glow of the Tesco beyond – would stumble upon us, rabbit-eyed teenagers in sweat-slicked hoodies, desperately trying to tackle each other for a Coke bottle top. They would eye us with the same suspicion we would eye them: like one animal had stumbled into the territory of a herd of others. A man and his girlfriend accosted us once, wobbling on their feet: 'You boys,' he said. 'You boys, you boys, you boys.' He unzipped his trousers and pissed in full view of all of us. 'Let me give you one piece of advice, boys,' he said, maintaining a startling virile stream throughout. 'All women – *all women* – are whores.' This is the folklore imbued into the very soil of Chesterfield. The Devil got inside this man and made him piss at us. He shook our hands, pissily, every one of us, then patted his girlfriend on the back and ushered her along with him. 'Good-*night*.' Then the rain came, sudden and total, and we stood in the yellow-white blur of the underpass we knew so well, rocking like we'd just been punched, staring out into the darkness as it lit up jagged with splinters of water, stunned into silence.

Chesterfield never felt like home to me when I lived there, and I always had this itching urgency to get out. I never understood why nobody else there had that: is this what you want? Does nobody here want to *leave*? But then I realised it offers something serene, and simple, and homely and safe. You can see why the Devil found a home here: Chesterfield doesn't challenge you and it doesn't ask for anything but a bit of respect back. Navigating it as an adult now is odd: we sold the family home a few years ago, and the last time I saw it there was a Hallowe'en pumpkin outside it and a plume of steam coming from a newly installed boiler exhaust, and I realised that the rooms I once knew so well – a room that felt like a bedroom, felt like a front room, the room out back with the big table where my mum used to smoke – had gone, been reshaped and repurposed by another family, who know it only as their own. When I go back I sleep on sofas and walk around town marvelling at the new shops that have opened there. When I go back I pull in backwards on the train and watch that old Crooked Spire creak into view. When I go back I feel nothing, really, just a few half-memories of big walks to Tesco, the flat where my dad died, an old factory that used to be here, the inexplicable amount of time I spent on a town's golf course where I don't really and never have played golf. Then I get caught in the rain without a jacket, and have to hide under an awning and watch a sudden curtain of rain fall in front of me, and there's that smell – the particular scent of cold sudden drops of rain falling on hot dusty summer air – and it's there again: there's that feeling I had so many times growing up. Home doesn't have to be a place, because places change: places get sold and exploded with dynamite in front of a watching crowd, and torn down and replastered and built anew, and sat on and contorted and bent. But then sometimes it's just something simpler than that: or for me it is, at least. Home is the smell of being dry beneath an underpass, watching outside as it rains.

MOUSTACHE RIDER

When I was a kid my dad had so much of a beard it was essentially the only defining feature of his entire head. Dad was defined – much like Groucho Marx, or Hitler – by the accessories of his face rather than the bone structure underneath it: perfectly round bald circle head, Homer Simpson-esque *M*s of hair on either side, a beard to join them, and glasses in between. I truly do not know if my father had a nose or not. Were there eyes behind the glasses? It is impossible to tell. Freckles, moles, scars, wrinkles? Honestly couldn't tell you. I would say once a year for the past decade-and-a-half I have been walking through a train station and seen a bald man with glasses and just gone, 'Ah, that is my dad then.' You see those heartbreaking viral videos, don't you, of orphan monkeys being given to a surrogate mother, and you think: 'How can the idiot monkey be so easily convinced that this baboon with tits is its true mother? Come on, baby monkey. Interrogate the information a little.' But honestly give me pints enough to reduce my faculties and introduce me to a bald man with glasses and I'll just assume he is my father, no questions asked. I'll curl up at his feet and ask him to tell me a story. I'll beg him not to leave me again. The scene, after a while, will actually become quite chilling.

My dad's beard was so intrinsic to him that the day he shaved it off it felt like a glitch in the matrix. I came home from school and he was just looking at me, smiling, and I looked at his face – a jawline I had never seen before in my life, a chin, oddly soft skin around the jowls – and my mind couldn't really process what it was seeing. 'Notice anything?' he said, and I said: 'There's definitely something.' We stared at each other for a minute or so. 'There's definitely *something* wrong with your face.' It was as if someone had yanked the sky away and I was just staring at the void left behind. Like skipping over a spelling error in an otherwise smooth-flowing sentence. My brain filled in the information that it couldn't truly see. 'I shaved my beard off,' he finally said, pointing to his nude, soft face, and I said: 'Dad, are you drunk again?'

He was, but that's irrelevant. The point is I dropped further from the testosterone tree than my dad did. I have a full head of hair – and thank almighty Christ that I do, honestly, because without it I would be nothing – so I am already one up on the man who went bald at 19 and, 23 years later, sproinged me from his loins, but facial hair has for the entirety of my pubic life been my bane. I didn't start shaving until I was 20, and it took a couple of years from that early scraping for a full filled-in face of stubble to occur. I stopped clean-shaving years ago because I have such a soft babyish face that I quite visibly revert to childhood when I do it, and off licences and bars stop serving me because they assume I am a preternaturally tall and confident sixth former trying to buy alcohol for his smaller and less pubescent classmates. I cannot grow a full beard because something in my genetic make-up won't allow it: at some point my stubble grows long enough to be scruffy but not significant enough to comb together into a beard, so I just look like George Michael after a couple of days spent tangled in the Hampstead Heath toilets, RIP. Essentially my facial hair grows in a liminal space between boyhood and true manliness, and I'm fine with it, I'm fine with it, but also I'm very much not fine with it.

At 30, I tried to grow a moustache. I have always been a fan of moustaches, ever since the England goalkeeper David Seaman stopped a penalty against Scotland during Euro '96 – the exact and precise, if you want to stop the universe and know exactly where it happened, moment I fell in love with football – and roared in celebration in a lurid yellow Umbro shirt and a lustrous brown moustache (before overarming the ball to Darren Anderton who set off the assist for the ensuing Gazza goal – truly, the greatest four minutes of football ever played in history). Tom Selleck had a moustache, sure, and about a hundred TV detectives, and also about 90% of sex offenders ever imprisoned in the UK or United States. But despite that they represent a sort of grizzled, world-weary version of manhood: a moustache says you are aged and wise, and know what a good cigar tastes like, and can fix or put up a shelf. Nobody is going to take a swing at a guy with a moustache, because they know he's going to swing right back. In an active hostage situation, are you (the bank robber) going to try and put a gun to the head of the dude rocking a 'stache? Like hell you are. You just fucking *know* that guy knows medium-to-basic kung fu, and will take the weapon off you before you can blink. The last few milliseconds of your life – as the bullet slowly crashes your skull apart, out from the back of it – will be spent thinking, 'I never should have underestimated the moustachioed man.' I had to have one.

Sadly, this took weeks. I tried to under-arm the new, Moustache Me into existence: I grew my stubble out as far as it would go, so everyone assumed I was just having a sort of ungroomed mental health break, then shaved down the sides and chin – just a little, just subtly – so the moustache area stood out a couple of millimetres more. At first, like my dad and the vacant beard, people noticed but didn't *notice*: 'Your face looks more ... ginger,' they would say, pointing to the curious orange-redness around my mouth, as if I had been sucking frenziedly from a rusted tap. 'There's something ... red about you.' I was kissing a girl in the red-pink glow of her bedroom after midnight and she pulled away, her arms still around me, and said sweetly: 'This tickles and we have to stop.' About three weeks later, one Friday, everything fell into place:

'Are you … growing a moustache?' three separate people asked me, and I told them: yes. 'Why?' they would say, and I ignored them. I felt manly for the first time in my life. I felt robust, like I could fix a motorcycle. Like I could hit the president over the head with a folded chair. Like I could be a medium-to-high famous Hollywood actor in seventies America. Like I could go into space and come back without choking in the vacuum of it, without my lungs exploding.

Life with a moustache was good, for a while. I took to nibbling on it when I was bored or thinking. I would flick at the long edges of it when I was watching TV. I've never smoked but always envied that smokers have something cool-looking to do with their fingers – they are always twirling a cigarette from one knuckle to another, or flicking and un-flicking a Zippo lighter, or unfolding a Rizla paper and rolling it up tight – and now I finally had something to occupy myself: an orangutan-red half-moustache that sort of looked like I was getting ready to go to my first prom with it. Then one day I woke up and looked at myself in a mirror and realised: ah, no. Good god, no. I looked like a substitute manager at a regional branch of CeX. Like I took Game Workshop very seriously as an adult. I looked like I had a 500-yard forbidden zone around every primary school in the country. Like I had opinions about motherboards that I express on special motherboard forums. I looked, as a man, as if I collected replica swords.

It had to go. I felt nothing as I trimmed it down to the

nub. Five weeks of ludicrous experimental growing, gone. The switch from 'ah, this moustache is good!' to 'get the horrid hair off my face' was not unlike the ugly feeling of regret you have after masturbating alone: shut the laptop lid, close out all the squalid porn, shave your moustache off and moisturise the area beneath. My upper lip was dry and caked with a dry skin residue under there. My face suddenly looked vacant without the addition of a third eyebrow. I started to detach from reality a little: if my face wasn't my face with the moustache, and it wasn't my face *without* it, then where did my face go? Who … *am* I? And then I realised that I'm a man who cannot experiment with the way his head and skull looks, at all. I can never pierce an eyebrow or get a teardrop tattoo. I am very dependent on my lustrous hairline and without it I look foolish. That I, too, don't have a discernible *face*, much like my dad: that I am a collection of notable features, mushed onto a sort of plain canvas backdrop. I learned a lot about myself, growing a moustache for a little bit. I learned a lot about who I am as much as who I am not. I am not, it turns out, capable of having a moustache.

RUNNING ALONGSIDE THE WAGON

1% A.B.V.

I don't remember how old I was exactly but I know I was a fucking dumbass, so that narrows it down slightly to anywhere between the ages of five and twenty-three. (For simplicity's sake I'm going to eyeball it and say I was seven, or eight.) I'd just got home from school. My school – as I now recognise as being some sort of fifties-era idyll in comparison to every other person my age alive – was just up the road from my house, so I was trusted to walk there and back on my own from a young age, like olden days, before child molesters were a thing. And when I got home from it my dad, as he ever was, was on the sofa.

Something was off, this time, though. Dad had his sofa that he shared with the dog, and Mum and I had ours. I think everyone's dad has a sofa. I do not know if this is something inherent to fatherhood – that the moment a baby is born, scalped with red blood and thin sacs of skin, and cords and screaming and yellow-orange liquids, origin unknown – something within the male psyche clicks and unlocks, and they go home and put A Real Ridge in a sofa cushion or their favourite chair, and they get antsy and agitated when they cannot sit in that chair, if guests are over for example, and they keep the butt ridge deep and maintained, something close to sacrosanct, a Shroud of Turin personal to their own dad-arse. I know I do not yet have this urge. But Dad always had his cushion – to the left of the sofa, to get a better angle on the TV – and this time he was slumped face down across the whole thing, orange and moaning slightly.

'Dad,' I said (this was the way I addressed my father). 'What's up?'

'*Mmrnnf*,' he said, or something like that.

And I noticed the pint glass he had on the floor, by his trailing hand. Again, you probably had this in your childhood home, but there was a hierarchy of glassware – beakers and tumblers that you, a clumsy boy or girl, were trusted with for your soda or squash; nice glasses, such as you may drink water out of at dinner with the dinner cloth down; then something crisp and crystal that might only be broken out if it was Christmas or a grandma was coming to stay. Dad had his special pint glass out – ornately formed, slightly blue-green in colour, and stemmed, sturdy but elegant at the same time – and it was filled with something see-thru, and sparkling. I was, and remain, a fat sugar-crazed gurgling idiot of a child, and I was jolted and ecstatic to see lemonade – previously considered contraband in our household – on full display.

'Is that ... lemonade?' I asked him. Dad paused for a second.

'Yes,' he said. 'That— yes. That is ... yes. Lemonade.'

And I drank the lemonade. And it wasn't lemonade. Dad was *drunk*.

2% A.B.V.

The thing with having an alcoholic father is you don't really realise you have an alcoholic father because even when you see other, non-alcoholic fathers, it doesn't exactly strike you as unusual. (It does not help, of course, that alcoholics are very famously reluctant to admit their alcoholism – I mean it very literally is Step One of The Program for a reason, people don't cheerfully roll around with an extended hand all 'Hi!' and 'I am an alcoholic! Nice to meet you! Please, if you have any port in the house, fucking hide it from me! My very bones are desperate to drink it!'). I suppose I did not notice anything was different until I was ten, eleven, say: that it wasn't the usual childhood rite of passage to come home from school before Mum did, to make black coffee for Dad, drunk in the afternoon, to shake him from his slumber, to pat him round the cheeks and try and make him more lucid, to come to. And I didn't realise, either, that in doing so I wasn't doing it out of any particular care for him, but rather for *me*: that making my dad sober, or at least a hollow impression of sobriety, meant the house might go an evening without an argument about how drunk he is, and

I would have a more peaceful life as a result of it. Draw a string from my dad cracking a cold one at noon on the dot and me in my room, cross-legged and playing Megadrive, trying to get Sonic through the Chemical Plant Zone and failing because the people downstairs keep shouting. My motivations were, as they ever are, very selfish. I never beat Robotnik and I squarely blame my father.

3% A.B.V.

He was dead at 15 (I was 15, not him) and I suppose you can blame the drink. I've been thinking about it for half my life now and I'm not sure I exactly do. He was found, prone and backwards, lifeless in his council flat, and for a while I thought he might have died while pissing, like a sort of unglamorous Elvis – the last time I'd seen him, he had a golf-ball-sized purple lump on the dome of his head, where, losing his balance while having a drunk mid-afternoon wee, he'd collapsed backwards and hit his head squarely on a jutting electrical socket directly in the hallway behind. 'Maybe this is how Golbys die,' I thought. '*Ridiculously*.'

But no, he'd died the normal way: his liver, fatty and engorged from years of cheap cider-shaped abuse, finally failed, and the rest of his body crumpled along with it. He and my mum had split a couple of years earlier – the arguments with the drink finally spiralling to breaking point, just as his marriage to his first wife had before me – and he ricocheted from one council flat to another, losing weight, incrementally, losing lucidity, growing ever less like a human being and more and more like a phantom. I never really knew him, I don't think. I only ever knew a symptom of a disease. When I ask people what he was like their eyes fill with a sort of sparkling joy when they tell me how bright he was, how talented, his eye for a photo, the art he could produce, the way he could do anything, really, if he put his mind to it. When I was nine or ten every boy at my school and I got simultaneously obsessed with penknives – so intricate! So many blades in one small space! So useful! Toothpicks! – and, to stave me off buying an actual knife and inevitably stabbing myself with it, he crafted me one out of wood: a balsa blade, slotting neatly into an off-shoot of curtain rod, fixed in place with a wooden peg so I could still flick it and softly threaten people with it. I played with it endlessly one summer. He could fix my lust for knife violence. Why couldn't he fix *himself*?

4% A.B.V.

Dad died at the age everyone at school got into alcohol and fingering, so he stole my formative drinking years away from me, because to be honest I associated alcohol with arguing and death, and that's a real boner-kill when you're trying to pass a bottle of Strongbow round a park with a group of your peers and do some artless hand-stuff with them ('Hey wow, a great long chug of the poison that killed my dad – thanks!' No.). This continued throughout my late teen years, and sort of pushed me to the edges of it a bit: my friends, a tight knot of whom have seen me through every major event of my life, were dabbling in beer, and weed, and clubbing, and getting off with girls, and I was just sort of very quietly eating pizza and staying in on Friday watching *Robot Wars* and scrolling through internet bulletin boards. Would I have fucked before the age of 20 if my dad hadn't died? No. You can't blame everything on your dead dad, you soft nerd.

5% A.B.V.

I don't remember my first beer, precisely, and I don't remember the first time I got drunk, either: often, people with that love–hate relationship with booze seem to be able to remember with remarkable clarity that first sparkling sip of it, how it danced on the tongue, how suddenly the pieces seemed to click into place, how they knew – right then – that this would be a long and stormy friendship. I remember my mum used to come home from nights out dancing – when I was old enough to be left alone in an evening and she was trying to piece her social life back together after the explosion of death through it, she would announce that she was 'out boogying' that night and spend like six hours getting ready for it, a cloud of perfume and that lipstick smell, leaving the house in a sparkly top, and then me, alone, with money for a pizza – and got in the habit of bringing me a single drink, drip-feeding it to me, hoping I would get the taste for it but not the thirst. Once she came home when I was still up

– *Vanishing Point* with Viggo Mortensen was on late-night TV and I had decided it was the greatest film ever made about driving your car for 90 minutes until you died – and she thrust at me an Irn-Bru flavoured vodka WKD, which I sat and drank while Viggo drove himself full pelt into concrete, and I thought: *I feel nothing. This does nothing for me*. As origin stories go, it's not a good one.

6% A.B.V.

When I was younger I was constantly paranoid that I would succumb to The Disease. It ran in my family, I was told – a cousin had struggled with it when I was a kid, distant grandparents 'liked a tipple', my sister quit abruptly when I was college-aged – and I always assumed I would take a sip of beer once and then one day, boom, wake up 40 years later, dazed and deranged on the sofa. One time, when Dad was out, Mum and I emptied an old cupboard, where we'd stored a case of continental beers left over from a New Year's Eve party (these are the beers mums buy for guests when they don't want them to at all drink beer, and so are always leftover, and in fact if you have a garage right now there is almost certainly at least 80% of a case of them left there, whether you bought them here or not: tiny 200ml brown-glass bottles of sour lager that are near impossible to enjoy, entirely useless things). Only, they weren't: when we looked closer we noticed every lid had been carefully pried off the bottles, which had been drunk and filled with water again then put back. Alcoholics do this, with booze, like cats kick their sand over shit: hide it, disguise that it ever happened, the flawed logic of a drunken fool. Can you imagine being that desperate for a beer that you would do that? I watched Mum heave the case onto the kitchen counter and dust her hands in preparation for the bollocking to come, and I thought: *that'll be me, one day. Drinking beer and pretending I didn't*. (Dad's excuse, by the way, was: 'Maybe that's how the shop sold them to us. You should complain.' He maintained this for over an hour. He even lifted the beer up and made motions to walk it back up the hill to Lidl before he gave up and promised to go to AA, again.)

7% A.B.V.

Every guide I read before I went to university told me that Freshers' Week was a sort of bacchanalian week – days of excess, where I would drink and fuck and make friends and fuck and drink and join a rugby club? For some reason? And fuck and drink and fuck and fuck and fuck and drink and fuck. The pamphlets mostly lied. Week One I was the victim of some sort of accounting error that meant my loans didn't come in, so I was living off a £20 note my mum left for me, and in the end bought one beer at an English department meet-up, vaguely hoping I would like the taste, more so hoping it would push me far out of my social comfort zone into the free-talking cool guy I always suspected I would become one day and never did, more so than that, hoping it would push me through various developmental stages of pubescence during the course of one 500 ml bottle and make me brave enough to talk to the tall brunette I spent the next three years silently lusting after – but never, very crucially, ever talking to – on my course. It didn't. I looked down at the bottle – Spitfire Amber Kentish Ale, I remember very vividly – dark and brown and nutty, foamy but not fizzy, out in the car park on a hill behind what would become the English dept go-to pub, looking out dark across the channel that separated mainland Wales from the island of Anglesey, perched from my position on the path towards an unillustrious 2.1 from Bangor University. It was cold, and the beer was sort of lukewarm, and there were no fuzzy lights or agitations to speak to anyone, and I kind of looked at everyone else jealously – they were all of them in the same smoking corner, bathed in yellow-white light and soft and relaxed with drunken giggles, and though they were a few yards over they may as well have been a million miles from me – and after that I went back to my dorm and ate three apples and went to sleep. Maybe I'd never catch the bug, I thought, for better or worse. Maybe I'd be alright.

8% A.B.V.

You can make chilli vodka a variety of ways but the way The Skerries in Bangor, North Wales makes it is like this: dozens, hundreds of dried chillies, left in a demijohn for months, years maybe, occasionally topped up with the most methylated clear vodka they can find. Nobody orders this shot because they don't want to die. The Skerries in Bangor, North Wales is an old man pub with a tatty pool table and fuzzy corner-mounted TVs showing uninteresting continental football and red-pink-faced men shouting catastrophically in Welsh. It does not like two boys who have spent the afternoon drinking cider crashing through that delicate atmosphere, ruining it. That is why they give them the shot.

By Year #3 of university I had discovered drinking. I do not recall where, exactly, or when – I remember a giddy, gleeful realisation that I was drunk one summer evening, sat next to my friend David after what must have been two or three pints of fizzy lager, euphoric with this odd new feeling (my arms were ... wow! My ... wow! I ... my head was ... ha-ha, wow!) – but when it became a regular habit I don't know: the tracks imperceptibly slipped, and I switched from one to another, and I never saw the join, like a skilled magician had guided it with unseen hands. I was living with a housemate who had two medical strikes against him – an allergy to gluten and a stewing, nascent alcoholism – and we would rail cases of cider together, splitting them halfway down the middle, to accommodate his allergy. 'If I get beer, I'll bulge up and go all red,' he would say, and I would look at him – bulged up, red – and think: *hmm, okay.* We would take semi-weekly trips to a pharmacist to pick up his doctor prescribed carbohydrates – crumpets, breads – then stagger back with heavy bags of them, deciding on the way that we deserved a pint.

The Night We Got Shot was a big one. We'd started early – splitting a case of Strongbow Dark Fruits between us, cracking the first can a little past noon, then staggering up to the off licence a few hours later for another. Friends texted us to say they were in a nightclub further up the town and that we should join them, and we decided to go: not changing from the jumpers and sweats we'd been drinking in all day, instead downing our cans and grabbing one for the road and staggering to The Skerries, the nearest pub to our house. 'One shot, please!' we said at the bar, and the barmaid said: of what? And we said: 'Surprise us!' And that was our first mistake.

The plan was to dip into every bar along the high street and have a shot in each, but that went out of the window as soon as the chilli vodka hit. The thing is, it didn't hurt at first: we made it maybe a hundred yards before the searing started, first in our mouths and then in our throats and guts, a sort of delayed pain I imagine (*Kill*) Bill experienced after the Five Point Exploding Heart technique, chest pumping and burning at the same time, tears streaming, snot just everywhere. There was a thin rain in the air, and we held our tongues up to it for solace: 'MILK!' we were crying, trying to gulp down drops of water from the clouds, 'WE NEED MILK!' One of us vomited in a bin. I think every hardened drinker has a story where they ruined, forever, one drink for the rest of their lives – some recoil at the smell of tequila, some can't do red wine after a sickness with it, some even beer – but that's the one for me. Not, oddly, chilli vodka. Waking up with the sickly medicine-fruit smell of Dark Fruits Strongbow in my house was enough to put me off it for life. Every time I see a can of it I am transported back to Bangor, back ten years again: me, alone, rain sodden, hands on the rim of a bin, begging an unyielding god for a sweet cold taste of milk.

9% A.B.V.

When I turned 18 my mum threw me a party, which was her way of getting out of buying me actual, proper presents. When your mum throws you a party it's very rarely the party you *want,* exactly: me and all my boyish mates were confined to the house's front room, where we played N64 and had arguments about whether the Foo Fighters were good or not, while at the front of the house a bunch of my mum's grown-up friends, plus an occasional handful of family, were milling around a buffet. Occasionally I was dragged forth to be shown off to my mum's work friends like some large, dumb prize – 'An 18-year-old boy! A large, hearty boy! I made that!' – then sloped off with a paper plate full of lasagne and birthday cake to go and get sugar-high and rowdy with my mates. When you turn 18 it's not for you, really. It's just an occasion where your mum can remember that time she turned her body inside out for you, the agony, the agony, and now look: you made it to adulthood, sort of, you might yet turn into something, all the gore and stitches might one day prove to be worth it.

I barely saw my mum that day – my teenage moodiness clanged against her life-of-the-party electricity – but when she said goodbye to some friends and stopped outside the front gate to have a fag I briefly joined her. 'I might have a beer,' I said, and she nodded. 'Well. You are 18.' I looked to my friends, inside, yelling at an ageing copy of *Mario Kart*, seemingly deep in a well of fun I couldn't quite tap into. 'I might get drunk.' And she stopped for a second, and looked at me, and it wasn't begging, exactly, in her voice – it was something more fragile than that – but it was weak, and naked, and human. 'Please don't,' she said. 'Please.' And she flicked her cigarette out into the road and walked inside.

10% A.B.V.

So I just woke up one day and my tooth was chipped. My tooth was chipped. My tooth! Was chipped. My tooth! You know how many teeth you get? *Not many*. Run your tongue across the front of your teeth. Are they chipped? No. Exactly. Mine is. Right side, front and centre, slight chip along the base. It's wild how much a small chip can throw off the feel of your whole mouth: once so pure, so smooth, like an inverse of a pebble, and now just a slight snag of jaggedness, lingering there, something you could catch a strand of cotton on. My tooth, forever chipped. I surveyed the room around me – blankets tied around my legs like a knot, the air in here warm and close, the whole room smelling like my breath, clothes discarded and thrown slumped in the wardrobe, all the signs of high drunkenness – and thought back: where was I last night? In the same pub we always went to after work. But why did— oh, right, yeah. Around my third or fourth pint I'd really swung the glass up to my face – that's *thirst*, baby – and clicked it against my front tooth. I guess it had chipped then. I ran my tongue along it again, sharp enough to just cut the flesh. *Fuck*. I cried a bit then got up and brushed what was left of my teeth and washed my face, then pulled on last night's jeans and headed to work. My dad's drinking injuries were always so extreme – the golf ball, the time he fell face-first down some train station steps and shattered his nose and his camera, that time his liver failed and he died – so I guess I got off lightly. But I still had to get off the bus halfway in and vomit on the side of the street. There was still a golf-ball-sized bulge on my *dignity*.

11% A.B.V.

People tell me I am a very charming drunk. My eyes go heavy-lidded and I have a placid smile on my face, and I really lean into the tell-people-what-you-really-think-of-them 'you know what, mate? I love you. And above that I *respect* you'-type pub chat, and I'm generous getting the rounds in and I'm not afraid to keep the party going if it starts to sag, and most importantly I'm me but with a few knots untied – day-to-day I can be quite uptight, a clenched fist vs my drunk version's open palm, day-to-day I can be tense and unapproachable, throwaway jokes sometimes come out mean and unnecessarily cutting. And then I'm drunk, and the gears shift down, and everyone likes me more. 'Hey,' they say, everyone, in one perfect chant in unison (this is how I remember it, sober remembering drunk). 'Fun Joel Is Here!' Apart from one goth kid's brother, once, at a bar in Chesterfield where he really wanted to fight me. And one extremely gnarly bouncer at a field in Leeds Festival that one time. A Deliveroo driver punched me quite recently, in front of some girls. But other than those three times and no other times at all: I think everyone likes me when I'm drunk, more so than they do when I'm not. Which, I suppose, if you think about it for more than one second, is part of the problem.

12% A.B.V.

My sister's mum was coming to stay. I'd just broken up with a girl and had to move house in a hurry and needed somewhere stable where I could write (this.) (this book.) and my sister was going on holiday and her mum had already agreed to house-sit for them so there was me, 30-year-old child-boy relentlessly checking his ex's Instagram account 30 or 40 times a day, and then there was my sister's mum, 70+ and new to Slimming World and the recipes therein (the key lime pie? Not bad!), and we were in a weird Odd Couple situation for a week or five days sharing a house and tending to the house and the cats in it, and then in the evenings we would eat vegetable stir-fry together and silently watch *QI*. And then one night I was like Hey, What Was My Dad Like, and she was like, Oh—

It's funny, actually, she said. She said: he was a brilliant man, really. He was a producer, when he had a career, a big player on the nascent advertising scene in London in the seventies. A golden boy, for a while. He could have done whatever he wanted. He had big offers from advertising houses all across Europe. And then he sort of ... fucked it up.

And I am thinking: *I hope my book goes well I hope my book goes well—*

She said: he just sort of, got carried away with himself. And then the drink set in, obviously. He lost a job directly because of his drink problem: even in advertising, seventies London advertising, he drank too much. *He drank too much for the advertising industry to deal with*. And then they had to move from the house they had in London – they had to sell it, she said, and she looked up how much it would be worth now and it made her shit – and out to Devon, back where she was from, and then he started to get worse: to make ends meet he was working in a pub, which wasn't ideal, bumbling home happy-drunk across country fields in the yellow–orange haze of a late summer sunset. And to think that, just a few months ago, he had been thriving, top of the world, a big hitter, a happy marriage with a young daughter. And now he was here. All his dreams shattered and no agitation to change.

And I thought: *god I hope the book goes well god I hope the—*

And things fell apart for them, a bit, afterwards. And he sort of moved back to London – he was sleeping on friends' sofas for a bit – but he never got back to where he was. And I thought of the man I knew – chronically unemployed, yellowing slightly, quite often snoozing lazily on the same sofa he used to sleep on, ruining another relationship in slow motion with his refusal to quit. And I looked at myself – single, beer with dinner, at the height of my personal success but also everything balanced perilously on a knife edge, it could all tumble beneath me, I could be the Jenga block that topples the tower it sits under – and said: *ha-ha, ha. Ha-ha. That's really funny.*

13% A.B.V.

For some reason I remember vividly the moment I realised I could just, like, buy a can. I was about 22, living in a shared flat in London but feeling alone about it, and I was doing my usual Friday night routine – home on the bus to an empty flat, nine episodes of *Seinfeld* and a chippy tea – when I realised, at the shop opposite, I could just: *buy a can*. Like: I could *buy a can of beer*. And nobody could stop me doing that. I didn't need to be at a party. I didn't need to be at a show. I could just: buy a can. I bought three, drank them alone with dinner, and thought: *I have the greatest creative mind in the universe. I just invented nirvana*.

95% A.B.V.

The ethnic make-up of Chesterfield is basically entirely working-class white apart from an old Italian community (there are: two Italian restaurants), a small Indian/ Pakistani following and, after a brief swell of immigration in the mid-aughts, a bustling Polish population. I never quite understood what it was that drove Poles *here*, exactly: I was English and didn't want to be there, much less travel across Europe for the chance of it, and most people outside the county didn't even know the town was there: how did Poland hear about it? And I had been to Poland, too: it's beautiful, and the pints cost £1, and they eat fat lumps of pork for every meal, surrounded either by high gothic architecture or rolling verdant hills, and I could quite happily live there, perhaps becoming a Legia Warsaw ultra, take a firm-faced Polish wife who hated me and everything I stood for. Why they came here – where the main thing in town was two Wetherspoons and a Frankie & Benny's – always baffled me to my core.

The point is when we – just about post-teenagers, thirsty boys with our first jobs and our first few flushes of cash and a hankering for a party – realised that the new Polish shop on West Bars offered the strongest vodka in town, and, well. We just had to see it for ourselves.

The tradition was this: every payday, we would all throw £20 into a kitty, and then walk clatter down town to The Polish Shop, then group in front of the counter staring at the vodka selection and saying 'errr?' for half an hour until someone took pity on us and helped us. We drank Zubrowka that way, Wyborowa. Lubuski and Soplica. We had a muddy-looking vodka that came served to us in the shape of a glass cockerel, its head coming off at the top like a shot glass. We tried herbal liqueurs and intensely concentrated fruit mixers. And then one day we came in and the shopkeeper looked both ways then went back, and I saw what he had in his hands and heard angels sing: Spirytus Duch Pusczczy, rectified spirit. The label literally had a ghost on it. A tiny half-litre bottle that would cost us most of our stash. But there, on the label, bold as brass: 95% A.B.V.

Rule #1, the shopkeeper told us, keeping both hands firmly on the bottle like it was a mogwai about to go crazed if fed after midnight: Rule #1 is, you don't drink it neat. Rule #2: you only have half-shots of it, never full (the cocktail he suggested was a Mad Dog, which is a half-shot of spirit, half-shot of blackcurrant liqueur and a shot of Tabasco: a shot that somehow manages to burn you three ways at once). Rule #3: keep it in the freezer at all times, to ... well, to hide the taste. You don't want to taste this, boys. It tastes bad. And Rule #4 is please stop coming to my shop.

Memories get fuzzy after this because – to reiterate – what I was drinking was 95% proof, which is essentially what Russian governments use to kill people. I remember our friend's younger brother telling us he was training in judo and was a reformed Christian, so we made him do high kicks in the garden until he fell on his tailbone and cursed God. I remember having one Mad Dog, then another. Then … I want to say I had six more? Deep dark night fell around us. My friend Party (we called him Party because he liked to Party) was looking a little worse for wear, and so I volunteered myself to walk him home. 'I reckon I'm the most sober one here, anyway,' I told the party. 'I'll sort him out.'

The walk to Party's house takes about 20 minutes each way but records on file from the time tell me I was gone somehow for two hours. At some point his brother, the Christian, spied some roadworks up ahead and sprinted towards them, clanging his fist on a shipping container that had been left there. Dogs barked, a cul-de-sac of lights came on around us. 'What,' I asked him, 'what in the fuck are you doing?' And he turned to me with deep, real fear in his eyes and told me: *The Devil's In There*.

And I said what, in there. That's a bulldozer mate. It's not The Devil.

And he said: It's The Devil. In there. I know.

And he pounded on the container – more dogs, more lights – shouting 'I KNOW YOU'RE IN THERE', before turning his ear to the still-ringing metal and going: oh, no. My bad.

He said:

There's nothing in there at all.

When I got back to the party things were starting to

peter out, so I went to get another Mad Dog to steady my nerves. My friend Chris stopped me. 'You know,' he said, 'you know you're not actually speaking, when you're trying to do speaking?' He explained: 'You've basically been making just animal sounds for a few hours now. I didn't know quite how to tell you.' I agreed with him that it was probably time to go home ('AUGHHGH! YUAUAHGHH!' – me) and I woke up at 3 p.m. the next day with my head ringing like a clanged bell. Even my mum, who liked to treat my more regular hangovers with the delicacy they deserved – i.e. dropping every pan she owned loudly on the floor of the kitchen while yelling 'GET UP!' – knew to leave me alone, so deathly ill I looked. I tried to turn over once in bed and straight up vomited. I tried to watch a Steve Carrell film and nearly sobbed. I was essentially paralysed for 24 straight hours after that one. Was it worth it? I nearly saw The Devil in a shipping container, mate. Hell yes it was worth it.

14% A.B.V.

There's a very particular clang that a bin full of empty cans makes when you decant it into a garbage bag. A clang on top of another clang. A very hollow, empty sort of clang – not a deep clang, like a gong, or a high alarming clang like a school bell – something weaker, more pathetic. I suppose I had emptied my bedroom bin out eight, ten times before I noticed. *Man,* I thought. *I drink a lot of cans*. After mum died I didn't really notice it but I started drinking more – something in the fuzzy, liminal space between my conscious and unconscious would tell me 'Hey, who's gonna tell you off about it?' – and my intake increased. At first I didn't notice it – the routine would be, in a house full of boys, that everyone would come up to my room to drink beer and play videogames. But then there were those odd Tuesdays where no one was home but me. The times near the ends of the month where I would decant change out of my change jar and take it to the shop to buy as many singular cans as I could afford. I got into Desperados, which is a cheap lager sweetened and strengthened with a shot of tequila, which I can now no longer stand. A relationship crumbled around me without me noticing. I got *fat* as *fuck*. And still I didn't really notice how unhealthy my bin-bag situation was. *Clank, clank*. A very specific noise of one empty beer can falling against another. There's no other noise like it. It was the sound of the monster tiptoeing in.

15% A.B.V.

I've had enough periods of sobriety now that I can see it less like a fun sort of challenge (I now understand my own psychology enough to know that I am electrifyingly turned on by maintaining streaks of good behaviour: if I weigh myself every day, or stick to a gym routine, or ride my bike five days a week, or don't eat meat for a fortnight. If I ever need to do something, I just need to give myself a time-dependent deadline on when I can do it *again*, and then

I can abstain.) and can actually pull out enough and self-examine why I do drink when I do. Fundamentally it's because it relaxes me: two pints in and the muscles in my shoulders unclench, my posture loosens, my heart rate slows, I flush gooey and warm, I talk more and without any mental gatekeeping on what I'm saying or who I'm saying it to. That's fine, but it's also possible to relax *without* putting two pints of very mild poison in your body (like: read a book, my guy. Have a warm cocoa and a snooze.), and learning that was a steep curve. Drinking to grease the rigid wheels of my own personality felt like a losing battle, so I also edited the *amount* I was drinking on nights when I was: switching from cans to bottles, pints to halves, pacing myself with soft drinks in between. Being drunk became less like the goal and more like the happy side effect: instead of racing after a hurricane I was falling backwards into a warm, soft swimming pool. You can do a lot of things drunk – charm, flirt, be funny, be open, be open to adventure, vomit in a bin, dance – and it's entirely possible to do all those things sober, too. Literally the only thing in the world you have to be drunk for first is karaoke. Everything else can be done after pounding a load of Diet Cokes.

16% A.B.V.

Friends have gone sober, and my attitude towards them has gone from hard to soft with it. In my early twenties, my friend Paul did a month off alcohol, and I was incredulous – 'Why, though? *Why*?' – and he shrugged and said: to see if

I can do it. And later, when I tried it myself, I understood: it's a feeling, of control and regulation, one my dad never got to feel and I did, and there's a curious powerful buzz to that. It helps that your skin clears, your sleep loosens, you lose that puff of extra weight, you have more money at the end of the month. I never had the actuality to analyse just how much alcohol was affecting my mood until, six weeks into a stretch of sobriety, my friend remarked how much he had been on it lately and how run down he was feeling as a result. 'It's probably all those litres of depression juice you pour into your body,' I said, and despite being the world's most sanctimonious hypocrite, I was mostly right: unmoderated alcohol input leads to a tight, spiralling, subverted feeling of unhappiness, one that's very hard to shake. But sobriety is the calm eye of a raging storm, and in my case it's still underpinned by fear: in real life I am pathologically, near serial killer-levels of calm and composed, but internally the way my thoughts bend and lean towards alcohol lean to chaos. In bed, in the blue-black darkness, six weeks clear of a beer, fingers kneading against each other as I drop into a pure dreamless sleep, I sit and wonder – *what if I'm not as in control as I think I am? What if it's all a ruse drunk-me is pulling on myself?* And then I can't shift it. And then I can't stop thinking about it.

0.5% A.B.V.

At first I started for a month to see if I could do it, then I read somewhere that that in itself is a sign of alcoholism, so then I extended it to two months, then ten weeks, to avoid that particular pothole. The thing is when you're not drinking people get incredulous about it so you need to come up with some excuses to sidestep any uncomfortable situations that might arise (you can only pretend you are on antibiotics, 'which will react very violently, with me, just vomit everywhere, honestly, the worst, so yes a Diet Coke is fine please', for so long). One way I word it is by saying, 'Oh, I'm not drinking ... *at the moment.*' It opens up this distant possibility that one day you will snap and go rage on the beers and tequilas and lines again, and you will open up and once again become fun, and not that the lid is tightly on you, forever, now. Another good tactic I've found is to order non-alcoholic beer, because holding it and drinking it and clinking it against others beers in a cheers-formation feels better, tickles the same synapses, as actually drinking does. I go bursts of not drinking, now: a couple of months here, a fortnight there, a big night out now and again. The worst realisation is, somewhere between 11 p.m. and midnight, everyone starts chatting *shit*: talking in circles, the same tired anecdote stretched long and repeated, awful, and they just want to keep going, everyone forgets every normal social cue, friends stop noticing you are disinterested hours before you can leave them. At a party at my house recently I went to bed at 1 a.m., clarifyingly sober, and when I got up at half-three for a 0.5% beer-induced piss there was a friend, on my sofa still, alone, fiddling with the AUX chord, looking for that one song, no honestly mate, you have to listen to this one *precise song right now*. I don't think I'll ever go sober-sober – too much of my social life, for better or worse, is tied in with drinking and going to the pub – but I've managed to screw the bottle from a different angle, now: I can say no to a beer, I never drink alone, I know when to order myself a taxi home, I haven't shattered one of my front teeth in ages. I call it running alongside the wagon: knowing when to hop on, when it is good for me to stop, when I need the mental breathing room. But also being able to jog alongside it enjoying a cool beer on a hot day.

0% A.B.V.

The one interesting thing about me, I tell girls on dates, is my birth was registered in a pub. You have 42 days to register the birth of a child in the UK, is the thing. And on Day 41, so the legend goes, my dad – instead of, like, phoning every registry office in the south London area – went to his local pub and loudly moaned about the situation to anyone who would listen. 'There's a massive fine,' he said. 'For fuck's *sake*.' Inexplicably, this tactic worked: I'm a registrar, a man three stools down said, and wherever my special registrar ink and registrar pen and registrar paper goes, well, that's a registry office. And my dad said: 'If I meet you here and lunchtime tomorrow and buy you a pint, could you register my large illegal son?' And the man thought for a moment and said: yes.

And so in the bright August sunshine, in the beer garden of Peckham's Clockhouse pub, so it came to pass: Yung Joel Golby, 42 precious little days old, soft and pink and snoozing, was legitimised under the eyes of the law. Apparently a circus walked past during the ceremony, which didn't move me. Apparently everyone got drunk. I slept through it. And I think of that, sometimes: the great irony, that I was birthed and notarised in the same liquid that would blight my life, forced under a curse that would never truly be lifted, and that 30 years later, I'm still struggling with it today. That my dad clinked ciders with men he'd lose touch with when he moved away from here to die. That my mum sat there and watched, not knowing what doom this spelled for us all. 'Raise a glass,' my dad said, 'to my son,' and the people cheered. How little they would know. How little they would know.

ACKNOWLEDGEMENTS

Love and appreciation to all of the following lads: Lain, Adam, Party, Paul, Lacey, Davio, Emma, Lizzie, Nat; Duncan Vicat-Brown's 35-hour 'Ambient Noise' Spotify playlist but not Duncan Vicat-Brown himself, he knows why; Christopher Bethell, Bekky Lonsdale, Michael Segalov, Ben Smoke; all of my VICE gang but most especially Jamie, Simon, Jack, Dipo, Tshepo, Wiegertje, Ryan, Nana, Toby, Angus, Kev Kharas, Amelia Abraham, Alex Miller and, of course, the Goblins; Max Brokman, my tall and emotionless brethren; John Saward, my hero and my mate; Carl Anka, and Jack Fitzgerald, but absolutely fuck Tom Bradley; Bill Stiteler, I am so sorry I have never sent you a single postcard in response to your many postcards but I hope this dedication goes some small way to healing the wound; Andy Riley, please see the bit I wrote for Bill; my family – Chris, Steph, Sam, Christina, Oscar, Elijah, Annie, and Val – you weird, weird, weird weird bastards; everyone who has ever put me up during the writing of this book but most especially Jemma and Arthur, you legends, sorry about all the mess I made; Stripes, Molly; Terri, Keith; Felix Cohen but more importantly Esme. Emily, Phoebe, and the cursed lurker 'Gabby LM'. James 'Jay' Driscoll, the only person who overtly requested his presence in the acknowledgements section. World's Greatest Illustrator™

Dan Evans. As a result of a lost bet I am legally obliged to present the name of the following acknowledgee as thus: '2K17 Monopoly: No Mercy Edition ultimate champion Kimeya Baker'. Sam Diss will be expecting a long sentence here saying how much he means to me as a friend and a brother – in fact I imagine this is the first page you have turned to, isn't it, you little prick, running your fat little finger thru the dense acknowledgements section to find your bit – but I refuse to give him the satisfaction. Dawn, Grant, and Nancy Diss, however, get my eternal gratitude and thanks. All The Lovely Lads At Mundial. Sacha, Sarah, Jasmine and Robocop. Monica Heisey, whose only feedback to reading the first draft of this was 'I'm sorry but my section in the acknowledgements was not long enough at all', so here, have this, you brat. Moon-faced shed shagger Oobah Butler and his vile accomplice Joe Zadeh. Emmeline Saunders, (who I don't even like but know will kick off most of all, out of everyone I know, if I don't put her name in here), as well as: Annesie, Jo, Jess, Rhiannon, Laurence and all the lads at heat. James Clee, my wife. Chardonné Cooper, meme lover, pasta fiend, friend to pigs. Mia, Ed and Max. Wiggy and Sam. Sweet Thomas Bellringer. Horrible, horrible Fred. Ella, Jamie, Janina, Caroline and John. P.C.S.D. David, David, and Peter. Bob Foster. Colin Brightwell. Everyone who helped the book get to where it is today: Jon Elek, Jack Fogg, Zoe Ross, Yaniv Soha, Dan Walker, Cara Reilly, Dolly Alderton, Mary Beth Constant. I would also like to thank myself, because I don't think I ever get enough due. Curses: as ever, curses go to my enemies. Apologies: apologies obviously go out to the many people above who I forgot. Thanks: thanks go out to any reader (you.) who has made it this far. That is the end, now. *Fin*.